ABOUT THE AUTHOR

Ambassador Johan Kaufmann, who joined the Netherlands diplomatic service in 1950, has since 1961 been Permanent Representative to the United Nations Office and other intergovernmental organizations in Geneva. He learned something about negotiating techniques during several years in private banking before the Second World War. Since 1946, when he entered the Netherlands Government service, he has been a participant in numerous international conferences. Some of these are the U.N. General Assembly, the Economic and Social Council, the Governing Council of the U.N. Special Fund (which Mr. Kaufmann chaired in 1959) and GATT trade negotiating conferences. His earlier *How United Nations decisions are made* (2nd edition 1962, written together with Mr. John G. Hadwen) attracted widespread interest and favourable comments. Mr. Kaufmann holds a doctor's degree (economics) of the University of Geneva.

CONFERENCE DIPLOMACY

CONFERENCE DIPLOMACY

An introductory analysis

by

JOHAN KAUFMANN

Foreword by
JOSEPH M. A. H. LUNS
Minister for Foreign Affairs
of the Kingdom of the Netherlands

A. W. SIJTHOFF—LEYDEN
OCEANA PUBLICATIONS, INC.—DOBBS FERRY, N.Y.
1968

Photographs for cover: United Nations

Library of Congress Catalog Card Number: 68-26727

© A. W. Sijthoff's Uitgeversmaatschappij, N.V. 1968

Printed in the Netherlands by A. W. Sijthoff, Printing Division, Leyden

To M.L.K. and R.M.K.

FOREWORD

The evolution of diplomacy in the last two decades has witnessed a phenomenal growth of international conferences. No week passes without a major international meeting becoming the stage for world or regional diplomacy.

Government officials of practically every type of government department become delegates to such conferences. Private citizens not connected with government services are frequently called upon to attend international meetings. Thus the expert has to be a diplomat at the same time. The professional diplomat inevitably finds that he spends a greater or smaller part of his career in international conferences.

Traditional handbooks on diplomacy and international law, even if they describe the legal or institutional aspects of the United Nations system or of other international organizations, do not usually concentrate on the practical details of international conferences.

Against this background and having often seen how bewildered events at international conferences may leave newcomers (and occasionally also old hands!) I believe that an introductory work on conference diplomacy will find many interested readers.

Johan Kaufmann, whose earlier *How United Nations Decisions are made* (written together with John G. Hadwen) provided a systematic review of United Nations decision-making processes, has now written a comprehensive outline of the significant elements of conference diplomacy. It alerts conference delegates to the sort of situations they may encounter. It shows tactical moves delegations may make. It demonstrates the varying possibilities for using the presidency of a conference. It elucidates the differing roles which secretariats and especially the heads of international organizations may play. It familiarizes the reader with what happens in the lobbies outside the formal meeting rooms, where much of the real conference work takes place.

Mr. Kaufmann's book will, I expect, prove to be both useful and interesting to all those whose work or studies may bring them into contact with international conferences.

The Hague,
December 1967

Joseph M. A. H. Luns
Minister for Foreign Affairs
of the Kingdom of the Netherlands

TABLE OF CONTENTS

Foreword by Joseph M. A. H. Luns, Minister for Foreign Affairs
of the Kingdom of the Netherlands 7

Preface 15

Abbreviations 19

I
Conference diplomacy defined; objectives of conferences

1. Conference diplomacy defined 21
2. Objectives of conferences 25

II
Decision-making in conference diplomacy: a general view

1. Debate, resolutions and voting; the normal procedure . . . 29
2. Some aspects of voting 36
   a. Weight of votes 36
   b. Quorum requirements 36
   c. Majority requirements 37
   d. Method of voting 38
3. Conference decisions by consensus 40
   a. Consensus with a resolution 40
   b. Consensus without a resolution. 42
Illustration I: Preparation, discussion and adoption of a resolution 35

III
Conference diplomacy—the organizational setting

1. The preparation of the conference 45
   a. General preparation 45
   b. Negotiated preparation 47
   c. Documentary preparation 47
2. Conference organization 48
3. The procedural situation; protocol 50

a. Rules of procedure 50
b. Protocol 52
4. Secretariat services 52
5. Conference rooms and lobbies 55
6. Scope of the conference 57
7. Size and membership of the conference 57
8. Periodicity and length 59
a. Periodicity 60
b. Length of meeting 61
9. Geo-climatological aspects 62
10. Hierarchical position of the conference 63

IV

Conference diplomacy—the human setting

1. Cooperation or conflict 66
2. Some principal categories of conflict 69
a. Political conflicts: the clash of the angry 69
b. Economic conflicts: the rich and the poor 69
c. Budgets and work programmes: the programmatic versus
the budgetary approach 70
d. Elections 73
3. Confidence and anger 75
4. Leadership 76
a. Leadership by individual delegations 76
b. Leadership by the president 78
c. Leadership by an "inner circle" 78
d. Leadership by groups; the activity of "fire brigades". . 79
e. Leadership by the secretariat 79
5. Publicity 79
a. Conference completely open to the public; informational
media active 81
b. The conference is public; informational media give only
limited attention 81
c. Public and informational media not admitted; access to
conference limited to participating and observer governments
and accredited non-governmental organizations 81
d. Access only to participating governments; public information media kept actively informed by delegations 82
e. Access only to participating and observer governments and
accredited intergovernmental organizations; occasional press
coverage 82

V
The role of presiding officers

1. General characteristics of presiding officers 83
2. Procedural functions 86
   The effects of a wavering attitude 88
   A case of firmness 90
   Presidential ruling reversed 90
3. The presiding officer and "irrelevant remarks". 92
   The case of the ILO General Conference: what is out of order? 92
4. Substantive functions of presiding officers 97
   a. The chairman permits time for informal negotiations . . 98
   b. The chairman actively promotes informal negotiations, but
   does not participate himself 99
   c. The chairman promotes informal negotiations and takes part
   in them himself 99
   d. Exploratory mediation 100

VI
Secretariats and conference diplomacy

1. Introduction 102
2. The constitutional position of the executive head 104
3. The personality of the head of the secretariat: Secretary or
   General? 107
4. Filling the vacuum: political conflicts 108
5. Filling the vacuum: activities of organizations 109
Illustration II: Secretariat Intensity 104

VII
Delegations and permanent missions; their general characteristics

1. What is a delegation? 113
2. The composition of delegations: (*a*) credentials 114
3. The composition of delegations: (*b*) nationality 115
4. The composition of delegations: (*c*) diplomats, pseudo-diplomats, experts, public or parliamentary members; summit diplomacy 117
   a. The leadership of the delegation is in the hands of foreign
   policy specialists (defined as either professional diplomats or
   Foreign Office personnel); the delegation has several members
   with other affiliations 117
   b. Leadership is in the hands of a minister or policy official

not connected with the Ministry of Foreign Affairs; the delegation consists mostly of personnel pertaining to the government department of the head of delegation 118
c. No foreign policy personnel involved; the delegation is composed wholly of specialists from certain government departments 119
d. The specialist attending a group of experts or rapporteurs in his individual capacity 120
e. Summit diplomacy 120
5. Permanent missions and permanent delegations 121
a. General liaison with the secretariat of the organization to which they are accredited 124
b. Preparation and follow-up of conferences 124
c. Participation in conferences 124
6. The internal organization and working methods of delegations 126
a. A good relationship between the head of the delegation and the delegation members including a sensible distribution of work 127
b. The delegation meeting 127
c. Reporting 128
d. The allocation of tasks 129

VIII
Conference diplomats—requirements and characteristics

1. The relevancy of traditional qualifications to conference diplomats 130
a. Truthfulness and honesty 131
b. Precision 132
c. Calm and good temper 133
d. Patience, modesty and zeal 133
e. Adaptability 134
f. Loyalty 135
g. Physical and mental endurance 136
h. Speed 136
i. Linguistic versatility 136
j. Courage 136
2. Characteristics of conference diplomats 136
a. The silent 137
b. The lobbyist 137
c. The orator 137
d. The procedural specialist 137
e. Old- versus new-timers 137

3. Professional background and conference diplomacy 138
   a. The lawyer 138
   b. The economist 139
   c. The political scientist 139
   d. The historian 139
   e. The parliamentarian 140

IX
Groups in conference diplomacy

1. Introduction and definitions 141
2. Types of groups 142
   a. Regional groups 142
   b. Political groups 143
   c. Groups based on formal international economic agreements 143
   d. Groupings based on a common level of economic development or some other common interest 144
3. Functions of groups 145
   a. To exchange information on all or part of the agenda of a conference, either in advance or during a conference . . . 145
   b. To develop common general positions on important agenda items, without definite voting commitment 146
   c. To develop common positions on certain agenda items or initiatives with agreement on how to vote 146
   d. To agree on candidates to be put forward by the group or on a common vote for candidates from outside the group . 146
   e. To agree on a common spokesman, and on the contents of the statement to be delivered 147
   f. To undertake joint action for or against a certain proposal 148
   Concluding observation 148
4. Groups and the negotiating process in conference diplomacy. 148
   a. Relations between various groups, and of groups with the president 148
   b. Relations between members of a group and the group . . 149
   c. Relations between groups and the secretariat 149
5. The effect of groups on the negotiating process 149

X
Tactics, instructions, speeches, and conciliation in conference diplomacy

1. Tactics in conference diplomacy 153
   a. Tactics to get a proposal adopted 153
      (1) Intellectual arguments 154
      (2) Promises 154

      (3) Over-asking or under-offering 155
    b. Threats and warnings 155
    c. Other tactics for opposing a proposal 157
    d. Lobbies, social functions and the exercise of persuasion. . 159
2. Instructions 160
    a. Everything dealt with in detail 160
    b. General position outlined 161
    c. Position related to that of other countries 161
3. Communications and speeches 162
    a. The significance of effective communication 162
    b. Types of speeches in conference diplomacy 164
      General debate statements 165
      General statements on specific agenda items 165
      Statements to introduce a draft proposal 165
      Statements commenting on proposals by others 166
      Statements on points of order and procedural motions . 166
      Statements in explanation of vote 166
    c. Length of speeches 167
    d. Conference diplomatic language 167
4. Conciliation 168
Illustration III: Conference Diplomatic Language 168

XI

*Case studies in conference diplomacy: trade, disarmament, aid
to a less-developed country*

1. Disarmament negotiations 172
2. Multilateral trade negotiations 177
3. A comparison of trade and disarmament negotiations . . . 183
    a. General features 183
    b. The role of the large powers 184
    c. The role of the smaller powers 186
    d. The role of United Nations organs and of the Secretariat 188
    e. Timing and organization of the negotiations 189
    f. The role of informal and formal groups 192
    g. Publicity and privacy 195
    h. The influence of the private sector 197
    i. The role of experts 198
4. A small intergovernmental conference: aid to a less-developed
country 200

Notes 204
Index 215

PREFACE

This book presents an attempt to provide a comprehensive analysis of conference diplomacy: diplomacy as carried out in and in relation to intergovernmental conferences. The analysis is concentrated on three principal sets of actors in conference diplomacy: delegations, representing governments, secretariats, in particular the executive heads, and presiding officers. The actions and inter-actions of these participants constitute the scene for conference diplomacy.

An effort has been made to keep the book concise. For every situation described different possibilities are given. Examples taken from a variety of conferences and organizations are meant to be illustrations and do not imply any evaluative judgement. Indeed, I have generally applied the principle of "analysis without judgement" to the entire theme of conference diplomacy as treated in this book. For this reason "Conclusions" have been omitted, since these would have transgressed into the banned realm of evaluation, while a mere repetition of points made in previous chapters seemed superfluous.

The book contains elements of international law, but apologies are offered to experts in this field who will find, I assume, errors and omissions. Similarly, the book does not pretend to be an exercise in "conference-ology", although it was felt necessary to explain certain principles and elements of conference organization. Nor does the book pretend to provide a systematic look at intergovernmental organizations, although many examples are derived from their characteristics and experiences.

Chapter I provides, by way of introduction, a discussion of the concept of conference diplomacy and describes various conference objectives. In chapter II a general view of the decision-making process in conference diplomacy is given, describing both voting procedures and methods of arriving at a consensus without voting. This chapter includes a description of the average process of preparation and adoption of a draft resolution. Chapters III and IV go into general aspects of intergovernmental conferences, somewhat arbitrarily divided into the "organizational" and the "human" setting. Chapter III describes certain conference techniques and such data as the state of documentation, and the rules of procedure, which are significant to conference diplomacy. Chapter IV, as a prelude to the rest of the book, first discusses "cooperation or conflict", as the dominating feature of most intergovernmental conferences, and then briefly analyses some other human aspects of conference diplomacy, such as the confidence factor, leadership, publicity and privacy of meetings. In Chapter V the role of presiding officers is discussed, and the various ways in which chairmen can perform their tasks, both those foreseen in the rules of procedure and other functions, such as assistance in the solution of conflicts. This chapter examines in some detail examples of a wavering and of a decisive attitude of a chairman and includes an analysis of the different interpretations given to the extent of presidential powers in annual conferences of the International Labour Organization. It is shown that the reality of conference diplomacy is determined at least as much by the particular political, economic or other conditions prevailing at each conference as by the written letter of constitutions or rules of procedure. Chapter VI examines the role of the Secretariat, in particular that of the executive heads of intergovernmental organizations. Different possibilities for the exercise of this role are reviewed, in the light of three factors dominating the secretariat role: the statutory role of the secretariat and its executive head, his personality in terms of taking initiatives, and the degree of confidence member governments have in the secretariat and its head.

Chapters VII, VIII, IX and X deal with the different aspects of delegations and their role in conference diplomacy. In Chapter VII a look is taken at the different ways in which delegations can be composed, and at the role of permanent missions to intergovernmental organizations. The functions of these missions in their dual relation to international organizations and their governments are analysed. If conference diplomacy is something distinguishable from diplomacy in general, it is worthwhile to reflect on the applicability to conference diplomats of traditional requirements demanded from diplomats, ever since diplomacy and "negotiating with princes" attracted the interest of writers. This is done in Chapter VIII. Some special requirements for conference diplomacy are also briefly discussed, as are the usefulness of different types of professional background or training. The chapter also provides brief sketches of frequently encountered types of conference diplomats. The behaviour, especially on voting, of the various groups active in intergovernmental conferences, has attracted a great deal of attention by academic and other observers. The role and function of groups in conference diplomacy are the subject of Chapter IX. The best known groups are briefly described. There follows an examination of the effect of groups on the negotiating process in conference diplomacy.

Chapter X discusses four specific aspects of conference diplomacy: tactics, instructions, speeches and conciliation. In the discussion of tactics it is shown that in conference diplomacy some specific devices are available to proponents and opponents of a proposal. Different types of instructions are discussed in this chapter. For some observers conference diplomacy is equivalent to speech-making. For this reason it is necessary to examine the significance of speeches. Some observations are made in Chapter X on conciliation processes with a description of a recent conciliation procedure in one of the U.N. organs.

Finally, in Chapter XI trade and disarmament conferences are compared, with a view to showing the relevance of some of the factors and aspects discussed in the previous chapters. The negotiating framework developed in the General Agreement on Tariffs and Trade (GATT) is compared with that of the Conference of the Eighteen-Nation Committee on Disarmament (ENDC).

This distribution of the material over chapters has caused different aspects of the same question to be discussed in different chapters. For example, while in Chapter V the functions of presiding officers are discussed, Chapter VIII has something to say on the possible loyalty conflict to which a chairman may be exposed. Readers familiar with international conferences may wish to go directly from chapter I to chapter IV.

To each chapter are added bibliographic references. In the first or second note to each chapter an effort is made to provide suggestions for further reading.

A book like this incorporates not only experience of a more immediate past, in my case twelve consecutive years of direct contact with conference diplomacy, but also more remote experiences which consciously or subconsciously mold ways of thinking and methods of analysis. Wartime years at the University of Geneva and Graduate Institute of International Studies, with the late professors E. Milhaud, W. Rappard and W. Röpke among my inspiring teachers, have no doubt deepened my interest in international affairs. My understanding of the world of diplomacy and negotiations has greatly benefited from guidance and advice received from successive superiors: Dr M. P. L. Steenberghe, the late Ambassador A. H. Philipse, Ambassadors E. N. van Kleffens, J. H. van Roijen, H. R. van Houten and C. W. A. Schurmann.

To Dr J. M. A. H. Luns, Minister for Foreign Affairs of the Kingdom of the Netherlands, I express sincere appreciation for his encouragement and for having contributed a foreword.

I am specially indebted to professor Chadwick F. Alger, of Northwestern University, who sacrificed part of the time of his sabbatical year at Geneva in giving advice on many points and commenting extensively on drafts. Comments on drafts were made by: Dr P. R.

Baehr, William Epstein, John W. Evans, Allan Gotlieb, Professor Pitman B. Potter, Professor A. J. P. Tammes, M. Weisglas. To all of them I express my gratitude, as also to all those, including colleagues in the Netherlands Ministry of Foreign Affairs and in the Netherlands Permanent Missions in Geneva and New York who have been kind enough to reply to my queries. Needless to say that the text of the book as it has now emerged is wholly my own responsibility.

Without the skilful and efficient assistance of Mrs. Joan Oppenheim this book would not have become readable. She not only corrected innumerable errors, but also in many cases found better ways of expressing my thoughts.

The typing and handwriting-deciphering dexterity of Miss E. D. Biegel, Mrs. J. M. Tj. Cergneux, Mrs. L. C. Philips, Mrs. M. Savoie and Miss C. C. Schade van Westrum has coped with numerous drafts.

Finally, the assistance and constant encouragement of my wife are gratefully mentioned.

Geneva, December 1967   Johan Kaufmann

ABBREVIATIONS

BENELUX	Belgium, Netherlands and Luxemburg Customs and Economic Union
BIRPI	Bureau Internationaux Réunis de la Propriété Intellec-tuelle
CERN	European Organization for Nuclear Research
ECA	Economic Commission for Africa
ECAFE	Economic Commission for Asia and the Far East
ECE	Economic Commission for Europe
ECLA	Economic Commission for Latin America
ECOSOC	U.N. Economic and Social Council
EEC	European Economic Community
EFTA	European Free Trade Association
ENDC	Eighteen-Nation Committee on Disarmament
EURATOM	European Atomic Energy Community
FAO	Food and Agriculture Organization of the United Nations
GA	U.N. General Assembly
GAOR	United Nations General Assembly Official Records
GATT	General Agreement on Tariffs and Trade
IAEA	International Atomic Energy Agency
IBRD	International Bank for Reconstruction and Development
ICAO	International Civil Aviation Organization
IDA	International Development Association
IFC	International Finance Corporation
ILC	International Law Commission
ILO	International Labour Organization
IMCO	Intergovernmental Maritime Consultative Organization
IMF	International Monetary Fund
ITO	International Trade Organization
ITU	International Telecommunication Union
LAFTA	Latin American Free Trade Association
NATO	North Atlantic Treaty Organization
NGO	Non-Governmental Organization
OECD	Organization for Economic Co-operation and Development
SUNFED	Special United Nations Fund for Economic Development
UN	United Nations

UNCSAT	United Nations Conference on the Application of Science and Technology for the Benefit of the Less Developed Areas
UNCTAD	United Nations Conference on Trade and Development
UNESCO	United Nations Educational, Scientific and Cultural Organization
UNICEF	United Nations Children's Fund
UNIDO	United Nations Industrial Development Organization
UPU	Universal Postal Union
WIPO	World Intellectual Property Organization
UNDP	United Nations Development Programme
WFP	World Food Programme
WHO	World Health Organization
WMO	World Meteorological Organization

I. CONFERENCE DIPLOMACY DEFINED; OBJECTIVES OF CONFERENCES

1. *Conference diplomacy defined*

"The gibers are beginning to say: Ah! Another Conference! Forty-five nations! A thousand experts! What folly! What extravagance! Yes, what extravagance—a thousand experts, financial, diplomatic, economic. They are cheaper than military experts. Their retenue is a smaller one".

This sort of criticism of international conferences, parodied as early as 1923 in the above words[1] of Lloyd George, has become more intense as the number and frequency of conferences has augmented. For some observers of traditional diplomacy modern intergovernmental conferences of the U.N. General Assembly or Security Council type are not diplomacy and essentially a waste of time, energy and money.[2]

To others, such conferences are an important outlet for diplomatic skills and for the achievement of foreign policy aims. Indeed, one of the first acts of newly independent countries is to establish a permanent mission to the United Nations in New York. The premise of this book is that intergovernmental conferences have importantly modified traditional diplomatic methods and that it is worthwhile to dissect diplomacy as conducted in such conferences into its component parts. Diplomacy has been defined as "the management of international relations by negotiation; the methods by which these relations are adjusted and managed by ambassadors and envoys; the business of the art of the diplomatist" (Oxford English Dictionary). Conference diplomacy can be defined as that part of the management of relations between governments and of relations between governments and intergovernmental organizations that takes place in international conferences. This definition covers not only relations between governments, but also those between governments and the organizations of which they are members. This latter type of relations has introduced new elements into diplomacy.

The term "conference" is used in its most general sense, discarding the old distinction between a conference and a congress, which latter term was used for gatherings at which sovereigns or their principal ministers were present.

In most intergovernmental conferences three main actors can be detected:
—the delegations, as representatives of their governments;
—the secretariat and its executive head;
—the presiding officer(s).

Sometimes others become actors in conference diplomacy, for example non-governmental organizations or journalists. However, the course of events at most intergovernmental conferences is determined by the actions and inter-actions of the three actors just mentioned. The analysis of the varying possibilities for these actions and inter-actions is the main object of this book.

Conference diplomacy must be distinguished from multilateral diplomacy and from parliamentary diplomacy. Multilateral diplomacy involves "negotiations between and among many states",[3] but is not necessarily conducted in the framework of an intergovernmental conference. Parliamentary diplomacy, a term derived from a certain similarity between international conferences and national parliaments, overlaps largely with conference diplomacy, and is described by Rusk as a "type of multilateral negotiation which involves at least four factors: First, a continuing organization with interests and responsibilities which are broader than the specific items that happen to appear upon the agenda at any particular time—in other words, more than a traditional international conference called to cover specific agenda. Second, regular public debate exposed to the media of mass communication and in touch, therefore, with public opinion around the globe. Third, rules' of procedure which govern the process of debate and which are themselves subject to tactical manipulation to advance or oppose a point of view. And lastly, formal conclusions, ordinarily expressed in resolutions, which are reached by majority votes of some description, on a simple or two-thirds majority or based upon a financial contribution or economic stake—some with and some without a veto".[4] This definition relates to the public meetings during international conferences. Thus, parliamentary diplomacy is a narrower concept than conference diplomacy because the latter covers not only public meetings, but also private, often informal meetings held before, during and after international conferences. Indeed, in many international conferences informal conversations, encounters and meetings, away from the publicity of the open meeting, form the most important part of the conference. In the modern conference system "open covenants" are arrived at through procedures and negotiations which are open only in their early and their final stages, and confidential or at least not "public" for the remaining, often the greater, part. Negotiations! For some the conference method is the very opposite of negotiation.

The word negotiation has caused a lot of confusion because of the differing content it is given. When the fifth Board session of UNCTAD (Geneva, September 1967) discussed the agenda and *modus operandi* of the second UNCTAD Conference (New Delhi, February/March 1968), a number of delegates emphasized that it should be a conference where concrete solutions to certain problems would be negotiated. This was disputed by other delegates who considered the conference essentially deliberative, with the power to make recommendations (but not more than that) to governments. There need be no disagreement on the significance of negotiations in intergovernmental conferences if one defines "negotiation" as the *sum total of talks and contacts intended to solve conflicts or to work towards the common objectives of a conference*.

This definition of negotiations is purposely a wide one in order to cover all sorts of contacts between delegations: a conversation on a single paragraph in a resolution may also be negotiation. Furthermore with this definition the existence of a conflict is not necessary to be able to speak of negotiations.[5] Many conferences have the character of a board of directors [6] meeting, where various matters of interest to the organization or the conference are discussed and subjected to decisions. The process of putting these decisions in best possible shape is often one of negotiation, but the participants would themselves deny the existence of a conflict.

It may be said that the Congress of Vienna was the first major conference with a number of characteristics reminiscent of contemporary conferences: the fight over the character of the conference, discussions as to who would be invited, the role of the "Great Powers" vis-à-vis that of the "Small Powers", the question of unanimity, the constitution of committees and the question of their membership, the establishment of "continuing machinery" to function after the Conference was over.[7]

The idea of systematic periodicity of conferences was already a feature in some of the older organizations, for example the Universal Postal Union, established in 1875. Conference periodicity received a strong impulse after the First World War with the League of Nations and with the International Labour Organization. The Covenant of the League of Nations (article 4) required the Council of the League "to meet from time to time as occasion may require, and at least once a year".

Even a superficial comparison between the period after the Second World War and the one before the First World War, with the interwar period as a sort of transition, shows a number of interesting developments:

(*a*) The number of international conferences has increased at a fantastic rate. In 1929 for one author "the most astounding fact in regard to post-war meetings has been their frequency. Never before in the history of internationalism have so many been held over so short a period of time. It is not surprising that an editorial appeared some time ago in one of our periodicals entitled 'Conferences and Conferences' ".[8]

What was an impressive development in 1929 has become an avalanche in 1967, as is confirmed by the following information from a U.N. report on the growth of the number of conferences over the period 1960-66: "The number of meetings has almost doubled over the past six years, and as far as Headquarters, New York, and the Palais des Nations, Geneva, are concerned, the facilities are used to capacity (between 2000 and 2400 annually for New York and between 4000 and 4300 annually for Geneva, including both United Nations and agency meetings); meetings held elsewhere have also increased—those held by the United Nations regional commissions increased from 770 to 1120 over the same period";[9]

(*b*) Gradually the old habit of arriving at decisions by unanimity has been replaced by majority decision-making.[10] As will be shown in chapter II, this can be done in various ways.

(*c*) Before the First World War international conferences were usually called by one, or sometimes several, of the major powers, or occasionally by one of the smaller powers after close consultation with the great powers. Between the two world wars the League of Nations system already had what might be called a self-propelling system for organizing conferences. After the Second World War most conferences have been convened in the framework of the United Nations or the specialized agencies. Conferences convened by individual countries have become the exception instead of the rule (an example of a recent conference convened by one country will be given in Chapter XI).

(*d*) A fourth important difference between international conferences before the Second World War and those held since 1945 is that economic, financial, social and cultural questions have increasingly become agenda items, whereas in the old days questions of peace and war dominated the international conference scene. Of course certain social questions found early international recognition. The work of the League of Nations in combating slave trade and traffic in narcotics is well-known. Indeed, slave trade was condemned as early as the Congress of Vienna of 1815. The 19th century international organizations, mostly called "Unions", dealt with postal matters, telecommunications, and meteorology. But the recognition of the problems of less-developed countries together with the general increase of international economic and social cooperation has overwhelmingly modified the average contemporary conference agenda as compared with the old days.

2. *Objectives of conferences*

There are various ways to distinguish international conferences. Some of these, based on specific organizational or human characteristics, are discussed in chapters III and IV. The simplest way to distinguish conferences is on the basis of their objectives.[11] If one wishes to make a broad division one can say that intergovernmental conferences are deliberative, legislative or informational and sometimes two or three of these at the same time:
—a deliberative conference concentrates on general discussions and exchanges of points of view on certain topics;
—a legislative conference endeavours to make recommendations to governments or makes decisions which are binding upon governments;
—an informational conference has as its main purpose the international exchange of information on specific questions.

A more detailed differentiation reveals the following seven categories of conference objectives:

(a) *To serve as forum for general discussion of broad or specific issues;*
(b) *To make non-binding recommendations to governments or international organizations.*

These two objectives can be found together in the annual conferences of the major organs of the United Nations and the specialized agencies. The U.N. General Assembly, the U.N. Economic and Social Council, the Assembly of the World Health Organization, the plenary conferences of the International Labour Organization, FAO, UNESCO, WMO, ITU, etc. all serve as a forum for general discussion and for possible adoption of non-binding recommendations to governments.

There are also conferences where general discussion takes place, yet where the practice of making recommendations to governments on the basis of draft resolutions submitted by delegations is exceptional. Examples are the annual meetings of the Governors of the International Bank for Reconstruction and Development with affiliated organizations (IFC, IDA) and of the International Monetary Fund. These serve as a forum for general discussion and as the place where a number of formal decisions, related to the operations of the IBRD and the IMF, are taken.

(c) *To make decisions binding upon governments;*
(d) *To make decisions giving guidance or instructions to the secretariat*

of an intergovernmental organization, or on the way in which a programme financed by governments should be administered.

These two objectives can be found in the periodic plenary conferences mentioned under objectives (a) and (b), and in the numerous bodies which supervise more directly than the plenary conference the work of an international secretariat and certain jointly financed programmes. The Governing Body of the International Labour Organization, the Executive Board of the World Health Organization and of UNESCO, the Executive Committee of the World Meteorological Organization, the Administrative Council of the International Telecommunication Union, the Executive Board of the International Bank for Reconstruction and Development and that of the International Monetary Fund, the Governing Council of the United Nations Development Programme, the Executive Committee of the Programme of the U.N. High Commissioner for Refugees, all are examples. One of the principal binding decisions taken, usually in the plenary conference of an organization, is the one approving the budget of the organization and the way it is assessed. Once this decision is made, every government is bound to pay its share according to the approved scale of assessment. This scale is periodically reviewed, if only because of the entry of new members.

(e) *To negotiate and draft a treaty or other formal international instrument.*

The following are a few from a long list of examples:

—The 1944 Bretton Woods Conference where the Statutes of the International Bank for Reconstruction and Development and of the International Monetary Fund were drafted;

—the San Francisco Conference of 1945 which decided on the text of the United Nations Charter;

—the International Atomic Energy Agency Statute Conference (New York, 1956), which on the basis of a draft prepared by an intergovernmental committee considered, modified and then approved the statute for a new international organization;

—the Law of the Sea Conferences of 1958 and 1960 which drew up draft treaties defining various rights, for example those of coastal states;

—the 1966 conference of the Legal Sub-Committee of the Committee on the Peaceful Uses of Outer Space, which agreed on a draft Treaty on Principles Governing the Activities of States in the Exploration and Use of Outer Space, including the Moon and other Celestial Bodies;

—the Stockholm Conference of 1967 where the convention establishing the World Intellectual Property Organization (WIPO) was approved.

Some periodic conferences also serve to negotiate international agreements. The U.N. General Assembly over a period of nearly 20 years drafted and then approved (in 1966) the International Human Rights Covenants (one on Economic, Social and Cultural Rights and one on Civil and Political Rights). The annual conferences of the International Labour Organization often consider and approve draft conventions concerning labour matters.

Conferences dealing with the establishment of a new organization and the elaboration of its statute are usually confronted with a series of separate, identifiable questions of considerable importance, such as:
—the criteria for admission as a member;
—the rules for voting;
—the relations to existing organizations working in the same or allied fields;
—the powers of the organs which will govern the new organization or programme.

Each of these various issues may give rise to differences of opinion. For example, on the question of membership certain countries advocate universality of membership with any country or state allowed entry. Other countries advocate a more limiting entry clause, excluding the states which are not members of the United Nations or any specialized agency nor a party to the statute of the International Court of Justice. On voting there are various systems to choose from, and each of them probably will have its supporters or opposers. If there is to be a clause that important questions shall be decided by a two-thirds majority vote, the definition of "important questions" can cause long and difficult discussions. There may also be efforts to write into the statute some sort of conciliation procedure prior to voting.

Discussion of the relations and the division of activities between existing organizations and the new body will find partisans of these organizations defending the latters' postulated interests. When UNCTAD was established, certain countries felt that the autonomy and work fields of GATT should be protected. The precise relationship between UNCTAD and GATT was, however, not spelt out in the resolution establishing UNCTAD. The result was a certain amount of continuing uncertainty as to the division of work between the two organizations. When UNIDO (United Nations Industrial Development Organization) was established (at the 21st session of the General Assembly in 1966), existing specialized agencies concerned with certain aspects of industrialization wanted to make it clear that their areas of activity should not suffer from the new UNIDO. For example, the International Labour Organization was anxious to make sure that its extensive activities in the field of vocational training would not be unfavourably affected. This assurance was obtained by a modification of the text of the draft resolution establishing UNIDO and, in addition, an interpretation to the desired effect by the chairman of the Second (Economic and Financial) Committee of the General Assembly.

The size and attributes of the organs administering a new body is another issue on which there may be a division of views. Some countries will prefer a maximum of powers to be given to the all-membership organ (the "general conference" or "assembly"), others wish to see the limited-membership "executive committee" or "board" given considerable authority. The preference of some countries for one or the other may be affected by their estimate of the likelihood that they will be elected to the "executive committee" type of organ.

(f) *To provide for the international exchange of information.*

All international conferences involve exchanges of information to a varying degree. Intergovernmental conferences specifically organized to exchange information on a certain subject or series of related subjects are somewhat similar in character to private scientific congresses. Examples are the U.N. Conference on the Application of Science and Technology to Less Developed Areas (Geneva, 1963), the U.N. Conferences on the Peaceful Uses of Atomic Energy (Geneva, 1955, 1958, 1964).

On a smaller scale, many committees, subcommittees and working parties of the U.N. and the specialized agencies work for the exchange of information.

(g) *To provide for the pledging of voluntary contributions to international programmes.*

For the U.N. Development Programme, the programme of the U.N. High Commissioner for Refugees, the World Food Programme and various other programmes, annual conferences are held, where governments announce their voluntary contributions for the next year. On the one hand such pledging conferences provide the necessary indication how much financial support a programme will have in the coming year and on the other hand they speed up the decision of each government on its financial contribution, since most governments prefer not to have to inform a pledging conference that they are not yet in a position to announce their contribution.

II. DECISION-MAKING IN CONFERENCE DIPLOMACY:
A GENERAL VIEW

Some conferences are not intended to arrive at decisions. They do not go beyond general debate or the exchange of information. Most inter-governmental conferences, however, end with decisions. The procedure by which decisions are taken and the form in which they are cast dif-fer from conference to conference, depending on the objective of the conference, its rules of procedure and traditional practices which may have been formed over the years.

In this chapter, section 1 covers the normal procedure for arriving at decisions on the basis of a draft resolution which is voted upon.[1] Section 2 discusses some important aspects of voting. Section 3 describes the process of arriving at a decision without voting, i.e. by some form of consensus.

1. *Debate, resolutions and voting; the normal procedure*

In the average conference of the United Nations or of one of the spe-cialized agencies draft resolutions are the centre of interest of all dele-gations. A draft resolution can be defined as the draft of a decision in a specific form: a preamble, setting forth the reasons why a certain ac-tion or recommendation is necessary, and an operative part, which contains the action or recommendation. Debate precedes the adop-tion of a resolution; the debate can be on the draft as a whole, as well as on portions of it, even on the significance of a single comma.

In some organizations there are almost no restrictions on the way in which resolutions are tabled, in others there are limiting rules. In the U.N. General Assembly the only real restriction on the freedom of delegations to submit draft resolutions is that in each of the seven Main Committees of the Assembly the chairman usually sets a closing date for the submission of draft resolutions.

In contrast to this the rules of procedure of the International Labour Conference, the all-member organ of the International Labour Organi-zation, provide that resolutions relating to a matter not included in an agenda item must have been deposited by a delegate to the Conference with the Director-General of the International Labour Office at least

15 days before the opening of the session (art. 17 of the Standing Orders of the International Labour Conference).

While in the U.N. General Assembly draft resolutions are dealt with in each of the seven Main Committees or in plenary sessions, in the International Labour Organization all resolutions not covered by agenda items are referred to a single Resolutions Committee. This committee selects by vote which five draft resolutions it takes up first, and in which order. If there is no time left, draft resolutions not included in the first five are not discussed, nor voted upon. On the contrary, in the U.N. General Assembly and most other U.N. organs a delegation can insist that its draft resolution, once submitted and circulated, be discussed and voted upon.

As an example of the average procedure for dealing with draft resolutions, let us assume that the agenda of a fictitious organization X includes the agenda item "the problem of . . .", and that there is a Secretariat report on the present state of the question. A representative (or perhaps the head) of the Secretariat will usually introduce the item, commenting upon or explaining the Secretariat report. The debate then opens with statements of varying length in which delegates give their views on the problem and possibly announce that they plan to introduce a draft resolution. During this debate delegation A may give informally to a number of delegations a piece of paper with the text of a proposal put in the form of a draft resolution. If the delegation wishes to underline the provisional and perhaps confidential character of its initiative, it will not even put its name on this draft. In many cases it will, however, put in the heading: "Text suggested by the delegation of . . ." or "Draft resolution proposed by the delegations of A, . . .". The space after A left open then indicates that delegation A would like to have co-sponsors.

The following is the fictitious text for the informally circulated resolution:

Preamble:	The . . . th session of the Assembly of the X Organization,
	1. *Considering* that the problem of . . . urgently requires a solution;
	2. *Believing* that the X Organization can make a constructive contribution to such a solution;
Operative Part:	1. *Endorses* the report of the Secretary-General on the question of . . . (doc. no. . . .);
	2. *Appeals* to all governments to take measures to cope with the problems dealt with in this report;
	3. *Requests* the Secretary-General of the X Organiza-

tion to make a further intensive study of the question of . . . and to draw up a report containing
concrete proposals designed to deal with it;
4. *Further requests* that the report referred to in par.
3 be submitted to the 25th session of the Assembly
of the X Organization.

Delegation A finds support for its proposal in informal explorations. Delegations B, C and D become co-sponsors. Often during this process
of securing co-sponsors the draft text undergoes changes demanded
by some of these potential co-sponsors. For simplicity's sake we shall
assume that the text as compared with the original draft of delegation
A remains unchanged, and is tabled as a formal draft resolution in the
name of delegations A, B, C and D. The Secretariat will circulate copies
to delegations in the working languages. It is normal, as for example
rule 80 of the General Assembly puts it, that "no proposal shall be discussed or put to the vote . . . unless copies of it have been circulated to
all delegations not later than the day preceding the meeting". This
requirement is waived if there is a unanimously expressed wish to go
ahead with a proposal presented the same day. The sponsoring delegations will agree that one of them will introduce (i.e. orally present in
a statement at a conference session) the draft resolution. Normally this
will be delegation A, the originator of the text. If for some reason
delegation A wishes to remain in the background, it will ask one of the
other sponsors to introduce the text. Another possibility is that delegation A makes the main introductory statement and that one or several
of the co-sponsors make a supporting introductory statement. This may
happen in particular if the draft resolution contains elements included
at the specific request of other sponsors.

The oral introduction of the draft resolution is normally brief and to
the point, clarifying any wording that could give rise to misunderstanding. The introduction may be somewhat lengthy in cases where no previous speech has explained the reasons for the draft resolution. It is
common and useful practice to give—after a general introduction—a
few comments on each of the paragraphs of the preamble and of the
operative part. The above example is simple and straightforward. Yet,
even though this may seem obvious to the sponsors, the introduction
should explain why the problem, as stated in the first paragraph of the
preamble, requires an urgent solution, and why, as stated in the second
preambular paragraph, the X organization is particularly suited to make
a contribution to the solution of the problem, and what sort of concrete
proposals the Secretariat might make in the report requested in the
third operative paragraph.

After the introduction by one or more of the sponsors, debate on the draft resolution can start. However, if it has been circulated only one or two days before, it may well be that there are no speakers immediately ready to start the debate. The chairman will then usually suggest that some other item of the agenda be taken up, with the understanding that "the question of. . ." remains "open for further discussion and for disposal of the draft resolution". Such a pause is—in most cases—useful. It can be put to good advantage by the sponsors to line up support for their draft resolution in informal conversations in the "lobby", or at luncheons, etc. If the sponsors sense some particular difficulty for other delegations, they may try to organize an informal meeting to deal with such difficulties. Such an informal meeting could lead to a revised text, to be submitted by the same sponsors, or with additional sponsors, whose suggestions have been incorporated in the text.

During the debate a number of speakers may indicate their support for the draft resolution. Some of them may announce that their delegation wishes to join the group of sponsors. It is normal that such a request to co-sponsor is immediately accepted and even welcomed by the sponsors. Other delegates may suggest amendments. Delegation L does not like the words "all governments" in the second operative paragraph. It wishes to see this appeal limited to governments which are members of the X Organization. Delegation L can either immediately move an amendment to delete the word "all" and insert before the word "governments" the word "member". The amendment will be circulated as a separate mimeographed document. Alternatively, delegation L may not move an amendment, but merely suggest the desired modification. It will then also hint at the possibility that the sponsors in informal contacts with delegation L work out a compromise solution. If delegation L opts for a formal amendment, the sponsors still have the possibility, usually permitted by the president until just before the vote, to incorporate the amendment in a revision of their draft resolution. The sponsors will do this if they realize that the amendment has overwhelming support (even though they themselves do not like it very much) and if they are desirous of having their draft accepted quickly with a minimum of voting on amendments.

Another amendment could be by delegation M, which proposes to insert in the third operative paragraph after the words "to draw up" the words "in close cooperation with other interested organizations". This amendment may lead to a so-called sub-amendment by delegation P, which proposes to replace the word "organizations" by the words "United Nations specialized agencies and the International Atomic Energy Agency". This would give additional precision. Unless delegation M declares itself willing to incorporate these words in its amendment, the sub-amendment will be voted upon first. If it is adopted, the amendment of delegation M includes the text resulting from the sub-amendment. It will then be voted upon in its modified form.

Before voting on the sub-amendment, delegation M could have withdrawn its amendment. Delegation P could then have decided to resubmit the amendment in its modified form. A similar withdrawal is also possible for a draft resolution as a whole: a resolution which is subjected to a great many amendments can be withdrawn before but not after those amendments are voted upon. The sponsors will do this if they realize that their original draft resolution has run into heavy opposition which can be detected in the number or contents of the amendments. If amendments have been adopted, the sponsors can no longer withdraw their resolution (see for example rules 82 and 123 of the General Assembly). They can, and sometimes will, vote against the amended draft resolution, which, heavily modified as it is, they no longer recognize as their own draft.

If two or more amendments relate to the same text, "the amendment furthest removed in substance from the original proposal" (rule 92 of the U.N. General Assembly, copied in many other rules of procedure) is voted upon first. Let us assume that in relation to the 4th operative paragraph of our example delegation R proposes to replace the words "25th session" by "26th session". Delegation S, which thinks that this is still too soon, proposes an amendment to strike out everything after the word "submitted" and replace it by the words "as soon as possible". The amendment of delegation S is then clearly furthest removed from the original text and will be voted upon first. If it is accepted, the amendment of delegation R is not put to the vote. If it is rejected, the amendment of delegation R is voted upon next.

According to the rules of procedure for most of the U.N. organizations (cf. rule 92 of the U.N. General Assembly) amendments must add to, delete from or revise *part* of a proposal. In the above example this would mean that if a delegation should propose an amendment to delete the entire operative part of the draft resolution, thus making it meaningless, the President would probably not permit the tabling of such an amendment.

A delegation which wishes to propose the deletion of a contested phrase or word need not submit an amendment. At the last moment, just before voting starts on an amendment or on a resolution as a whole, it can ask a separate vote on a paragraph, part of paragraph, the whole preamble, a single comma, in short it can ask for a separate vote on any portion of a draft resolution. This is called a "motion for division". If the result is rejection of the portion separately voted upon, it is deleted from the draft resolution as finally put to the vote as a whole. It is, however, fairly rare that the delegation asking for the separate vote succeeds in its effort to obtain deletion. The reason is that, in most cases, if the delegation really thought it could obtain the deletion of the incriminated words, it would have proposed a normal amendment and lobbied for it. The "request for a separate vote" usually indicates that the delegation wants to demonstrate its dissatisfaction with the words in question, by abstaining or voting "no" in the separate vote.

Under the rules of procedure of most organizations "explanations of vote" are permitted before or after voting (see p. 166).

Illustration I summarizes the procedure just described.

Illustration I. **Preparation, discussion and adoption of a resolution**

1. *Preparation of text*
   a. In capitals (Consultation with other governments)
   b. At conference site (Consultation with other delegations and/or with Secretariat)

2. *Informal circulation of text*
   a. Among selected delegations
   b. Among groups
   c. Possible revision of text
   d. Constitution of group of sponsors

3. *Deposit of draft resolution with Secretariat*

4. *Official conference circulation in working languages*

5. *Oral introduction by one or more sponsors*

6. *Debate (statements by other delegations)*

7. *Introductions of amendments*

8. *Debate on amendments*

9. *Sponsors decide whether amendments are acceptable*

10. *President may constitute negotiating group*

11. *Possible deposit of revised draft resolution*

12. *Debate on revised draft*

13. *Voting on subamendments*

14. *Voting on amendments*

15. *Explanations of vote*

16. *Voting on draft resolution*

17. *Explanations of vote*

2. *Some aspects of voting*

In any conference where voting takes place it is important for delegations to be conversant with four aspects of voting: weight attached to each vote, quorum requirements, majority requirements, the method of voting.

a. *Weight of votes*

In most conferences the system of "one country—one vote" prevails. In the few conferences with so-called weighted voting, where one country has several votes, according to some constitutional formula, delegations must of course be familiar with the precise voting situation. In the U.N. group of organizations weighted voting exists only in the International Monetary Fund and in the International Bank for Reconstruction and Development and affiliated organizations. The number of votes of each member of these organizations is related to its share in the capital. In plenary sessions of the ILO with its tripartite structure the governments have two votes (to be cast by two physically present representatives), the employers and the workers one vote each. In the Committees of the ILO, where participation is wholly voluntary (no nameplates by country are provided!), it is agreed at the outset of each series of meetings during a given annual conference how much weight is to be attached to each representative's vote. This is done in such a way that the constitutionally prescribed equilibrium 2-1-1 between governments, employers and workers is not disturbed. In the Council of Ministers of the European Economic Community a system of weighted voting exists. Under the provisions of the Rome Treaty this Council must decide on many questions by a qualified majority, which is determined as follows (art. 148 of the Rome Treaty): The Federal Republic of Germany, France and Italy have 4 votes each, Belgium and the Netherlands have 2 votes each, and Luxemburg 1 vote. Out of this total of 17 a majority of 12 is required in cases where the Treaty prescribes (as it frequently does) that the Council can only take a decision upon the proposal of the European Commission, while in cases where such a proposal is not required there must be a majority of at least 12 votes, cast by at least four members.

b. *Quorum requirements*

The rules of procedure of most conferences provide that a specified minimum number of members or participants must be present. During debates this requirement is often not enforced. For voting it is usually essential. Any delegation believing that the requisite minimum is not present can request the president to verify whether this is the case. The quorum is determined by a count of delegations who must be represented by at least one person. If there is no quorum, no vote can take place, or, if taken, its validity could be challenged. For example, rule 69 of the General Assembly provides that "a majority of the members of the General Assembly shall constitute a quorum". In the International Labour Conference "a vote is not valid if the number of votes cast for and against is less than half the number of delegates attending the conference and entitled to vote" (art. 20 of the Standing Orders of the ILO Conference). The main difference with the quorum requirement of the U.N. General Assembly is that abstentions do not count: on the basis of an assumed membership of 100 a draft resolution voted with 21 in favour, 19 against and 60 abstentions would have been adopted in the U.N. General Assembly, but rejected in the International Labour Conference on account of the absence of a quorum.

c. *Majority requirements*

In most conferences decisions are normally made by a majority of the delegations "present and voting". This means that those who abstain from voting, who are absent or who cast an invalid vote are not counted. For example, if on a total of 120 delegations, 30 abstain or are absent, those "present and voting" number 90. The required majority, usually stated by the chairman or the secretariat in announcing the result of the vote, then is 46, so that the proposal is adopted if the number of "yes" votes is at least 46, the number of "no" votes no more than 44. If there are 45 votes in favour and 45 votes against, the proposal is rejected.

It exceptionally happens that a delegate remains silent during a roll-call vote. In that case he is registered as "absent", even though he is physically present in the conference room.

Other possible requirements are:

—*two-thirds majority* of those present and voting. Again abstentions or absentees are not counted. Those in favour of a proposal must be at least twice as numerous as those against. Example: present 100 members, abstentions: 10, present and voting: 90, required majority: 60. The proposal is adopted if there are 60 or more votes in favour, 30 or less against; it is rejected if there are 59 or less votes in favour, 31 or more against.

The statutes of the various organizations prescribe what questions are to be decided by a two-thirds majority. The U.N. Charter (art. 18) and, based on it, the Rules of Procedure (rule 85) of the General Assembly indicate that "important questions" are to be decided by a two-thirds majority. Some of these are: recommendations with respect to the maintenance of international peace and security, the election of the non-permanent members of the Security Council, the election of members of the Economic and Social Council, the admission of new members and budgetary questions. Additional categories of questions to be decided by a two-thirds majority can be determined by a simple majority vote of the General Assembly.

—*unanimity:* unknown in U.N. organs as a requirement, it does exist in certain other intergovernmental organizations. A well-known example is the Organization for Economic Cooperation and Development (OECD), whose statute states that "unless the Organization otherwise agrees unanimously for special cases, decisions shall be taken and recommendations shall be made by mutual agreement of all the members" (art. 6 of the Convention on the OECD). In the EEC the Council of Ministers can amend proposals of the European Commission only by a unanimous vote (art. 149 of the Rome Treaty).

—*agreement or absence of disagreement by specified members:* the best example is the proviso that the negative vote of any of the five permanent members of the Security Council invalidates a decision, even if favourably voted upon by the required majority.

—*dual voting:* in some conferences a majority is required not only of all members, but also of specified classes of members. For example in meetings of members of commodity agreements producers and consumers (or exporters and importers) may separately have to approve certain important decisions. The International Coffee Agreement contains such a stipulation.

d. *Method of voting*

The principal methods of voting are:

1. *By a show of hands.* This is the method most frequently applied. The presiding officer asks: "All those in favour of the proposal contained in document . . . will raise their hands". A member of the secretariat counts the hands raised. The same procedure is applied to the votes against and the abstentions. A vote by a show of hands makes it easy for those who wish not to take part in the vote. Such non-participation remains unnoticed during a vote by a show of hands, except to the immediate neighbours. In the case of a vote by a show of hands it is not officially known how delegations voted. Therefore, delegations wishing to know how all or certain delegations voted, must post observers in strategic positions in the conference room, each quickly taking notes.

2. *By standing.* This method, provided for in the rules of procedure of the General Assembly, is not applied in practice.

3. *By a roll-call.* The roll-call or record vote is a method whereby each delegate is called upon and asked to reply "yes", "no", or "abstention" (rule 89 of the U.N. General Assembly). In some conferences mechanical voting (by pushing a button, causing a large illuminated board to flash the vote cast) has been introduced. In the U.N. General Assembly and other organs any single representative can ask for a roll-call vote. In the International Labour Conference a roll-call vote, which the ILO Standing Orders call record vote, must be asked for (by a show of hands) by a minimum of 50 delegates. The record vote is mandatory in the ILO Conference in all cases where a majority of two-thirds of the votes is required by the ILO Constitution.

A roll-call or record vote will be requested when the sponsors deem it important to know exactly what each government's position is. They may also have speculated that, forced to take a stand, certain delegations which might otherwise have abstained or not participated in the vote, will vote "yes".

The way each delegation voted in a roll-call or record vote is stated in the official record of the meeting. Accuracy is therefore absolutely necessary in casting one's vote in a roll-call. The rules of procedure of most organizations and conferences do not permit modifying one's vote once cast. Therefore, a statement by a delegation that it wishes to be considered to have voted differently from the way it actually has, is inserted in the record of the meeting, but does not modify the result of the voting.

4. *By secret ballot.* The secret ballot type of voting is reserved in most organizations and conferences for elections. The rules of procedure of certain conferences, for example of the World Health Assembly, provide that a secret ballot can be taken on other matters by a majority decision of the members present and voting. In case of a secret ballot delegates deposit their ballot papers in a box; a count is made by secretariat members joined, usually, by two tellers chosen, just before the balloting starts, from among the delegates on the proposal of the president. If the tellers do not agree, they will count again until they agree. A secret ballot often means the filling in of a name, or the putting of a cross near a name. If this is not done in the right way, a ballot paper may be declared invalid. The tellers may disagree whether a spelling mistake or another minor irregularity does or does not invalidate a ballot paper. They communicate the result of their count to the president who then announces it to the meeting.

5. *Postal ballot.* Some organizations, in particular those whose principal bodies meet infrequently, have a system of postal balloting. In GATT postal balloting is used for votes having a legal effect, such as decisions to have new countries accede to GATT as contracting parties.

The ballot paper is mailed out to members who fill in "yes", "no", or "abstention" and send it back to the secretariat. A ballot paper not sent back is equivalent to non-participation in the vote.

3. *Conference decisions by consensus*

Because voting is so conspicuous, conference diplomacy is sometimes condemned as an inferior method of decision-making, where large majorities, using the "voting machine", push through the resolutions they insist in seeing adopted. This view neglects the fact that in practice a great many decisions are arrived at without any voting, through a process of consensus.

If the consensus is laid down in the form of a resolution, a unanimous vote will reflect the agreement reached. Even if there should be some abstentions, a proposal is, according to the rules of procedure of most conferences, adopted unanimously if there have only been votes in favour, no votes against. As Tammes pointed out "unanimity is reached by making the retreat for dissenting delegations easier. They are permitted to have their objections fully recorded in the minutes. They are exempted from the rigid alternative of either subscribing to what is hardly acceptable to them, or defeating what may present itself as the hope of Mankind. It will not be considered irregular, therefore, if they abstain from the vote. Abstentions not being counted in ascertaining whether there is common acquiescence, the principle of unanimity is outwardly saved, but under that veil, as was the case in mediaeval communities, majority decision is virtually introduced. . . When something substantial has emerged from the early discussions, when amendments have been added and compromises inserted in order to meet the opposition, the final product is the work of the whole, rather than of the majority, and minorities may find it more and more difficult completely to deny or reject that product when, in the course of the successive legislative stages, it gains in weight and approval. The argument will be used that you cannot permit the result of long preparations, of laborious discussions and of happily reached compromises to be entirely lost in sight of the harbour." [2]

a. *Consensus with a resolution*

Under this category come the numerous cases, encountered in many organs, where a resolution is completely non-controversial. The non-controversiality can have been demonstrated by unanimous adoption in a lower body. The plenary session of the U.N. General Assembly each

year approves many resolutions without voting because they have previously been adopted unanimously in one of the seven Main Committees of the General Assembly. The President of the Assembly will in such cases state that, as can be seen from the report of the committee, the resolution was adopted unanimously, that he assumes that the Assembly will wish to adopt the resolution unanimously, that he sees no objection, and that he declares the resolution adopted. This is also called adoption by acclamation. This "no-objection" procedure received a peculiar sort of application at the 19th session of the U.N. General Assembly (1964-65). At that session a severe dispute had arisen between the Soviet Union and other countries on the one hand, and the United States and others on the other hand, on the applicability of article 19 of the U.N. Charter. This article states that a Member of the U.N. which is in arrears in the payment of its financial contributions shall have no vote in the General Assembly if the amount of its arrears equals or exceeds the amount of the contributions due from it for the preceding two full years. The United States claimed that this situation had arisen for the Soviet Union and others as a result of their refusal to pay their assessed shares towards the costs of the U.N. presence in the Middle East and in the Congo. The position of the Soviet Union was that such assessments were unlawful and that there was therefore no question of being in arrears. The United States had made it known that it wanted to force a "show-down" vote on this issue. In order to avoid this, (the wish of many U.N. members) it was agreed after long negotiations that there would be no voting at the 19th session. This meant that only absolutely non-controversial draft resolutions could be adopted and that only unavoidable elections would be held. This feat was performed by a procedure under which the President privately consulted member countries on their positions and then communicated the result of his consultations to the plenary sessions. Some resolutions were wholly uncontroversial, such as that establishing the U.N. Conference on Trade and Development (resolution 1995 (XIX)). But in other cases the consultations took the form of a vote behind closed doors. For example, after two seats on the Security Council had been filled without difficulty, because for each of them there was only one candidate, the consultations (in fact a private vote in the President's office cast successively by the representative of each country) had to be continued for the third seat, for which Jordan and Mali were candidates. These consultations had not produced the required two-thirds majority for either of them. Finally, the President noted that Jordan had more "votes" than Mali and proposed that Jordan would occupy the seat in 1965 and Mali in 1966. This proposal was accepted without objection.[3]
Most of the more routine consensus-with-resolution decisions relate to

matters which come up every year. Many organs in the United Nations must "approve" or "take note of" decisions or reports of lower organs. This happens in a great majority of cases without a formal vote.

On the other hand a resolution may have been negotiated with so much difficulty, that the president himself is requested to propose it. He will usually only be prepared to do this if he is assured that the text in question will not be challenged by some delegation which insists on a vote. Examples of this category of consensus promulgated under auspices of the presiding officer are given in chapter V.

b. *Consensus without a resolution*

This is the procedure for agenda items which are either extremely routine or so important, and at the same time controversial, that delegations prefer to avoid both debate and the adoption of an explicit resolution. In all cases of consensus without a resolution it is extremely important that the chairman sums up in the right way, giving the exact reflection of the presumed consensus, which must then be incorporated in the record or report of the conference. An example of a routine decision is that taken with regard to the notification by the Secretary-General of the U.N. (in conformity with art. 12(2) of the U.N. Charter) to the General Assembly of matters relative to the maintenance of international peace and security. This notification is in the form of a report to which the President of the Assembly draws attention and on which he states that the Assembly "will wish to note this report" or words to that effect.

In many conferences another item thus dealt with is the adoption of the agenda. Such adoption constitutes in itself the first item of the provisional agenda. The president (or temporary president, in case the president must still be elected) draws attention to the provisional agenda, asks if there are any observations and if there are none, declares the agenda adopted.

Consensus decision-making without a resolution is also normal practice in organs which have to approve technical assistance or other projects, so that there is no text involved. The Governing Council of the U.N. Development Programme approves most projects unanimously on the simple motion of the chairman. On some projects a delegation notes for the record that, if there had been a vote, it would have voted against approval or would have abstained; only in extreme cases (mostly on instruction from its government) a delegation would insist on a vote.

In most technical committees of the United Nations and the specialized agencies there is no voting but a habit of arriving at consensus decisions without a resolution. The same applies to most of the sub-committees of the Economic Commission for Europe, the so-called Industrial Commissions of the International Labour Organization, various organs of the General Agreement on Tariffs and Trade, and the U.N. specialized agencies generally. In the WHO special "Rules of Procedure for Expert Committees and their Sub-Committees" provide (rule 3) that "purely scientific questions shall not be submitted to a vote". If there is no agreement, diverging opinions are included in the report.

Although the consensus method often seems to come about naturally, without a conscious, explicit decision, there are other cases where such a decision by the conference as a whole, or by an important majority, appears to be at the origin of the consensus method. For example, the U.N. Special Committee on Peace-Keeping Operations, which started to meet in 1965, explicitly agreed "to reach agreement by general consensus without voting. It was understood, however, that a vote would be taken whenever any member felt, and the Committee agreed, that such a procedure was necessary".[4]

At the 1966 session of the Special Committee on Principles of International Law concerning Friendly Relations and Co-operation among States, the representative of Lebanon, speaking on behalf of the non-aligned countries (14 countries in total) represented in the Committee, stated that ". . . in order to facilitate general agreement in the Special Committee . . . the non-aligned delegations have not sought to utilize their comparative majority . . . and have refrained up until now from resorting to a vote".[5]

If there are two or more competing draft resolutions on a question, neither of which has much chance of getting the required majority, a consensus decision to have no vote on either of them (only possible if the sponsors are willing to withdraw their texts), may be the logical way out. This happened at the 12th session (1957) of the General Assembly in regard to two competing draft resolutions on a border dispute between Syria and Turkey. As Bailey recalls "the matter was considered in a rather strident atmosphere at six plenary meetings of the Assembly during . . . two weeks. Syria proposed that a commission be set up to investigate the situation on the spot. Canada and six other States submitted a draft resolution which would have expressed confidence that the Secretary-General, in the exercise of his responsibilities under the Charter, would be available to undertake discussions with the parties. Throughout the period of the public debate, there took place intensive private consultations in an effort to ease the tension and assist the two countries to compose their differences. At the conclusion of the debate, the Indonesian representative appealed to the parties to the dispute and to the sponsors of draft resolutions not to press any of the proposals to a vote. Syria, Turkey and the seven sponsors of the second draft resolution agreed to the Indonesian proposal; the President of the Assembly stated: 'I feel sure that the Assembly will regard this ... as a satisfactory outcome'; and the Assembly proceeded to other business".[6]

The consensus-without-resolution procedure is sometimes characterized by the absence of debate. This, of course, saves a certain amount of time. However, if delegates get the feeling that they are more or less forced to give up the opportunity of debate and to forego the adoption of a resolution, the result may be the opposite of what is desired, because a long debate will take place on the procedure to be followed. It would then have been simpler if the decision to have a normal debate had been taken immediately.

Summing up, one can say that the consensus procedure without a resolution is appropriate in the following situations:

(*a*) The action to be taken follows directly and in a non-controversial way from the debate. Many procedural decisions announced by the chairman are in this category.

(*b*) The action to be taken is more or less agreed, but the drafting of a specific text would cause insurmountable difficulties. Summing up by the chairman in sufficiently vague or general language is then the way out. In the U.N. Security Council this method of proceeding is repeatedly used. It avoids sharp differences of views on drafting specific texts.

(*c*) Decisions arrived at in negotiating conferences which are in fact the result of some sort of consensus. Typical examples are the 1964-1967 GATT trade negotiations and the disarmament and arms control negotiations in the framework of the Eighteen-Nation Disarmament Committee (ENDC), to which we shall revert in chapter XI.

(*d*) Decisions to postpone an agenda item to a later session.

It must be stressed that whether or not there is a resolution, all decisions taken without a vote require the careful judgement of the chairman. If he errs in his judgement, which must reflect what has been agreed privately, a procedural wrangle may well break out and the chairman's prestige will suffer to some degree.

III. CONFERENCE DIPLOMACY—THE ORGANIZATIONAL SETTING

The organizational setting [1] can be divided in:
1. The preparation of the conference
2. Conference organization
3. The procedural situation
4. Secretariat services
5. Conference rooms and lobbies
6. Scope of the conference
7. Size and membership
8. Periodicity and length of the conference
9. Geo-climatological aspects
10. Hierarchical position of conferences

1. *The preparation of the conference*

a. *General preparation*

The preparation of conference services has become a professional job. The following quotation from document E/4276 of the U.N. Secretariat indicates the required facilities to be supplied by a host government for the "International Symposium on Industrial Development" (Athens, 1967):

"(*a*) A plenary hall to seat 155 groups of five participants each, including 127 governmental delegations and participants from eleven specialized agencies, ten inter-governmental bodies, and seven international non-governmental organizations, with at least one desk seat per group and two back-up seats for advisers; a table to seat six précis-writers and press officers, and extra seating for 200 persons in a public gallery and 50 persons in a press section;

(*b*) One conference room for committees of the whole to seat 155 groups of three participants each, including 127 governmental delegations and participants from 11 specialized agencies, 10 intergovernmental bodies and 7 international non-governmental organizations with at least one desk seat and one back-up seat per group; a table to seat six précis-writers and press officers, and seating for 90 persons in a public gallery and 30 persons in a press section;

(*c*) Two meeting rooms for working parties to accomodate 70 to 100 persons, including 50 desk seats;

(*d*) All rooms listed above are to be equipped for simultaneous interpretation into four languages with a microphone at each position at the conference table and a booth for the sound technician;

(*e*) Sound equipment for recording discussions in the plenary hall and conference room;

(*f*) A suite of offices for both the President and the Secretary-General of the Conference and office space for: 93 précis-writers, translators and revisers, 74 secretary-typists and 52 substantive and administrative staff members;

(*g*) Seventy-four typewriters, preferably electric, of which twelve should be Russian and the remainder trilingual;

(*h*) A delegates' lounge, an interpreters' lounge, a dining-room and related facilities for all Conference participants;

(*i*) A documents reproduction area with equipment (mimeograph machines, etc.) and staff (except for supervisory staff to be provided from Geneva) capable of producing 300,000 page-units per day of in-session documentation and summary records daily for distribution to Conference participants;

(*j*) A document distribution area equipped with pigeon-holes for distribution of documents to participants and with shelving for storage and ready access to all papers;

(*k*) A public lobby provided with information and protocol desks; a cable office, a post office, overseas telephone facilities, a travel bureau and a clinic;

(*l*) A press working area to accomodate a staff of twenty; a briefing room for correspondents; radio-television broadcast booths overlooking the meeting rooms; radio-television studios for interviews and programme preparation; short-wave radio transmission facilities;

(*m*) Staff for reproduction of documents (see (*i*) above) and for their distribution, messengers, clerks, typists, security, transportation, cleaning, etc.;

(*n*) Automobiles for the President of the Symposium and senior Secretariat officials;

(*o*) Hotel accomodation to be provided on a payment basis near the Conference site, or easily accessible by means of public transportation, for an estimated 1,300 participants, including delegations, Secretariat, correspondents and observers".

Without adequate preparation of the necessary conference services and facilities, chaos and confusion, possibly complete failure of the conference are difficult to avoid.

b. *Negotiated preparation*

The amount of preparation of a conference resulting from prior negotiations may differ considerably. At one end of the scale one finds the conference which tackles its subjects more or less from zero: no or few advance negotiations have taken place. The Bretton Woods Conference of 1944, where the statutes of the IBRD and the IMF were drafted, was approximately in this situation in relation to the statute of the IBRD on which, contrary to that of the IMF, few prior negotiations between governments had taken place.[2] At the other end of the scale are conferences so well prepared through prior negotiations (often in another conference) that they have little else to do but give final approval to what has been thus negotiated. An example of this may be found in the negotiations on the accession of Poland to GATT, which took place in a special working party, and in informal discussions. When the Council of GATT received the report with recommendations of the Working Party (July 1967), its task was limited to approval of the results, i.e. to recommend them for adoption by the Contracting Parties of GATT, with the aid of a postal ballot.

For most conferences the situation falls somewhere between these two extremes.

For conferences that fall within the negotiating category, i.e. those that are supposed to produce some international agreement or treaty or understanding, it is indispensable for some prenegotiation to take place between the major powers whose support is considered essential. Such prenegotiation is usually carried on through a series of meetings of a preparatory committee, sometimes supplemented by the exchange of diplomatic correspondence. Also, group meetings of like-minded countries may be held to prepare common positions to be advanced at a conference (cf. chapter IX).

c. *Documentary preparation*

The documentary preparation may be "weak" or "strong". It is weak if papers or conference documents are available only shortly before or during the conference, so that delegates have had no time to study them. It can be called strong if conference documents are available several weeks prior to the conference. In any case even more important than the quantity of reports is their quality.

With few exceptions, all conferences start out with a provisional agenda, preferably annotated, in which the Secretariat provides a guide to the status of and the documents distributed for each agenda item. Without a provisional agenda long drawn-out discussions on the agenda may be unavoidable.

Too many documents available before a conference starts may be nearly as bad as the complete absence of any reports. An example of "over-documentation" was to be found in the 1964 United Nations Conference on Trade and Development: hundreds of reports totalling thousands of pages were undigestible for even the most eager delegate. Fortunately, the Secretary-General of the Conference, Dr. R. Prebisch, provided a summarizing analytical report of his own, and this report proved to be almost the only one constantly referred to and used as a basis for discussion by the delegates.

Effects of careful preparation

Even careful preparation and the subsequent success of a conference do not guarantee the full accomplishment of the objective. For example, the 1948 Havana Conference to negotiate the Charter for an International Trade Organization was excellently prepared. It had been preceded by preparatory committee sessions in 1946 and 1947, so that the Conference started out on a prenegotiated draft for a charter on which a considerable measure of agreement existed. The Conference duly produced the Charter, but it did not obtain the required ratifications and thus was never put into operation.

On the other hand, the establishment of the International Atomic Energy Agency provides an example of complete success. Its statute was carefully prepared by the major powers and a draft, negotiated in a preparatory committee, had been submitted to the founding conference held in New York in 1956. Although numerous amendments were submitted and discussed and in some cases accepted, the Conference was in a position to produce an agreed draft statute, which was duly ratified by the required majority of states. The IAEA started its work in 1958.[3]

2. *Conference organization*

Most conferences are subdivided into plenary meetings, committees "of the whole" (of which all conference participants are members), subcommittees with a restricted membership, working parties, drafting groups. The success or failure of a conference will depend to a considerable degree on the activities in these various committees. Their fulfilment of any deadline set by the president is particularly important.

The optimum number of committees for any conference is the one which will give the conference maximum efficiency: it should be neither too large nor too small. Too many committees and subcommittees will have a stifling effect: overworked delegates running from one meeting to another may find it difficult to decide where to go first. Also, with too many meetings none of them will start even remotely on time and an atmosphere of disorder may get the upper hand. On the other hand, too few committees or none at all may overtax the capability of the plenary sessions faced with a long agenda.

The larger the conference agenda, and the wider the scope and variety of this agenda, the more need there is for committees and possibly sub-committees working in conjunction with the plenary sessions. A very large conference with a very narrow agenda might be able to go ahead in plenary sessions, without subcommittees. If it has a legal or drafting task to perform, it will possibly meet with the same membership as "committee of the whole", a method that makes it possible to have all texts discussed twice by all delegations participating in the conference: first in the committee of the whole and then for a second (and final) reading in the plenary sessions. The Statute Conference for the International Atomic Energy Agency met mostly as committee of the whole, which was called "Main Committee". Each article adopted received a second reading in the Main Committee and a final, more formal reading in plenary session.

A conference with a relatively small attendance but with a wide agenda will find it necessary to split itself up in a certain number of committees. The Economic and Social Council, which can be put into this category, with 27 members, traditionally sets up at each session (inter alia) an Economic Committee, a Social Committee and a Co-ordination Committee. Not all of the usually long list of agenda items of ECOSOC go to one of these committees. Many items are first discussed in a general debate in plenary sessions, then go to a committee for elaboration of a draft decision, after which this draft decision accompanied by a report goes back to the plenary session for final action. A less time-consuming arrangement is that the item goes to a committee without prior debate in plenary session.

Often plenary sessions will take place at the same time as committee meetings. The U.N. General Assembly splits itself up in seven Main Committees: First (Political), Special Political, Second (Economic and Financial), Third (Social, Humanitarian and Cultural), Fourth (Trusteeship and Non-Self-Governing Territories), Fifth (Administrative and Budgetary) and Sixth (Legal). Some items are dealt with in plenary alone, but most are divided over the seven committees and reported back with, or without, draft decisions to the plenary sessions. In the annual general conferences of the International Labour Organization a continuous general debate takes place. The fact that each national delegation consists of three autonomous parts, namely a governmental, a workers' and an employers' delegation, each of which wishes to make a general statement, prolongs the general debate, which occupies most of the four or five weeks scheduled for the ILO Conference. During the ILO Conference there are a number of committees, including a Resolutions Committee, to which all draft resolutions are referred, and the important Committee on the Application of Conventions. These Committees are open for participation by all who register in advance. The World Health Organization's annual conference, called the World Health Assembly, has, besides plenary sessions, a Committee on Programme and Budget and a Committee on Administration, Finance and Legal Matters.

3. *The procedural situation; protocol*

a. *Rules of procedure*

It is possible to find cases of intergovernmental conferences operating without rules of procedure, the outstanding example perhaps being the Conference of the Eighteen-Nation Disarmament Committee (cf. page 176). However, practically all intergovernmental meetings operate under rules of procedure, even though in some cases they are hardly ever referred to. For periodically held conferences, such as those of the organs of the United Nations and of the U.N. specialized agencies, rules of procedure exist in the form of permanently available documents, which are from time to time revised. For *ad hoc* conferences provisional rules of procedure are either circulated in advance of the conference, usually drafted by the organ which is mainly responsible for the convening of the conference, or they are submitted by the secretariat at the beginning, in both cases for final approval by the conference.

Most rules of procedure cover the following topics:

(*a*) the general organization of the meeting:
—date and place of the meeting;
—the way the agenda is approved;
—composition and credentials of delegations;
—official languages;
—whether meetings are public or private;
—what records are held;
—duties of the secretariat.

(*b*) general and specific powers of the president:
—opening and closing of meetings;
—keeping order;
—according the right to speak;
—ruling on points of order and procedural motions;

—announcing and closing lists of speakers.

(*c*) specific rights of delegates:

—the right to make a procedural motion;

—the right of reply to another delegate;

—the right to make a point of order.

(*d*) the methods of making proposals and taking decisions:

—how proposals and amendments must be submitted;

—voting rights and majority requirements;

—methods and counting of voting, and conduct during voting;

—rules on elections.

It is essential for the conference diplomat to be aware of the exact procedural situation, which is determined both by the contents of the rules of procedure and the way in which they are applied.

The rules of procedure of the General Assembly and those of certain specialized agencies based on it (for example of the World Health Assembly) make a distinction between procedural motions and points of order.

A procedural motion as provided for in the General Assembly rules is related to the suspension or the adjournment of the meeting. Rule 79 of the General Assembly lays down the order in which procedural motions have precedence over all other proposals or motions before the meeting:

(*a*) to suspend the meeting;

(*b*) to adjourn the meeting;

(*c*) to adjourn the debate on the item under discussion;

(*d*) for the closure of the debate on the item under discussion.

A point of order is "basically, an intervention directed to the presiding officer requesting him to make use of some power inherent in his office or specifically given him under the rules of procedure. It may, for example, relate to the material conditions under which the meeting is taking place. It may be a request that the presiding officer should accord the speaker some privilege which it is in the officer's power to grant. Under a point of order, a representative may request the presiding officer to apply a certain rule of procedure or he may refer to the manner in which the presiding officer should apply a given rule, or the rules of procedure as a whole".[4]

For practical purposes the distinction between "points of order" and "procedural motions" has disappeared to the extent that a delegate will, lifting his hand or delegation-namecard in order to get the attention of the president, in both cases say or shout "Point of Order!". A procedural motion must immediately be put to the vote by the president. In practice, however, presidents often permit a series of conflicting procedural motions to be made: one delegate may move to adjourn debate and another delegate may move immediately thereafter suspension of the meeting. A more or less confused procedural discussion will then result. Another deviation from the literal application of the rules of procedure is that under a "point of order" a delegate will not ask for a ruling from the President but either exercise his right of reply or make some remark on the way things are going without specifically asking for a presidential ruling. While such deviations may be regrettable, they are so frequent that conference diplomats have to take them into account as something nearly normal.

"Procedure" and "substance" of a conference are supposed to be two separate things. In practice, however, procedural devices are used to obtain a substantial result and procedural debates often turn out to be debates on substance. In this book we shall encounter several examples of such situations (cf. chapters V and X). The alert conference diplomat will see to it that his objectives are not thwarted by procedural moves by others, or as a minimum he will recognize such moves for what they really are.

b. *Protocol*

In bilateral diplomacy the protocol regulating the precedence of heads of diplomatic mission (usually in the order of arrival at their post) and various other formal details play an important role, although certainly less than in previous centuries. In multilateral diplomacy protocol in the old sense is almost wholly absent. Seating of delegations in most conferences is in alphabetical order (French or English).[5] Before the beginning of the U.N. General Assembly lots are drawn to determine the country that will occupy a certain seat on the front row of the Assembly Hall, in relation to which all other delegations are seated, in the English alphabetical order. The order of countries thus fixed is also used during the General Assembly as a device to determine the precedence of delegates at formal luncheons or dinners, i.e. their placing at the table in relation to the host. The secretariats of most international organizations include a protocol office, which renders various individual services to permanent missions and delegations, such as advice on order of seating at luncheons or dinners, acting as intermediary on administrative matters with the host country, etc.

4. *Secretariat services*

The quantity and quality of secretariat services are of obvious and direct significance where the conduct of conference diplomacy is concerned. For example, if summary or verbatim records of meetings are produced, it is essential that they become available in the shortest possible time after the meeting takes place.

Summary records in their provisional version will contain an annotation that corrections, if any, are to be submitted to the secretariat within a certain number of days. U.N. General Assembly records feature the following note:

"Corrections to this record should be submitted in one of the three working languages (English, French or Spanish), preferably in the same language as the text to which they refer. Corrections should be sent *in triplicate within three working days* to the Chief, Conference and Meetings Control, Office of Conference Services, Room 1104, and also incorporated in mimeographed copies of the record. As this record was distributed on (date), the time-limit for corrections will be (date 3 working-days later). Publication of the final printed records being subject to a rigid schedule, the co-operation of delegations in strictly observing this time-limit would be greatly appreciated".

Occasionally a delegate, reading a summary of his statement in print, will regret part of what he has said. He will then submit a correction to the secretariat. The secretariat will accept real corrections, but normally refuses modifications which alter the essence of the actual statement made. At the U.N. General Assembly and at some other meetings tape recordings are made, which can be used by the delegate or the Secretariat. On rare occasions these tapes are also used when a delegate strongly denies having said something attributed to him by another delegate.

The absence of records of meetings, which prevails in numerous subordinate United Nations committees, need not be a subject of concern as long as delegates are fully aware that no records will be made. Indeed, the absence of records may have beneficial aspects: there is no need to make speeches for the record and hence the discussion may become more business-like. On the other hand it has happened that without records delegations become excessively critical of other delegations (knowing that in the absence of a record they can easily modify their remarks later). This may have a bad effect on the climate of the conference.

Whether there are records or not, for almost every conference a report is drawn up, approved at the last meeting (or occasionally in parts at earlier meetings). In some cases the report assumes the form of a "Final Act". If no records of individual meetings of the conference have been issued, there will be a tendency to include summaries of the positions of individual or groups of delegations in the report. Even if records have been issued, the reports will often contain such summaries.

The matter of reports very much depends on habits formed during the early life of an organization or series of conferences. The annual report of the Economic and Social Council to the General Assembly is limited to an indication of actual accomplishments with a minimum number of summarized discussions. Moreover, this report is not approved *in toto* by the Council which limits itself to approving the arrangements for completing the report. These arrangements consist in authorizing the President of the Council to approve the report, if necessary after having modified the draft prepared by the Secretariat. The U.N. General Assembly does not draw up a report on each session. It does publish for each session a volume of resolutions adopted as well as volumes of proceedings which contain not only the summary records of the meetings, but also the reports of the seven Main Committees of the Assembly and the main documents examined by the Assembly. These committee reports are factual like the ECOSOC report, stating draft resolutions, votes and decisions. Occasionally, they contain interpretations or other background facts not immediately visible from the texts; in such cases the substantive value of a report may be quite important.

Sometimes it is the secretariat instead of the delegations in whose name the report on a meeting is issued. This happens occasionally when the meeting has dealt with controversial questions or when there was no time for the conference itself to approve the report. Of course the secretariat should enjoy the confidence of the delegations; otherwise this task will not be entrusted to it. A number of committee meetings held under the auspices of the GATT are reported in this way. These reports are headed: "Secretariat Note on the Meeting of the . . . . Committee, held from . . . to . . .". The Secretariat also often assumes the responsibility for completion of the report in the case of very large conferences, where it is physically impossible, or would require an amount of time which is simply not available, to have the report discussed and adopted in the conference itself. Thus the U.N. Conference on the Application of Science and Technology to Less Developed Areas (UNCSAT, Geneva, 1963), where some 1500 delegates exchanged information on a very wide range of subjects, has been reported in a series of eight volumes prepared by the Secretary-General of the Conference, assisted by an editorial committee of six scientists.

Reports are not infrequently completed with the help of a rapporteur, elected from among the delegates, whose task it is to see to it that reports drafted by the secretariat correspond to the facts. He takes the responsibility of submitting the draft report for approval to the committee or conference. The exact wording used in a report can be of considerable importance. In some cases a delegation is willing to withdraw a controversial proposal, provided the report will mention the contents of the proposal together with a summary of the debate, and the fact of the withdrawal. The rapporteur will then see to it that the report reflects what is acceptable both to the delegation in question and to the conference as a whole.

A frequent point of disagreement in the discussion of a draft report is whether certain conclusions more or less agreed upon should be preceded by "the committee agreed . . .", or "the conference concluded that . . ." or that the words "many members agreed that . . ." or "several members believed that. . ." or "there was a fairly general consensus that. . ." should be used. Obviously, this problem arises only in relation to questions on which no resolutions have been adopted or rejected.

Within the secretariat interpreters form a semi-autonomous unit. Directly audible, more or less visible to the delegates, they are envied for their celerity, and on rare occasions rebuked, if something is alleged to have been wrongly interpreted. The ideal interpreter will not only render the equivalent of a speech, but also follow the intonation and emphasis of the speaker.

The précis-writers are responsible for drafting summary records. If a prepared text exists, copies will always be distributed to the précis-writers (and also to the interpreters) in order to facilitate their work. If there is no prepared text available, the précis-writer makes careful notes from which the summary record is later composed.

Translators, working behind the scenes, are charged with the translation of documents, including draft resolutions, into the working languages of the conference. Since they work under great time-pressure, it may happen that a translation unintentionally differs in minor respects from the original. A correction is then promptly issued.

The documents officer, who normally sits in the conference room, has a supply of documents relating to the agenda item(s) under discussion on that particular day. As delegates sometimes forget to bring their documents to the meeting, this officer becomes an essential wheel in the conference mechanism.

5. *Conference rooms and lobbies*

The physical conference facilities are of greater significance than is sometimes realized. Many an international conference has suffered greatly from inadequate conference rooms and insufficient space where delegates can meet informally. Such shortages create an atmosphere of claustrophobia. Delegates are hampered in their lobby activities and have difficulty in contacting each other. The ideal conference room will have its seats arranged horseshoe-wise or in the shape of a U with square corners, the chairman sitting at the shortest side of the table. Behind each delegate at the table there should be sufficient space for at least one adviser, but preferably for more. With horse-shoe or U-type tables, and consequently one end open, an adviser can sit directly opposite the delegate. At certain times, for example shortly before a vote is to be taken, it may be essential for a delegate to slip a note to another delegate. It is irritating if this can only be done by climbing over the knees of other delegates.

The efficient lay-out of the conference room is also highly important for the many informal conversations which delegates have with each other during meetings. Such inter-action [6] is an indispensable part of the negotiating process.

What has been said about the conference room equally applies to the lobby or lounge, where delegates meet before and after, and occasionally during the meeting. The lobby is normally adjacent to, or at least very near, the conference room. The New York United Nations building has in this respect a nearly ideal arrangement with its large lounge in the immediate vicinity of the conference rooms. "The fine art of corridor sitting"[7] came to full development in the principal lounge and the other lobbies in the United Nations building in New York. The main delegates' lounge in the Palais des Nations in Geneva is smaller and serves less as a focal point than the lounge in New York. This is caused by a com-bination of circumstances: the horizontal layout of the Palais des Na-tions as a consequence of which some conference rooms are located too far from the lounge, the operation of a second lounge area during large conferences and also the fact that the Palais des Nations at any one time serves some four or five meetings, each being completely separate from the other and related to different organizations. This introduces an element of disunity contrasting with the situation at the United Na-tions Headquarters in New York, where all permanent missions serve a single organization. The building of the International Labour Office in Geneva has a fairly small, but effectively located delegates' lounge, adjacent to the principal conference room. The same is true for the World Health Organization building in Geneva.

Restaurants must be considered part of conference facilities, if they are in the conference building. Luncheons offer an important opportunity for conversation, clarification and negotiation on conference issues. As a conference moves towards its final phase, delegates get pressed for time, and the availability of restaurants, including the cafeteria type, in the conference area becomes of considerable importance.

6. *Scope of the conference*

It makes an important difference whether a conference concentrates on one specific subject, for example the I.T.U. World Administrative Radio Conference (Geneva, 1967) which dealt with matters related to the so-called maritime mobile service (especially radio regulations for ships and coast stations) or with a broad agenda of items, as in the Economic and Social Council or in most of the seven Main Committees of the U.N. General Assembly. Generally speaking, it is easier to persuade a conference with one or only a few items on its agenda to stick to its assigned task than a conference with a very long list of questions to be dealt with.

The scope of a conference is closely related to its duration, a broad-scoped conference usually needing more time than one with a very specific subject.

A rough division of conferences based on their scope follows:

	Examples:
broad:	U.N. General Assembly; Annual plenary conferences of specialized agencies; U.N. Economic and Social Council
specific:	Annual meetings of U.N. regional economic commissions; Negotiating conferences for international commodity agreements (cocoa, sugar, etc.); U.N. Conference on the Standardization of Geographical Names (Geneva, 1967).

The scope of the conference has obvious implications for its organization, for the composition of delegations and for the duties of the chairman and of the secretariat, both of whom will have a more voluminous task in conferences with a wide scope.

7. *Size and membership of the conference*

A division as to size might be as follows:
Small (up to 20 delegations): U.N. Security Council; Eighteen-Nation Disarmament Conference

Medium (20—60 delegations):   U.N. Economic and Social Council

Large (over 60 delegations):   U.N. General Assembly;
plenary conferences of specialized agencies;
U.N. Conference on the Application of Science and Technology to Less Developed Areas;
U.N. Conferences on Trade and Development.

These distinctions as to size are from the 1967 point of view. Fifty years ago a conference with sixty participants would have been considered very large. Gradually, conferences have been getting larger.

In most cases increased size means decreased efficiency for a conference. There are, however, numerous exceptions to show that a large conference can be efficient and a small one inefficient. The WMO plenary session, which takes place only once every four years, is a good example of a large efficient conference.

Since most conferences are nowadays called under the auspices of an international organization, the question of participation is settled either by the constitution or other basic instrument of the organization or by a decision *ad hoc* of the organization. In resolutions of the U.N. General Assembly providing for the convening of an *ad hoc* conference one often finds the stipulation that participation shall be open to any state member of the "United Nations, the specialized agencies or the International Atomic Energy Agency". Special mention is made of the latter organization, because legally it is not a U.N. specialized agency. Membership in a single specialized agency, e.g. the Universal Postal Union, is thus sufficient to qualify a state as a participant. At the 1963 United Nations Conference on the Application of Science and Technology to Less Developed Areas and at the 1964 United Nations Conference on Trade and Development several small states or governments, such as Monaco, San Marino, Liechtenstein and the Holy See appeared as full participants under this rule. Another, more recently used, formula, found for instance in General Assembly resolution 2166 (XXI) with regard to the International Conference on the Law of Treaties to be held in 1968 and 1969, reads "Invites States Members of the United Nations, States Members of the specialized agencies, States Parties to the Statute of the International Court of Justice and States that the General Assembly decides specially to invite to participate in the conference".

The status of observer to a conference is also dealt with either in the constitution or other basic instrument of the organization, or in an *ad hoc* decision. In the United Nations system many meetings with a restricted membership are nevertheless open to any member government that wishes to participate as an observer.

Sometimes there are special procedures to determine conference participation. Thus for the Fifth World Meteorological Congress (Geneva, 1967) all member governments of the WMO were asked to nominate, before a certain date well in advance of the Conference, one or more non-member country(ies) to be invited to attend as observer. The list of countries so proposed was then submitted to a postal vote of the entire membership, as a result of which some of the proposed countries were permitted to send observers.

A special complication arises when the country where a conference is to be held proves to be refusing visa to delegates from certain countries whose governments it does not recognize. This usually leads to the last minute transfer of the conference to another site.

Apart from government delegations many conferences are attended by representatives of other intergovernmental organizations. The agreements between the United Nations and the specialized agencies provide for the mutual right of attendance of meetings. As soon as work programmes or matters of direct interest to them are discussed, the specialized agencies will participate actively in informal discussions and sometimes make statements.

Non-governmental organizations also attend most conferences. In the case of ECOSOC their right to take the floor or submit papers is regulated in detail.

The question of participation in a conference must not be confused with that of credentials (cf. p. 114). Situations may arise, e.g. if there has just been a revolution in a country, that two delegations present themselves, each with seemingly valid credentials. In that case the credentials committee has a knotty task.

8. *Periodicity and length*

Periodicity and length are related. A conference held at frequent intervals will usually not last very long, while a conference meeting once a year, or once every four years, will meet for several weeks. Although there is a direct relation between periodicity and length, it is not a proportional one: the annual plenary sessions of the World Health Organization and of the International Labour Organization last about one month. This is also the approximate duration of the plenary assembly of the World Meteorological Organization which is convened only once every four years, while the last Plenipotentiary Conference (plenary conference, which meets only once every six years) of the International Telecommunication Union (Montreux, 1965) lasted almost two months.

a. *Periodicity*

Some of the possibilities are these:

Completely *ad hoc*; only one conference provided, no repetition specifically anticipated	U.N. Conference on the Application of Science and Technology to Less Developed Areas 1963; Conference on the Conservation of the Resources of the Sea 1954 Paris Peace Conference of 1919
Repetition, because legal instrument can not be negotiated in a single conference	Conferences on the Law of the Sea, 1958, 1960
Periodicity (annual or other) based on statute or other decision of international organization	Plenary conferences of all members of specialized agencies
Periodicity partly self-determined	Conference of the Eighteen-Nation Disarmament Committee

The distinctions made here are of obvious importance. The conference with its own statute-prescribed or self-determined regular periodicity will fairly quickly assume a life of its own, a corporate character. If periodicity is not prescribed by the constitution or other international instrument, but self-determined as is the case for the Eighteen-Nation Disarmament Committee (cf. Chapter XI), the agreement of the major powers is essential where the date of reconvening a meeting is concerned.

There has recently been some discussion on the desirability of decreasing the number of meetings held by certain bodies. The Ad Hoc Committee of Experts to examine the Finances of the United Nations and the Specialized Agencies, which was established by General Assembly resolution 2049 (XX) to study the activities of the U.N. and the specialized agencies, recommended that those specialized agencies whose plenary conference is held annually should consider the possibility of holding such a conference once every two years. Other organizations (FAO, UNESCO) already have their plenary conference every two years.

Once the periodicity of a certain conference is firmly established, it is exceedingly difficult to modify it so as to meet less often: many delegates who come back year after year will resent such a modification. It is therefore important that a new organization planning the periodicity of its meetings begins with too few meetings rather than with a relatively large number. It is easier to add a few meetings than to get rid of them when they have become an established routine.

The date on which a meeting starts is sometimes fixed by tradition (the General Assembly normally begins the third Tuesday in September, the ILO Conference the first Wednesday in June), sometimes at the end of the previous meeting. In other cases it is decided by a higher body, or by an executive organ. An example of the latter is the Council of GATT, which periodically fixes a calendar of meetings, including the date of the plenary session of the contracting parties of GATT. In practice the fixing of dates for convening GATT meetings is left to the discretion of the presiding officer (if he continues in office) in cooperation with the Secretariat. Thus, meetings of GATT committees are often postponed on the proposal of the Director-General after consultation with the presiding officer (if he has already been elected) and the principal delegations involved. Since GATT is essentially a negotiating organization, its meetings must take place "when the time is ripe", which usually means that some prior negotiation behind closed doors has preceded formal meetings.

b. *Length of meeting*

A somewhat arbitrary division might be:

	Examples:
Short: less than a week	ECE Committees; Council and Committees of GATT
Medium: up to three weeks	Executive Board WHO; Governing Body ILO
Long: more than three weeks	U.N. General Assembly; Plenary conferences of most specialized agencies

In all cases the time factor plays an essential role in conference diplomacy, if only because of the time limitation inherent in any conference. Experience teaches that it is not possible to establish an automatic and generally valid causal relation between the length of a conference and its degree of success or failure. What can be said is that the chairman, the vice-chairmen and the delegates should have a clear idea how to organize their work in terms of available time. A conference with a fairly heavy agenda lasting for one week must make, immediately after its opening, a careful allocation of the various items over the available conference days. A one week conference is in fact a five day conference, or at most five and a half days. Irritation is bound to break out when at the end of the fourth day it becomes clear that the conference is hopelessly short of time. A conference scheduled to last for a fairly long period, say three or four weeks, suffers from a phenomenon that might be called "conference myopia": attention is focused on the immediately following days; the weeks beyond appear far off and plenty of time seems to be available to deal with the agenda. Suddenly the last week has arrived, time is running out and tempers get correspondingly short. Like students preparing for an examination, delegates will make careful use of the time available to prepare for the moment of truth, the last days of the conference when the principal decisions must be taken.

Is there an ideal length of time for an international conference? Each conference has an ideal duration of its own, which is the length of time needed to get the conference objectives accomplished. It may not even be best to crowd as many sessions as possible into each conference day so as to shorten the total duration of the conference. Giving enough time for informal consultations among delegations and for individual delegations to consult with their capitals will often be time gained, not wasted.

9. *Geo-climatological aspects*

Two aspects are important in relation to the place of a conference:

a. *Is the conference, if periodically held, taking place at its normal site?*

The answer will be in the affirmative for most conferences held under the auspices of an intergovernmental organization. In that case it is relatively easy to maintain a normal routine, to which those delegates who are old-timers are accustomed. Occasionally, however, an organization decides to meet away from its headquarters. Certain organizations have even adopted a pattern of periodically convening elsewhere. The annual meeting of the Governors of the International Bank for Reconstruction and Development and of the International Monetary Fund meets every other year away from Washington D.C., the headquarters site. A meeting away from headquarters, unless prepared with special care, may create a temporary amount of confusion, because the normal conference procedure somehow has not immediately taken root in the new environment. This danger can be overcome by combined action of the host country and the secretariat, as a result of which delegates are aware, immediately after arrival, of various practical details and any special procedures. Even with fully adequate services and facilities on the part of the secretariat and the host country, a certain uneasiness resulting from the unfamiliarity of the conference site may persist and unfavourably affect smooth conference activity.

If a conference is held away from its normal site, there may also be a certain loss of conference time because the physical attractions of the city where it is held will absorb some of the attention and time reserved for the conference; the host country will usually offer one or more excursions. The larger the town is where the conference is held, the greater the possibility it offers for distracting the average delegate from attending the conference, and so the general efficiency of the conference is lessened.

Occasionally a conference is held on purpose in a specific place directly related to its subject. For example, a WMO/UNESCO Symposium on Hydrological Forecasts met in 1967 in Surfers' Paradise, Queensland, Australia. In a wider sense it is felt to be useful that certain periodically held conferences are occasionally convened in an environment where the delegates can observe some of the problems they are dealing with. Thus, UNCTAD, which deals with problems of less-developed countries, held its second Conference (1968) in New Delhi.

b. *What is the weather during the conference?*

Extremely hot or cold weather will affect conference activity. In particular, meetings in hot, non-airconditioned rooms may slow down conference activity or lead to a flare-up of tempers. At the eighth session of the Economic Commission for Latin America (Panama, 1959) a heated exchange of views on the problem of inflation between the Executive Secretary and the representative of the IMF may have been brought about, or intensified, by the extremely hot weather.

10. *Hierarchical position of the conference*

Many conferences are important in their own right and each organ has its own intrinsic importance, so that it is hazardous to attempt to classify them as "lower" or "higher". For example, it has sometimes been argued that the Economic and Social Council is lower than the U.N. General Assembly. Both, however, are principal organs of the United Nations with well defined distinct tasks under the U.N. Charter. The same is true for the Governing Body in relation to the ILO General Conference.

Those conferences which are related to a higher, lower or parallel organ will find their decision-making influenced by this position. Sometimes the task of a conference is made easier if its terms of reference specified by the higher organ are neither too detailed nor too vague, or if a higher organ receives a ready-made report with conclusions from a lower organ. At other times the task may be more difficult, because an organ may throw back an unfinished piece of business to a lower or higher body. An example of this is the problem of East-West trade, which offers many difficult economic and legal riddles, and which for years was tossed around between plenary sessions of the Economic Commission for Europe, the ECE Committee on the Development of Trade, Ad Hoc Groups of Experts, and various committees of government representatives.

A committee may have a relation with another committee on a parallel "horizontal" level. For example the Legal Sub-Committee of the Committee on the Peaceful Uses of Outer Space has occasionally passed on a subject to the Technical Sub-Committee (the two subcommittees did not meet simultaneously).

The hierarchical position of a conference influences the tactics and positions of delegations. A group of experts who know that their recommendation must be approved by a series of other meetings, including meetings on the governmental level, will be fairly relaxed in coming to an agreed solution because, working largely on their own responsibility, they do not commit their governments. An intergovernmental conference, knowing that its recommendations will come close to engaging governments (even if such engagement is circumscribed by the legal freedom not to implement a recommendation, or not to ratify an initialed treaty), will operate in an atmosphere of "protecting one's position", where every delegation is careful not to commit itself prematurely.

In many cases a conference is both an instruction-receiver and an instruction-giver. The Economic and Social Council frequently receives requests from the U.N. General Assembly and itself transmits requests of its own to the regional commissions or the so-called functional commissions, all of which come under its supervision. A regional commission such as the Economic Commission for Europe has to approve the work programmes of a series of subcommittees working under its aegis, just as its own work programme must be approved by the Economic and Social Council.

In certain international organizations reference to the executive body by the plenary conference of proposals, which are either too controversial or too complicated to be dealt with by the conference, is fairly normal procedure. For example, at the tenth regular session of the General Conference of the International Atomic Energy Agency, (Vienna, 1966), six delegations jointly submitted a draft resolution on the future of the International Centre for Theoretical Physics at Trieste. This draft resolution requested the Board of Governors to take measures to ensure that the activities of this Centre would be continued in the coming years, and also requested the Director-General to initiate negotiations with the Italian and other member governments and with UNESCO and interested foundations with a view to determining the extent of their financial contributions to the Centre. After some discussion another draft resolution, tabled by one country, was adopted, simply requesting the Director-General to communicate to the Board of Governors the text of the first draft resolution together with the records of the discussion.[8]

The Executive Board of the IBRD regularly receives decisions from the annual meeting of the Board of Governors (the plenary conference). On some of these the Executive Board reports back proposed action to the Board of Governors, on others it is itself empowered to do what is necessary.

IV. CONFERENCE DIPLOMACY—THE HUMAN SETTING

The human setting of international conferences is made up of a great many factors varying from political to intensely personal reactions which may affect delegations' positions at the start as well as during the conference. The specific influence of presiding officers is discussed in chapter V and that of the secretariats and their executive heads in chapter VI.

In section 1 the conference setting is discussed against the background of the dominant feature of the conference: cooperation or conflict.

In section 2 some principal categories of conflict or cooperation are reviewed: political conflicts, economic controversies, disagreements on budgets and work programmes, election struggles.

Section 3 draws the attention to confidence, anger and other human emotions as factors in conference diplomacy.

In most conferences some lead, and others follow. The question of leadership is examined in section 4.

The rules of procedure of most conferences establish whether meetings shall be open to the public or not. The formal decision on public or private meetings may, however, deviate from the degree of publicity actually surrounding a conference. The varying possibilities will be discussed in section 5.

1. *Cooperation or conflict*

In principle international conferences are supposed to serve—in various forms—international cooperation, i.e. cooperation between sovereign governments.[1] In practice conflicts of various types are found at conferences:

(*a*) A conflict may be related to a question on the agenda of a conference, with no or only some cooperation towards its solution forthcoming. Certain of the international disputes which for years have been before the U.N. Security Council and the U.N. General Assembly fall into this category. Partial cooperation could consist in some agreed activity to mitigate the effects of a conflict, such as the sending of a U.N. observer group or the stationing of a military force.

A conflict between two states brought before the Security Council may have the effect of some countries siding with one party to the conflict, some with the other party and some staying neutral. If the Great Powers, which each have a veto in the Security Council, are divided, no international cooperative action is possible, and one can say that on top of the conflict between the countries directly concerned, a second conflict between others has been created. Alternatively, the Great Powers and with them a majority of the Security Council may be able to agree on some action, even though the basic conflict remains unsolved. The agreement on the U.N. Peacekeeping Force in Cyprus is an example.

In the economic sphere the existence of so-called residual quantitative restrictions on imports, contrary to the rules of the General Agreement on Tariffs and Trade, has created and maintained a conflict between countries imposing these restrictions and those opposing them. Some cooperative mitigation of this conflict has taken place through the willingness of most countries concerned to examine jointly in the GATT framework the effect of these restrictions and the possibilities of removing them.

(*b*) Without being explicitly on the agenda, a conflict can become apparent during a conference by severe disagreement on the fundamental aspects of a question or inability to agree on a text even though the substance of the matter is agreed. The disagreement thus arisen may disappear after a longer or shorter period. Exceptionally, a conflict may lead to the premature ending of a conference: in 1964, the ITU African Broadcasting Conference had to end when the Secretariat withdrew its services from the conference after a vote, which the Secretariat considered illegal, to exclude two countries from participation.

(*c*) Dissension may break out during a conference on a procedural matter, or between two delegations because one delegation had made an observation to which the other delegation takes exception. In most cases this category of conflicts can and will be solved during the same conference session.

Conflicts of the sort mentioned under (*b*) and (*c*) can be avoided by prior agreement between the principal countries concerned, and with the cooperation of the chairman and the secretariat, on how to deal with certain disputed questions. For example, at the annual plenary sessions of the Economic Commission for Europe there has been advance understanding between the Eastern and the Western members that two speakers (from Eastern European Countries) will speak in favour of attendance by the German Democratic Republic (not recognized as a state by the Western countries), and two other speakers (from Western countries) against such attendance. These statements are summarized in the report; no vote is taken. At the beginning of the 1956 Statute Conference on the International Atomic Energy Agency it was informally arranged between the United States and the Soviet Union that the question of attendance by the People's Republic of China would be briefly dealt with through a few statements for the record. Thus a long and probably acrimonious debate, and possible voting were avoided, and the harmonious atmosphere which characterized that conference was not endangered.

It is important to distinguish between "pre-fabricated" disagreement on issues for which delegates are prepared to agree to disagree and sudden, unexpected anger about some non-anticipated incident or speech. It is this latter type of anger that can play havoc with the efficient conduct of conference diplomacy.

The intensity of a conference conflict or disagreement is influenced by psychological factors. Elements of mass psychology play an important role: the strong feelings of a few may easily capture those of the group to which they belong or even of participants belonging to other groups. In this connection the harmonious small conference, with friendliness the dominating feeling, is remarkably different from the large conference, where strong feelings, expressed vigorously, reflect diametrically opposed positions of delegations or groups of delegations.

The psychological atmosphere of a conference will be strongly influenced by the mood in which delegations arrive. If no severe differences of position exist on the more important points of the agenda, the conference can start on a harmonious note. Barring dissensions during the course of the conference, such a feeling of harmony becomes a factor in its own right. "Let us not disturb the friendly atmosphere of this conference" will be the prevailing thought to be encountered in informal lobby conversations or in formal statements in the conference.

A continuously peaceful conference may be an inactive one, where many decisions are postponed. Some of the Economic and Social Council conferences in the period 1959-1965 seemed on a sizeable portion of the agenda imbued by such a spirit of "false harmony". During those years, several initiatives which might have started in ECOSOC came from the General Assembly.

The distrust of some of the new U.N. member countries not represented on the Council and the tendency of some of the specialized agencies to consider the Council a bothersome organ whose incessant calls for "coordination" were unnecessary, jointly caused the relative inaction I have called "false harmony". An objective analytic inquiry would probably show that even in its less active years the Economic and Social Council produced certain initiatives and performed numerous tasks which, although more or less routine, were indispensable to the smooth functioning of the United Nations system.

2. *Some principal categories of conflict*

a. *Political conflicts: the clash of the angry*

Within the U.N. conference system the U.N. General Assembly and even more specifically the U.N. Security Council are the organs where political conflicts are discussed, and occasionally brought to a satisfactory solution. It is hardly necessary to recall the wide variety of political disputes, some of them accompanied by armed intervention, which have come before the world forum. Any of these conflicts may be brought before the Security Council as a threat to the peace, breach of the peace, or act of aggression. The position of each government confronted in a conference with the need to take a position on a political conflict will be influenced by a series of considerations and factors, some of which are:
—whether the government is somehow involved in the conflict, for example through a treaty of friendship or mutual assistance with one of the conflict countries, or because of geographic proximity;
—whether its parliament and public opinion take a vivid interest in the question;
—whether it feels that it must try to play a mediating role;
—whether it has an established standard policy which it wishes to apply to the conflict (for example in regard to colonial questions).

b. *Economic conflicts: the rich and the poor*

Many disagreements in contemporary conferences are caused by differing views on how to deal with various aspects of the problem of accelerating the economic development of less-developed countries. Proposals are often made in regard to trade, aid or domestic economic policies, to be followed by developed countries. Even though the adoption of such proposals means legally no more than the adoption of a recommendation, not binding on governments, many developed countries do not wish to accept recommendations which, they fear, if followed up, will limit their freedom of action too much or impose policies or financial burdens which are deemed unacceptable.

A good example of such non-binding recommendations can be found in the so-called "General and special principles to govern international trade relations and trade policies conductive to development" discussed and voted upon at the first UNCTAD Conference (Geneva, 1964). Each of these was voted upon separately. Although by and large less-developed countries voted in favour and developed countries sometimes in favour, while at other times they abstained or voted against, there was no uniform voting pattern. On certain principles one found a few less-developed countries among the abstainers. Bloc and group cohesion was strong for the less-developed countries and the Soviet bloc, but much less for the Western developed[2] countries.

Disagreements at intergovernmental conferences on problems of less-developed countries also illustrate clearly the clash between what many, if not all, governments admit is desirable in the long run, and what is possible in the short run. Taking a long term point of view almost everybody would agree that liberal trade policies of developed countries permitting maximum exports of less-developed countries are desirable, and that the flow of public and private funds to less-developed countries must be increased. Hence, recommendations to this effect would seem logical. Yet, in the actual formulation of such recommendations (whether in the U.N., GATT, UNCTAD or elsewhere), all sorts of short-term political, economic (protection of one's own industrial and agrarian interests) and financial (budgetary limitations) constraints cause difficulties. The result is that recommendations concerning less-developed countries in intergovernmental organs are often couched in general terms: the more general the formulation is, the larger the built-in escape clause for those who do not want to follow up the recommendation. For example, general exhortations to increase the flow of funds to less-developed countries easily found unanimous support, and appeals that such flow must constitute 1% of the total national income of all developed countries caused some difficulty, but gradually found common acceptance. However, a recommendation that each economically advanced country, taken separately, should endeavour to supply financial resources, as nearly as possible amounting to 1% of its national income was adopted (Annex A. IV. 2, part III, to Final Act) at the first UNCTAD Conference, only after prolonged discussion and negotiation, and then only on the understanding that the flow of funds to which the recommendation referred included not only transfers by governments, but also private investments.

c. *Budgets and work programmes: the programmatic versus the budgetary approach*

The average delegate to conferences of the United Nations, the specialized agencies or other organizations will often find himself confronted with budgets and work programmes in the general sense, i.e. a budget or work programme for a specific period covering all or most activities of the organization in question. Usually the "budget and work programme for the year. . ." has first been drafted by the secretariat, is then submitted in the name of the head of the secretariat to a body which in an advisory or in a decision-making capacity approves the budget and programme, after possible amendments. It then goes to the plenary organ for final approval. In the World Health Organization the sequence is that a draft programme and budget, divided by regions, for say 1969, goes first to the various regional organizations of WHO which meet in the autumn of 1967, then in January 1968 to the Executive Board, which gives an opinion on the programme and budget. Finally, the programme and budget are submitted by the Director-General, in the month of May 1968 in our example, to the World Health Assembly, which has a Committee on Programme and Budget. In the ILO it is the Governing Body which approves the programme of activities and the budget. It is submitted to the annual Conference for final approval. In the United Nations itself programmes emanate from a large number of separate organs, including ECOSOC, the General Assembly and many committees coming under one of these two principal United Nations organs, including the regional economic commissions. The financial implications of all U.N. programmes come before the Fifth (Budget and Finance) Committee of the General Assembly in the form of a large document entitled "Budget Estimates for the Financial Year . . . and Information Annexes". After publication this document is supplemented by separate "Supplementary budget estimates", each of them the result of a programme recommendation in some organ. All these budget proposals are first considered in a small committee of experts (elected by the General Assembly) called the Advisory Committee on Administrative and Budgetary Questions (ACABQ), which reports its comments on the secretariat proposals to the Fifth Committee.

Different motives affect the position of delegations on programmes and budgets:

(*i*) programmatic considerations will lead delegations to support or oppose a proposal. For example, population questions, including birth control, have come into the foreground in recent years in several intergovernmental organizations (especially the U.N., WHO). Some governments have opposed far-going activities, such as technical assistance on birth control, family planning and related matters, on the ground that international organizations should not get involved in what to them seemed a delicate matter, with political and religious implications. To others, the pressing problem of overpopulation in certain areas of the world was of overriding importance and called for concerted international action.

Certain countries will give priority consideration to the programme aspects of any proposed new activity. For them the financial implications are secondary.

(*ii*) Distinctly opposed to the programmatic, sometimes called the functional approach, is one which gives priority to budgetary and financial considerations. Certain governments, for example, believe that the annual percentage increase of the budgets of international organizations should be limited in some way, for instance by linking it to the annual average national income increase of a representative group of countries, or simply by prescribing a fixed percentage ceiling which normally cannot be exceeded. It has in the course of time become evident that, with inflation or in any case continuing price increases having become a normal feature of to-day's world, the budgets of intergovernmental organizations show annual increases even without any expansion of their programmes and activities. These are called the "mandatory increases", since they relate to inevitable rises in salaries and other costs. In most organizations contracts carry a clause providing for salary increases geared to the rise in the cost of living.

A minority vote against a programme or budget adopted by a large majority has not much more than symbolic significance in organizations where members' shares of the budget are assessed according to a predetermined mandatory scale. The negative vote does not liberate the member from his obligations.

In voluntarily financed programmes, i.e. programmes for which annually (or with some other periodicity) a so-called pledging conference for the announcement of voluntary governmental contributions is held, governments which feel that the programme is going in the wrong direction may diminish or at least not increase their contribution for the next year. These programmes depend on the confidence of the principal contributing governments. It is therefore no coincidence that voting takes place only exceptionally in the committees administering such voluntary programmes (the Governing Council of the U.N. Development Programme, the UNICEF Executive Board, the Executive Committee for the Programme of the U.N. High Commissioner for Refugees, the UN/FAO Intergovernmental Committee for the World Food Programme).

d. *Elections*

Elections give rise to some of the fiercest contests of conference diplomacy, involving personal reputations and/or governmental aspirations and prestige. Perhaps this is also because the issue is usually fairly simple and does not call for the elaboration of a draft resolution or the approval of expenditures. Also, in the case of an election the decision, by whatever majority achieved, is certain to be implemented. This contrasts with a resolution on any subject adopted with a small majority as a result of which implementation will often run into difficulties. Experience shows that the mere fact of having been elected by a small majority does not have adverse consequences.

Most campaigns for elections to some disputed office or seat have the common characteristic of starting well in advance of the actual election time. Yet the government wishing to push a candidate must be careful not only to start its campaign not too late, but also not to start too early, in order to avoid "over-campaigning" which may provoke irritation. Also, a candidature advanced too early leaves ample time for competing candidatures to come forward. A sense of timing is therefore all-important. If the candidate is personally and favourably known to the electoral body, he has an advantage over any competing candidate who is only known by description, reputation, the propaganda efforts of his sponsors and possible adverse comments of any opponents.

The government which starts a campaign to have Mr. X elected (to whatever office) must not only point out his personal qualifications, but also stress other reasons which make it logical and desirable that Mr. X be elected, such as the fact that the government in question has never had a citizen occupying the post to which it aspires. If the candidature is solidly backed up by a group to which the person or country belongs, the group may be able to advance some of the same arguments. When Romania submitted, well in advance of the 22nd session of the U.N. General Assembly the candidature of its Foreign Minister for election to President of that session, it was strongly supported by the group of socialist countries (the Soviet Union and its allies), which was able to stress that never had anyone from its group been elected to the elevated position of President of the General Assembly.

Elections to bodies with a restricted membership, where a country may compete with seven other countries for five posts, require very careful manoeuvering. Usually there is a requirement that those elected must have at least the simple majority of all "present and voting". In the case of election of the non-permanent members of the Security Council and of the members of the Economic and Social

Council a two-thirds majority of the G.A. is required. This has led to some election contests for seats on the Security Council, where even after several ballots neither of two candidates had obtained the required majority. In the end after the President's mediation a compromise solution was found where two countries would split the two-year term normally applicable to non-permanent members of the Security Council. Governments which are candidates for a restricted membership body will carefully weigh their chances. Sometimes it is deemed wiser to withdraw at the last moment rather than risk defeat and "lose face". If such withdrawal is partly caused by heavy pressure from other governments, the country may be able to obtain informal promises of support at a future election of the same kind. Once defeated, it is too late to obtain such promises. An example was the election for the presidency of the General Assembly for the 1957 session, when at the last moment the candidature of Dr C. Malik (Lebanon) was withdrawn at the request of several important governments. The next year Dr Malik was elected, having had promises of support from many countries.

A recent development is the application of election procedures to the choice between different locations for headquarters of international organizations. This started in relation to UNCTAD (see p. 88) and was repeated when the headquarters of UNIDO (United Nations Industrial Development Organization) were chosen at the 21st session of the General Assembly.

A relatively new election method is for a basic resolution to provide exactly how many states from a certain region or from a certain economic grouping should be members of a restricted-membership body. In regard to the Governing Council of the U.N. Special Fund General Assembly resolution 1240 (XII) directed that its membership should be equally divided between economically more developed countries, having due regard to their contributions to the Fund, and less-developed countries, taking into account the need for equitable geographic distribution among the latter members. The elections for this body (now merged with the Technical Assistance Committee into a single Governing Council of the U.N. Development Programme) therefore took place in two phases, separately for each of the two groups.

In chapter X we shall see examples of groups functioning for the specific purpose of furnishing candidates for membership of certain bodies.

3. *Confidence and anger*

Confidence is probably the most important human feeling directly affecting the course of a conference. The 18th century writer François de Callières, in his *De la manière de négocier avec les Souverains,* (1716) already stated that open dealing is the basis of confidence and that sound diplomacy was to be based on the creation of confidence. The following categories of confidence can be picked out, and are likely to affect the conduct of conference diplomacy:

(*a*) Confidence of delegations in each other. The degree to which such confidence exists is influenced by the state of relations between the governments of these delegations and by the personal contacts between heads (and members) of delegations. For example, two governments may be on pretty bad terms, may perhaps have broken off diplomatic relations; yet if the heads of their delegations to a conference happen to have known each other for years, a certain amount of confidence and trust may come to exist at that particular conference between the two delegations.

(*b*) Confidence in the presiding officer. If the chairman is trusted, his decisions will be respected more easily than if he is distrusted.

(*c*) Confidence in the secretariat. If certain delegations do not have confidence in the secretariat, believing for example that it systematically tries to favour certain other delegations, latent or open disagreement between delegations will be fostered. Reports or other documents emanating from a secretariat which is not wholly trusted by certain delegations, are scrutinized much more critically and lengthily. On the other hand, a secretariat that has the full confidence of all delegations can have considerable influence towards cooperative action of the conference.

Confidence is a psychological trait which can exist as a collective feature of a conference. Ideally confidence emanates from the conference as a whole and is reflected in the behaviour of individual delegations.

Most emotional outbursts at international conferences will come from the individual delegates and then—sometimes—spread over the conference. Annoyance may start by something small. A delegate may have included in a statement some—in his own eyes—relatively minor critical observation on the deeds or inactions of another government. The delegate of the criticized government may react with vigor and soon an antagonistic debate breaks out. Resentment can arise not only between individual delegations, but also between groups of delegations. During meetings in 1965 and 1966 of the U.N. Trade and Development Board (permanent organ of UNCTAD) accusations were made mutually between the developed countries as a group and the less-developed countries as a group. The latter felt strongly that the developed countries were not doing enough to implement the recommendations of the 1964 United Nations Conference on Trade and Development. The developed countries as a group felt that the less-developed countries were giving too much attention to this question of implementation and that there were other more urgent tasks with which the Board should deal. Caustic arguments were made by both sides leading to a bad atmosphere.

From irritation to anger is mostly a matter of how intensely feelings are hurt. At the 1963 General Conference of the International Labour Organization anger erupted among delegates from African countries when the employers' representative of the Union of South Africa contrary to their wishes (but in conformity with the rules of procedure) was allowed to speak. In protest they left the conference room. The president resigned and a new president was elected.

Caution and fervour are two other emotional traits of importance in conference diplomacy. A general atmosphere of caution will impress upon a conference its own stamp of relative inaction, just as a general atmosphere of fervour, of enthousiasm, can produce constructive results.

4. *Leadership*

Conference diplomacy is directly and often decisively influenced by the exercise of leadership. Leadership in conference diplomacy can be defined as taking the lead towards realizing or preventing some specific objective within the framework of an intergovernmental conference. It can be exercised by delegations individually, by the president of the conference, by an "inner circle", by groups of delegations, by the secretariat, or by some combination of these. It must be stressed that not every intergovernmental conference produces examples of leadership. Many intergovernmental conferences accomplish (or fail to accomplish) their task without any recognizable leadership actively pushing and pulling the conference on its path. In such cases it is the chairman, or the chairman with the secretariat, who actually are leading the conference. Some of the leadership situations in conference diplomacy follow:

a. *Leadership by individual delegations*

A delegation which introduces a proposal in a conference and sees it through to a successful conclusion by having it adopted can be said to have exercised leadership. Leadership by an individual delegation can make itself felt if the proposal put forward is so attractive to the conference membership and so well formulated that it has easy sailing, even though the form in which it is finally adopted may, after amendments, differ from the original proposal. The essential contents, however, must have been maintained, or one cannot speak of a successful conclusion. Single-delegation-proposals of the sort here discussed are often proposals for studies of some kind, with appropriate action only following later.

Intellectual leadership of a single delegation can be combined with a financial donation to implement the idea in the proposal. An example is an initiative of the Netherlands Government, which proposed in 1962 that the U.N. should give more attention to studying the relationships between economic and social development. It offered an amount of $ 1 million to finance research to be done by a special institute in this field. This initiative was welcomed by the General Assembly and ECOSOC. The result was the establishment of a semi-autonomous U.N. Research Institute for Social Development (Geneva) which started its work early 1964. The amount offered sufficed for the first three years. Towards the end of that period its work had proved so important that other Governments took over the financing of the Institute, to enable it to continue its work. A single-delegation-initiative can thus trigger off continuous support by other countries.

A clear example of a successful single-nation-initiative was that of Ireland at the 16th session of the General Assembly (1961) on the prevention of the wider dissemination of nuclear arms. With a letter of August 16, 1961, the Government of Ireland had asked for the inscription of a special agenda item on this subject. In conformity with rule 14 of the General Assembly the item was automatically placed on the agenda. On November 17, 1961 the delegation of Ireland tabled a draft resolution, calling on all States, in particular those possessing nuclear weapons, to use their best endeavours to secure the conclusion of an international agreement under which the nuclear States would refrain from relinquishing control of nuclear weapons and from transmitting the information necessary for their manufacture to non-nuclear States, and under which the latter would undertake not to manufacture or otherwise acquire control of such weapons. The resolution came up for discussion in the First Committee of the General Assembly on November 30, 1961, in the two meetings held that day. After an oral introduction by the representative of Ireland, several speakers indicated their agreement with the draft resolution. At the end of the discussion the chairman did not have to ask for a vote: he noted that in the absence of any objection the Irish draft resolution would be considered as adopted unanimously. On December 4 the plenary session of the Assembly acted likewise (resolution 1665 (XVI)). It was in later discussions always referred to as "the Irish resolution". When on August 24, 1967 the United States tabled in the ENDC a draft non-proliferation treaty, the text of which had been negotiated with the Soviet Union, the United States representative referred to the unanimous adoption of the Irish resolution as "an important initial milestone" (ENDC/PV. 325). This initiative brought the Irish Government no other benefits than a certain amount of prestige and the satisfaction of seeing one's proposal adopted; it shows how a small nation can be successful in conference diplomacy if it comes with the right proposal at the right time.

b. *Leadership by the president*

The president of a conference can exercise considerable leadership in a variety of ways: by effective chairmanship, by insisting on the observation of time schedules for plenary and committee meetings, by picking the right moment for the establishment of informal groups to negotiate on a disputed issue or proposal, by acting as mediator. We revert to this role in chapter V.

c. *Leadership by an "inner circle"*

Inner circles, although formally consisting of delegations (or occasionally delegations plus secretariat) exist frequently as a group of individuals who, by their experience and through the activity of their delegations, exercise leadership in a conference. ECOSOC during the years 1950-1960 had such an inner circle of delegates who had been coming back year after year, knew each other well, trusted each other, and discussed new initiatives and the best way they could be handled. With the expansion of ECOSOC membership, first through the widening of the membership of its sessional (Economic, Social and Co-ordination) committees by nine countries, and then of the Council as a whole after ratification of the Charter amendment (increasing its membership from 18 to 27), the old inner circle was gradually replaced by a new one.

In conferences held to negotiate an international convention or treaty, possibly establishing a new international organization, the delegations of countries which have been members of a preparatory committee will often become a kind of inner circle trying to steer the conference in a certain direction. This was for example the case with the Statute Conference of the International Atomic Energy Agency. A Preparatory Committee of 8 (later 12) members had prepared a draft statute which was submitted to the conference, attended by 82 countries. Not unnaturally the governments which had been members of the Preparatory Committee felt that they had a certain responsibility to make "their" draft acceptable to the conference. This made them into an inner circle at the conference.

d. *Leadership by groups; the activity of "fire brigades"*

Increasingly groups of various kinds submit proposals or take other initiatives in intergovernmental conferences. Chapter IX discusses in some detail the functioning of groups in conference diplomacy. Here it is necessary to acknowledge their role as leaders in conference diplomacy. A special kind of grouping, somewhat overlapping with an inner circle, is the one often referred to as a "fire brigade": an *ad hoc* group of delegations which in a severely violent conflict makes efforts to obtain a compromise solution, or at least the agreement of the disputing parties to some set of interim measures. The term became generally used after the successful efforts of Canada and the Scandinavian countries to obtain General Assembly approval for the creation of the U.N. Emergency Force after the Suez crisis of 1956.

e. *Leadership by the secretariat*

In many conferences the secretariat is the dominating actor, preparing and influencing decisions to be taken. The secretariat leads, the delegations (governments) follow. This indeed is more and more common in conferences held under the auspices of an organization with a permanent secretariat. As the organization grows more complex and the membership bigger, the secretariat represents the permanent force, able to prepare accurately those decisions which delegations are expected to take. In some conferences the secretariat will also provide chairmen of meetings. This is frequently the case in meetings of the General Agreement on Tariffs and Trade. In chapter VI the role of secretariats in conference diplomacy is dealt with more fully.

5. *Publicity*

Conference diplomacy is equated by many observers with open, public diplomacy. The outsider can easily be misled into believing that conference diplomacy means the full application of the first of President Wilson's famous fourteen points: "Open covenants of peace, openly arrived at, after which there shall be no private international understandings of any kind but diplomacy shall proceed always frankly and in the public view".[3]

In actual fact conference diplomacy is conducted at least as much in private as in public.

The publicity surrounding many intergovernmental conferences has provoked a great deal of criticism, along the lines of the following view given by Nicolson: "These conferences do little to satisfy the vague desire for what is called 'open diplomacy'; but they do much to diminish the utility of professional diplomatists and, in that they entail much publicity, many rumours, and wide speculation,—in that they tempt politicians to achieve quick, spectacular and often fictitious results,—they tend to promote rather than allay suspicion, and to create those very states of uncertainty which it is the purpose of good diplomatic method to prevent".[4]

This view overlooks the fact that public intergovernmental conferences can very well provide the stage for the practice of "quiet diplomacy". As Hammarskjöld wrote in 1959: "The experiences of the past thirteen years have demonstrated that there is need to redress the balance between the public and private procedures of the United Nations if we are to make better progress in peace-making. By private procedures I mean the methods of classical diplomacy as applied within the new framework provided by the Charter and the institutions of the world organization".[5] The U.N. Scientific Advisory Committee (on which seven nuclear scientists sit and advise on the peaceful uses of atomic energy) and the Advisory Committee on the United Nations Emergency Force (which gave advice to the Secretary-General on the activities of that force which for several years helped to keep the armistice line between the United Arab Republic and Israel more or less calm) were examples of the injection of quiet methods into United Nations diplomacy.

The principal objectives which delegations may have in transmitting information to public information media are:

(a) transmitting information will very often serve the simple purpose of "public relations" of the delegation, in order to improve its image in the country where the conference is held, in its own country, or in the world in general.

(b) A delegation will transmit its point of view to the press with the specific purpose of getting favourable comments, and so improving its negotiating position. Or it may try to give unfavourable information on one or more other delegations whose unreasonable position is criticized. This sort of attempt to influence the press was frequent during the latter stages of the 1964-1967 GATT trade negotiations (the so-called Kennedy Round).

(c) A delegation transmits a specific piece of information containing a suggestion or proposal as to how to deal with a certain question. The idea is that delegations of other countries will react to such a "feeler", or "trial balloon" through comments similarly given to the press. This avoids, at least temporarily, a direct confrontation in a negotiation. The method may also be useful in a situation preceding possible negotiations, or where diplomatic contacts are non-existant or difficult. For example, after the war of June 1967 between Israel and the Arab States various spokesmen for Israel made public statements on how to deal with the problem of establishing peace with the Arab countries. The type of reactions which these statements produced could provide provisional guidelines as to the sort of negotiating framework and possible solutions for this problem.

In practice each conference has its own particular "mix" of publicity and privacy. It is important to look at the actual situation of each conference, which may not correspond to its official status. A conference open to the public may in practice attract no attention whatsoever, and therefore in fact resemble a private meeting. A conference closed to the public may be so widely reported through public information media, that it thereby becomes "public". The following situations represent some of the practical possibilities:

a. *Conference completely open to the public; informational media active*

Under this category come the General Assembly and the Security Council of the United Nations and certain parts of the all-membership conferences of the specialized agencies. The public is free to attend such conferences in the public galleries. The press covers the proceedings, in particular if there is a severely disputed question under discussion.

b. *The conference is public; informational media give only limited attention*

A large number, probably most, meetings in the U.N. system are public, but rarely attract the attention of the informational media, except perhaps for brief notices at the beginning or the end of a conference. Most meetings of the Committees of the U.N. General Assembly, the Economic and Social Council, the plenary conferences of the specialized agencies, and many *ad hoc* conferences of various kinds fall in this category. Of course an occasional agenda item or an acrimonious political discussion may attract so much attention that the situation described under (a) prevails.

c. *Public and informational media not admitted; access to conference limited to participating and observer governments and accredited non-governmental organizations*

This group comprises certain committees of the United Nations and the specialized agencies. Examples are the subcommittees of the Economic Commission for Europe and other regional commissions (their plenary sessions are public), committees of the Governing Body of the International Labour Organization (sessions of the Governing Body itself are public), the Council of the Intergovernmental Committee for European Migration. Non-governmental organizations play an important role in certain conferences and organizations, for example those related to refugee work, to human rights and to health questions. Sometimes special arrangements are made to consult the non-governmental organizations. During the 11th session of the Intergovernmental Committee for the World Food Programme (Rome, 1967), a special meeting was organized to enable the government representatives to meet with four non-governmental organizations cooperating with the WFP.

d. *Access only to participating governments; public information media kept actively informed by delegations*

A typical example is the Conference of the Eighteen-Nation Disarmament Committee. It meets in private, but much publicity surrounds its proceedings, because delegations hand out texts of their statements to the press as well as background information. In the case of the ENDC provisional verbatim records are kept private pending possible correction, after which the final records are released for public circulation. Meetings of the EEC Council of Ministers, although closed to all but the participating governments, are extensively reported in the press.

e. *Access only to participating and observer governments and accredited intergovernmental organizations; occasional press coverage*

This category comprises negotiating conferences with a specific objective, such as the trade negotiations conferences held under auspices of the General Agreement on Tariffs and Trade and the commodity agreement conferences held under U.N. auspices. The difference with the conferences under (d) is that these conferences are fully confidential. No communication to the press is supposed to take place, except through press releases agreed at the conference, usually at the end. Yet in practice leaks to the press, emanating from delegations, are not exceptional, as will be seen in Chapter XI.

V. THE ROLE OF PRESIDING OFFICERS

1. *General characteristics of presiding officers* [1]

The ferocity with which many governments and sometimes individuals pursue the election of chairmen of an international conference or committee could give the impression that the position of presiding officer denotes enormous power, influence and prestige. In fact, the position of chairman bestows—in varying degrees, depending among other things on the importance of the conference—prestige and honour on the person and his country. However, the amount of power and influence of presiding officers is, as a rule, rather limited.

The importance of a chairman's role is governed by the following factors:

—the experience and intelligence of the chairman, including his grasp of the rules of procedure;

—the degree to which the delegates constitute a homogeneous group vis-à-vis the subject matter before the meeting, or are antagonists whether politically, or in relation to the substance of matters to be discussed.

—whether the chairman can operate as a team with the secretariat, the vice-chairmen, and the rapporteur.

The ideal chairman is able to keep delegates' statements within reasonable length, limits himself to an occasional observation in order to remind delegates of the subject before them, will summarize occasionally but not too frequently lest he be accused of talking too much. The good chairman will also give rapid and correct rulings on procedural questions. He will keep in touch with delegates through conversations before and after sessions, in informal meetings at which he may be present, and at the various social events to which he is invited or which he himself organizes. If there are a number of committees or subcommittees functioning under his supervision, he will see to it that he keeps in touch with these committee chairmen.

During the U.N. General Assembly session the President has a weekly business luncheon with the chairmen of the Main Committees. Usually the Secretary-General and a few other secretariat members also attend. A. W. Cordier, who was for many years one of the main organizers of General Assembly sessions, has commented on these luncheons: "This instrument has proved, under active Presidents, to be most helpful. Each of the chairmen gives an oral report on the current work of his Committee and sets forth some of the problems that the Committee faces and upon which he may want guidance".[2]

Jessup defined the requirements for a president: "A skillful presiding officer seeks to avoid clashes in which his authority is challenged, but there is a nice line between the role of a firm and persuasive conciliator and that of the timid wavering chairman who always seeks to throw the responsibility to the group which is sure to speak with discordant voices. The wise and experienced chairman usually can 'feel' the temper of the meeting and will known when to assert his authority firmly and when to allow a procedural discussion to continue until a solution emerges. He should be able to detect the difference between a sincere argument about the procedure which the delegate believes will lead to the most satisfactory disposition of the business before the meeting, and the tactics of obstruction or the stubborn insistence upon a point of view which the delegate will not abandon but which the group clearly will not accept. The more the chairman allows himself to be drawn into controversy, the less does he act in a judicial capacity and the less successful he is apt to be in discharging his duties".[3] Or, as another observer said in regard to the U.N. General Assembly: "It is difficult to exaggerate the extent to which good chairmanship can facilitate, and bad chairmanship can obstruct, the work of the Assembly. It is true that a good chairman cannot prevent a United Nations organ from getting into a procedural tangle on occasions, since some procedural situations that arise are unpredictable and complicated. But an incompetent presiding officer can, singlehandedly, create procedural chaos if he does not understand the Rules, or does not enforce them, or acts in a dictatorial or partisan manner".[4]

Once elected, the chairman is "denationalized": he does not vote, another member of his delegation takes his place as head of the delegation (if he was the head) and he has to serve the collective membership of the conference which has elected him to his office. Yet in practice it happens fairly frequently that a president finds it embarrassing to accord the right to speak to a delegate representing a government not recognized by his own government. The usual method of getting round this obstacle is that the president asks one of the vice-presidents for whom this difficulty does not exist, to take his place.

The vice-president's only statutory function is to be available to replace the president, a vice-president acting as president having the same powers and duties as the president. The president together with the vice-presidents and any rapporteurs constitute the "bureau" of the conference. The significance of the bureau varies from conference to conference. In the case of the U.N. General Assembly the President, the Vice-Presidents, and the chairmen of the seven Main Committees constitute the General Committee. Its main task is to make recommendations with regard to the agenda and to the organization of the session (rules 38 to 44 of the General Assembly).

In small conferences, it is not wholly unusual for the chairman to continue to represent his government. If and when he speaks as his country's delegate, he has to make this quite clear.

In the Security Council the presidency rotates monthly in the English alphabetical order of the member countries of the Council. It has become customary for the president to continue to represent his own country. Rule 20 of the (still provisional) rules of procedure of the Security Council stipulates that the President must temporarily vacate the chair whenever he deems that for the proper fulfilment of the responsibilities of the presidency he should not preside over the Council during consideration of an item with which the country he represents is directly connected. This rule has occasionally been applied and has in some instances given rise to difficulties, when a president was challenged by a member to withdraw from the chair, and refused to do so.[5]

A special situation exists when apart from the presiding officers there are so-called co-chairmen constituting a steering committee. Chapter XI will give examples.

Occasionally the chairman is not the representative of a government, but a secretariat official, possibly the head of the secretariat. Normally this is proposed by a delegation. However, the statute of the IBRD provides that meetings of the Executive Board will always be chaired by the President of the Bank, who is the head of its staff. As will be seen in chapter XI, committees formed in connection with the GATT trade negotiations have been presided over by GATT secretariat officials. A secretariat official functioning as chairman probably operates under even more restraints than a chairman elected from among the delegates, since any error he commits can backfire and lessen confidence in him or his secretariat. Also the possibility for the chairman to turn to the head of the secretariat, usually sitting at his side, for authoritative advice, has *ipso facto* disappeared when the secretariat head is himself the chairman.

In analysing the functions of a chairman, it is useful to distinguish between those which follow directly from the rules of procedure of the conference, and those, of a more substantive nature, not usually provided for in the rules of procedure. Functions derived from the rules of procedure, i.e. from the chairman's role as presiding officer, will be referred to as *procedural functions,* while those which do not follow from the rules of procedure will be called his *substantive functions*. The latter are mostly related to assistance in solving conflicts between delegations.

2. *Procedural functions*

The procedural functions of a presiding officer can be divided in duties and rights.

His duties comprise the opening, closing, or adjourning of meetings, "giving the floor" to delegates (i.e. allowing them to speak), the prompt ruling on any points of order made. Among the rights of a chairman can be included the general power to make proposals for the efficient conduct of business, the calling to order of speakers who are wandering too far from the item under consideration. Unlike certain national parliaments, the presiding officers in the U.N. system of organizations have little disciplinary power. An exception is the ILO where, as will be seen in the analysis starting on p. 92, the President may require a speaker who is making irrelevant remarks to stop speaking.

In a normal meeting of an average U.N. organ, there is no great problem in assuring the orderly development of the conference. Over the years the rules of procedure of the General Assembly have come to serve as a model for not only other U.N. organs, but also for most specialized agencies. This has gradually introduced an amount of uniformity and procedural stability that has greatly facilitated the task of presiding officers.

Although mostly not specifically provided for in the rules of procedure, presiding officers will also maintain external order in public meetings, seeing to it that the public does not interfere with the orderly behaviour of a meeting. If there are demonstrations on the public gallery, the president appeals for calm, and if this appeal is not heeded, he may close the meeting to the public.

Another presidential function which is more implicit than explicit in the rules of procedure of most organs, is that of replying to requests for clarification from individual delegates. Such a request may simply relate to the order in which questions will be taken up or, more importantly, to questions of voting. Fairly frequent is the question, just before voting: 'Mr. Chairman, I am sorry, but can you repeat once again what exactly we are going to vote on?' Well known is the case of a motion for division, i.e. a motion to vote separately on some disputed part of a draft resolution (see p. 33). Such a motion may itself be put to the vote (G.A. rule 91), in which case the chairman has to explain that because the vote is not directly on the text, those who are in favour of retaining the words in question must vote 'no' and those against 'yes'.

In an average quiet conference, the presiding officer operates somewhat as follows: once he has been elected (and after a vice-chairman and possibly a rapporteur have been elected) he announces, after advice from the secretariat, which in turn is based on consultations with delegations, the plan for the conference. In many conferences an arrangement of business is proposed in a secretariat document. Unless already taken care of by an earlier decision or by well established tradition, he may then discuss with the conference whether or not any sessional committees or working parties should be set up. If there are already previously determined deadlines for the submission of draft proposals, he will remind delegates of such deadlines. He then takes up the items of the agenda in their numerical order, unless, as often happens, there is agreement to modify this order or to combine certain agenda items. Certain items require little or no debate, others more, some end up with a formal resolution with or without voting, others with a simple summing up. The chairman must know or find out how the conference prefers to deal with an agenda item. In many conferences voting on one or more draft proposals is the final stage of the consideration of an agenda item. The rules of procedure provide how voting is to be conducted. The chairman must take care to see that these rules are observed.

The chairman may at times, especially during a procedural debate, wish to consult with the secretariat. It is important that he turns off the microphone during such consultations. This will avoid the embarrassing situation found in the minutes of the second meeting of the ITU Plenipotentiary Conference (Montreux, 1965), where a delegate, protesting the fact that the chairman had interrupted another speaker, was able to say: 'An indiscreet microphone which you had not switched off let us hear the following piece of advice which was given to you: This is no question to discuss.'

The chairman will try to make sure that in announcing the order of voting on proposals or amendments, he is not going to run into protests from delegates. Sometimes such objections against the order of voting may be inevitable, in which case the chairman will immediately request the meeting to decide the matter by a vote. It can happen that a chairman shows irritation when his ruling is challenged and will "debate back" with the meeting, in an attempt to show that he is right. This, experience shows, is in the main unwise, because the protesting delegate is psychologically not in a mood to admit his error. The chairman, on the assumption that he can rely on being backed up by the meeting as a whole, does best to ask immediately for a vote on his ruling, when challenged.

The combination of disagreement between governments, the lack of a firm attitude of the secretariat and a certain amount of wavering by a chairman is a sure way of delaying decision-making. An example is provided by the discussions in the UNCTAD Board on the question of the location of the Secretariat of UNCTAD, the U.N. Conference on Trade and Development, which had been established by General Assembly resolution 1995 (XIX) of December 1964.

The effects of a wavering attitude

At its first session, held in New York in April, 1965, the Board, after considerable discussion, unanimously adopted a resolution providing for the establishment of the UNCTAD Secretariat in Geneva. After this the secretariat did not immediately move to Geneva. As a result certain governments who still preferred a site other than Geneva (Addis Abeba, Lagos, London and Rome were candidates) decided to reopen the entire question at the second Board session (Geneva, August 1965). Since the resolution on the establishment of the Secretariat in Geneva was in the nature of a "recommendation", with no binding force upon governments, there was no legal obstacle in the way of such reopening. The question was in any case included in the agenda of the second Board session under the heading "Progress Report by the Secretary-General of the Conference relating to the questions surrounding the location of the Secretariat of UNCTAD".

The debate quickly revealed that several less-developed countries wanted the Secretariat of UNCTAD to be located in a less-developed country. Others supported Geneva, in conformity with the first Board resolution, and again others implied that the capital of a large developed country, close to the centre of decision-making, might be a suitable headquarters.

The representative of Tanzania proposed at the 42nd meeting that a vote by secret ballot be taken on which capital should be the site of permanent headquarters of UNCTAD. The President then stated that the first step should be to vote on whether or not the Board could modify a previous recommendation which had been adopted unanimously. As he did not actually proceed with the vote discussion continued. At the next (43rd) meeting, the President, replying to a question, stated that the resolution of the first Board session remained valid unless and until the Board rescinded it by a formal decision. Later he added that such rescinding could be done either by explicitly annulling the previous decision to establish the Secretariat in Geneva or implicitly by adopting a resolution recommending another site. At the 44th session two draft resolutions were discussed. One, sponsored by Brazil and other countries, proposed that the Board vote to determine the Secretariat site: the vote would be in the form of an "election", the several proposed sites being "candidates". The other draft resolution, sponsored by Nigeria and the United Kingdom, proposed to postpone a decision until a later Board session.

The delegate of France then launched a proposal, in the form of a draft resolution, that there was no need to reconsider the resolution of April 1965 which had recommended Geneva as the Secretariat site and that therefore no vote should be taken on the substance of the two proposals just mentioned. He claimed priority for his proposal under rule 56(2) of the UNCTAD Board rules of procedure, according to which motions requiring that no decision be taken on the substance of proposals be considered as previous questions and be put to the vote first. The French motion was criticized by certain delegates as to form, because it was phrased as a draft resolution and not as a simple motion. Its substance was also criticized because its adoption would have been tantamount to a reaffirmation of the decision to establish UNCTAD in Geneva. To meet the first point, on which the Chairman at his own initiative might have given an immediate ruling, the French delegate —after a long discussion—reintroduced his proposal as a simple motion not to vote on the two proposals submitted. After a lengthy procedural discussion the French motion was defeated by 33 votes to 12, with 7 abstentions. On a motion of the delegate of Chile at the 44th meeting the debate was declared closed, but at the 45th session the Board decided by a vote to reopen it. Such reopening of debate after it has been closed is not provided for in the rules of procedure and therefore of doubtful legality, except according to the often heard precept: 'the Conference is the master of its own procedure'. At the 47th meeting a new combined draft resolution was submitted by the group of 31 less-developed countries represented on the UNCTAD Board, proposing that new offers for a Secretariat site were to be submitted till September 30, 1965, and that the Board should meet on October 28, 1965, to elect a site from among the ones proposed. The previous drafts (of Nigeria and United Kingdom, and of Brazil c.s.) were withdrawn and the 31-power-draft was finally adopted with 47 votes to none, and 5 abstentions.[6]

The discussion of this question was interrupted several times by procedural votes. The Chairman, with a few exceptions, did little to influence proceedings while the Secretariat apparently adopted a passive, neutral attitude. The entire episode was an example of international non-cooperation. Efforts to arrive in informal talks at a generally acceptable compromise were, if they took place at all, without result. On the agreed date (October 28, 1965) the vote was strongly in favour of Geneva. The net result was therefore identical with that recommended in the original Board resolution of April 1965. Had the Chairman kept a firmer hand on proceedings, the governments been more willing to negotiate a compromise and the Secretariat displayed a less passive attitude, these lengthy discussions might have been avoided as well as six months of uncertainty about the site of the UNCTAD Secretariat.

A case of firmness

In contrast to this lengthy procedural wrangle, the following example shows that a determined chairman by intervening immediately is in a position, even without waiting for a point of order from a delegate, to avoid a lengthy procedural debate. At the fourteenth session (October/November 1965) of the Executive Committee of the High Commissioner's Programme, which is the governing body for the activities of the U.N. High Commissioner for Refugees, a draft resolution was discussed, which in its first paragraph had the Executive Committee take note "with appreciation of the effective action taken by the High Commissioner in promoting resettlement opportunities for refugees." The observer for an Arab country then pointed to the fact that 1.3 million Arab refugees wished to return to their native country. He proposed to add to the paragraph just mentioned the words "and of any help granted to refugees who insist on repatriation to their native country and oppose resettlement elsewhere. . ." The Chairman then immediately stated that "the problem raised was an important one, but that the responsibility for dealing with it lay with other United Nations organs and the committee could only make progress if it continued to seek inspiration in humanitarian principles and to refrain from entering into political matters".[7] The Chairman subsequently stated that the problem was not on the agenda, and suggested that it should not be discussed. This proposal was agreed to without a vote and without discussion.

Presidential ruling reversed

At the Plenipotentiary Conference (plenary session) of the ITU (Montreux, 1965), the United Arab Republic delegation submitted on behalf of the African group a draft resolution (document 110) which would exclude the Union of South Africa from the conference. This gave rise to a lengthy debate on whether, under the constitution, called Convention, of the ITU the conference was competent to exclude a member country from the Conference. Finally, on September 17, 1965, the representative of the United Kingdom proposed that "any questions of competence . . . shall be settled before a vote is taken on the substance of the matter under discussion". The chairman then put this proposal to the vote, stating: "The question was whether the Plenipotentiary Conference was competent to vote on the resolution . . . (document 110). Those who considered that the Conference was competent should vote "yes" and those who considered that it was not should vote "no". The result of the vote, by secret ballot, was: 53 in favour, 53 against, 3 abstentions, 9 absent, 2 invalid. The record then goes on to say: "In the light of the results of the ballot, the Chairman announced that. . . the proposal was rejected". He did not specify which proposal was rejected. Immediately thereafter the meeting adjourned. At the next meeting (September 20, with a weekend in between) it turned out that there were two versions as to which proposal had been rejected. To some, including the chairman, the vote meant that the Conference had decided that it was not competent to vote on the draft resolution in document 110. To others it meant that the conference had not adopted the proposal that the Conference was incompetent to deal with the substantive matter raised in document 110. Therefore, according to this latter view, the Conference should proceed with the consideration and voting on the draft resolution in document 110. A playback of the tape recording of the relevant part of the previous meeting did not bring these conflicting views any closer. At the meeting of September 21—after another lengthy debate—the delegate of the United States submitted the following proposal: "That this Conference is not competent to take the action proposed in the draft resolution of the United Arab Republic (document 110)" This proposal was rejected by the following vote: 51 in favour, 58 against, 2 abstentions, 10 absent, so that the Conference had decided that it was competent to deal with the draft resolution. Thus the Conference had in fact reversed the earlier ruling of the chairman. At the next meeting the proposal in document 110 was adopted, with 59 votes in favour, 27 against, 7 abstentions, 2 invalid and 15 delegations not taking part in the vote, because they considered it illegal.

The confusion on the "competence" question had arisen because of the long delay before someone submitted a motion declaring the incompetence of the conference to deal with draft resolution 110. Instead the chairman had put to the vote a proposal by which the conference would affirm its competence to go ahead. Many delegates were, however, under the impression that what had been voted upon was a motion to declare the ITU's incompetence in the matter; and that this was what had been rejected. This sequence of events [8] shows how important it is for a chairman to make crystal clear what is being voted upon.

3. The presiding officer and "irrelevant remarks"

Rule 70 of the General Assembly provides: "The President may call a speaker to order, if his remarks are not relevant to the subject under discussion". Similar rules are found in other organizations. What is or is not relevant, however, is one of the most disputed questions, not only in the U.N. but also at other conferences. Especially in the many "general debates" in various organizations, where broad questions are discussed, the line is difficult to draw. It is fairly rare for a president on his own initiative to call a speaker to order, requesting him to refrain from making certain observations. It is, on the other hand, rather common for a delegate, immediately after a statement by another delegate or even interrupting the speaker, to rise on a point of order and ask the president to rule that the remarks just made by the delegate of X are completely outside the agenda item under discussion and therefore out of order.

The actual significance of rules of procedure can only be understood against the background of the realities of the conference where they are used, including the inclinations of the presiding officer and possible officially agreed interpretations. These realities may lead to different interpretations of the rules of procedure in the course of time. The following (incomplete, but—it is hoped—typical) analysis of differing interpretations of apparently quite clear rules of procedure is offered as an illustration.

The case of the ILO General Conference: what is out of order?

The rules of procedure of the ILO, established in 1919, are in part based on those of the British Parliament, and are called "Standing Orders". The three directly relevant provisions on declaring a speaker out of order are:

Article 13, par. 2: He (the President) shall ... accord or withdraw the right to address the Conference. . .

Article 14, par. 4: The President may require a speaker to resume his seat if his remarks are not relevant to the subject under discussion.

Article 14, par. 6: Except with the special consent of the Conference no speech, whether by a delegate, a visiting minister, an observer or a representative of an international organization, shall exceed 15 minutes exclusive of the time for translation.

At the ILO annual conferences there habitually is a general debate. Officially, according to the agenda, this is the debate on the "Report of the Director-General". This report, although usually focusing on a specific topic, is at the same time sufficiently general to permit speakers to touch upon almost any question. Everything can somehow be related to "labour" by a speaker who likes to comment on a large variety of subjects. The fact that the ILO Convention speaks about "peace", makes it possible to dwell on peace and war. During the forty-sixth session of the ILO Conference (1962) the President summed up his repeated rulings as follows: "I should like to explain for the benefit of delegates that it was decided by the officers of the Conference that, while criticism in a general way of a social or political system might not be ruled out of order, criticism of a political nature of a named or identifiable government would not be in order".[9]

By literally interpreting this ruling certain speakers nevertheless succeeded in expressing themselves in the way they wanted. For example, one speaker, when called to order after he had mentioned "the Chiang Kai-Shek clique", argued that he had not mentioned a government, and another speaker, who had criticized measures against strikers in certain Spanish provinces, stated that he had not mentioned the Spanish Government.

In 1963 there was one appeal to delegates by the President "to desist from making references of a political nature" and one reminder by the President "that political subjects are forbidden in this discussion".[10]

During the 48th session (1964) of the ILO Conference a delegate criticized certain arrests made in British Guiana by order of the British Government. This led to an interruption on a point of order by a Government Delegate of the United Kingdom who protested against the discussion of a matter outside the scope of the ILO. The President ruled that "it is not proper for us to get involved in a discussion of these internal matters of different member States" and he asked the speaker to limit himself to the matters raised in the Report of the Director-General.[11]

At the 49th ILO Conference (1965) the President ruled that "Heads of State shall not be attacked in any manner and, if a delegate resorts to such remarks in future, I shall . . . be constrained to request him to resume his seat. I must add that my position will be the same should any delegate refer to any theatre of war in any part of the world, as this is a purely political matter, is a subject which falls within the competence of the United Nations and the Security Council and is, in any case, not relevant to the subjects under discussion here".[12] At one point the President tried at the request of a delegate, to rule on what was and what was not "relevant to the subject under discussion" in the following terms: "My ruling on this point of order is that the President has the discretion to require a speaker to resume his seat if his remarks are not relevant to the subject under discussion. There are subjects which can be squarely placed in a particular compartment, either political, economic or social; there are other subjects which are on the borderline; and there are certain subjects which comprise two or three aspects. Therefore, it is not very easy to be precise and exact and say that a speaker is digressing from the objectives.

Therefore, I propose to appeal again to speakers to confine themselves to the subject which we are discussing; but if there are speakers who choose to digress, I propose to exercise my discretion, as referred to in paragraph 4 of article 14 of the Standing Orders, only if I feel that they are using unparliamentary or abusive language. Apart from that, I do not propose to exercise the discretion merely if I do not agree with them or think that what they are saying is beyond the scope of this Conference".[13]

At the 50th ILO Conference (1966), after the Acting President had first ruled that "political discussions should be left to other international organizations", the President made a declaration, from which the following is quoted: "The duties of the President and the rights of speakers are covered by article 13 of the Standing Orders of the Conference as regards the duties of the President, and by article 14 as regards the right to address the Conference. . . Apart from the time limit, the right of delegates to address the Conference is not subject to any other restrictions under the Standing Orders. The President can withdraw the right to speak only if the speaker departs from the item under discussion and ignores an appeal by the President to adhere to the agenda. The source of the next and last limitation concerns keeping the substance of the debate at an appropriate level with a view to ensuring the maximum effectiveness of the discussion. This is a question of the form of speeches, which must be consistent with accepted parliamentary form. It follows that intervention by the President will in most cases relate to the inappropriate form of a speech, and that the President will not intervene unless the speaker slanders a Head of State or unless he insults another delegate personally in expressing his criticisms and opinions with reference to certain circumstances or events to which he may take exception. . . There remains the question of cases where the speaker departs from the subject under discussion. . .
. . . I am not entitled . . . to withdraw a delegate's right to speak when, although in my opinion or that of anyone else at this Conference he is quite wrong, he respects the proper form in drawing attention to facts or events which in his conviction are in conflict with the ILO's task of strengthening world peace, since the problems of peace and social justice are fundamental to the ILO's activities. Nor am I entitled to intervene when the speaker refers, for example, to the right of all human beings, irrespective of race, creed or sex, to pursue their material well-being and their spiritual development in conditions

of freedom and dignity, of economic security and equal opportunity, particularly since clause (b) of article II of the Declaration of Philadelphia regards the attainment of the conditions in which this shall be possible as the central aim of any national and international policy, which therefore applies in the highest degree to the policy of our Organization".[14]

The second 1966 ruling was by far the most elaborate, because contrary to previous rulings, it went into considerable detail on the sort of statement which the president did *not* consider out of order.

At the 1967 ILO Conference a new situation came into existence. In the interval between the 1966 and the 1967 Conference the Working Party of the Governing Body of the International Labour Office on the Programme and Structure of the ILO had studied and discussed the question of "debate in the International Labour Conference in relation to political matters and the role of the President of the Conference."

The Working Party approved certain general principles as follows:

"54. Freedom of speech is the life-blood of the International Labour Organization. The Declaration of Philadelphia proclaims the principle that freedom of expression and of association are essential to sustained progress; it thereby treats freedom of speech as the corollary of freedom of association in the context of the fundamental principles on which the International Labour Organization is based. There is no immunity from criticism for anyone—a government, an employer or a worker—in the ILO.

55. Freedom of speech includes freedom to reply; he who criticises must expect those criticised to defend their views and conduct and must be prepared to accept similar criticism of his own views and conduct.

56. The fundamental purposes of the ILO, as defined in the Constitution and the Declaration of Philadelphia, embrace so wide a range, including social justice as a contribution to lasting peace and the right of all human beings, irrespective of race, creed or sex, to pursue both their material well-being and their spiritual development in conditions of freedom and dignity, of economic security and equal opportunity, that the limits of debate in the International Labour Conference can never be narrowly circumscribed. The ILO has a continuing responsibility to focus attention on these objectives and criteria of policy irrespective of political considerations.

57. There is nevertheless an essential distinction to be made between the purpose and proper scope of such debate in the International Labour Conference and the discussion of political matters in such organs of the United Nations as the Security Council and the General Assembly,

which are entrusted by the Charter with responsibility for political decisions in the United Nations system.

58. In periods of acute political tension the ILO has a twofold responsibility—to uphold the values of human freedom and dignity enshrined in its Constitution, and to circumscribe rather than extend the area of international tension by ensuring the fullest possible degree of continued co-operation in pursuit of the objectives of the ILO. Every delegate to the International Labour Conference therefore has an obligation to the Conference to keep these considerations constantly in mind, and the President has an obligation to ensure that the Conference does not lose sight of them."[15]

At the beginning of the debate on the Report of the Director-General on June 9, 1967, the president of the Conference made a statement of which the following is quoted:

"We begin this morning the debate on the Director-General's Report. In accordance with a recommendation of the Working Party of the Governing Body on the Programme and Structure of the ILO, which has been approved by the Governing Body and communicated to the Conference, I wish, before this debate begins, to draw attention to certain principles and considerations set forth in the report of the Working Party which are of vital importance for the fruitful conduct of our business. I have already had an opportunity of consulting my colleagues the Vice-Presidents and am now speaking on behalf of all of your presiding officers in indicating the principles which we propose to apply with the greatest possible measure of uniformity to all statements made by any speaker whomsoever.

All delegates to this Conference have an obligation to the Conference to abide by parliamentary language and by the generally accepted procedure, to be relevant to the subject under discussion and to avoid references to extraneous matters. It is the duty of the presiding officer to enforce these standards and none of us will hesitate to do so. In particular, if a speaker slanders a Head of State or a Head of Government or insults another delegate personally in the criticisms and opinions he expresses with reference to circumstances or events to which he may take exception, the presiding officer will immediately intervene.

We will be guided in determining the limits of debate by the principles unanimously approved by the Working Party which are set forth in paragraphs 54 to 58 of its report." [16] He then drew special attention to the text of paragraph 58.

The statement by the President, which was tantamount to a ruling, was repeated in the bulletin issued daily with the programme of meetings.

While this seemed to settle the matter, a number of speakers included in their speeches comments to which other delegates, rising on points of order, took exception under the presidential ruling of June 9. In a few cases the President, when a speaker ignored his appeal to omit certain references, asked a delegate to resume his seat. In other cases certain references to political questions deemed to be too offensive were deleted from the record by the President in consultation with the Vice-Presidents of the Conference. In still other cases political observations, some including the word "aggression", used with reference to a named government, were permitted in the record. Both the deletions from the record and the maintenance in the record of certain accusations provoked protests, which were duly recorded.

The only possible conclusion is that the recommendations of the Working Party and the presidential ruling based on it were sufficiently vague to permit representatives to insist on the correctness of their own interpretation of the sort of comments permitted in speeches in the ILO. Roughly, the Conference was divided between delegates who wanted unlimited freedom to criticize others, even on any political matters, and those who believed that such criticism should be circumscribed.

However, there was no effort by one side to impose on the other side its views of what was or was not out of order. It was therefore not surprising that the President, confronted with this situation, steered a middle course. If he had tried to enforce his ruling rigidly, he would have run into efforts to overrule him, and probably added to the acerbity of proceedings. It seems clear that in spite of the efforts of the Governing Body and the President to bring uniformity to the interpretation of rules of procedure, these have been interpreted differently from year to year, and occasionally even during one and the same Conference session.

4. *Substantive functions of presiding officers*

The procedural functions of a chairman are the ones which will normally take up most of his time. However, under certain circumstances his substantive functions become quite important. One task which presidents often perform on an *ad hoc* basis is the appointment of countries or individuals to a new committee. Usually the resolution setting up the committee will contain the relevant request to the president. In carrying out this request he will consult the principal delegations concerned and make sure that those to be appointed will accept the nomination. For example, at the 21st General Assembly session a resolution (2239 (XXI)) was adopted on the "Pattern of Conferences", which created a Committee on Conferences of fifteen members to be designated by the President of the Assembly for a period of three years. The President subsequently appointed fifteen states to this Committee.

The most important potential substantive function of a presiding officer is undoubtedly his role in mediating between conflicting views, and thus assisting a conference towards a conciliatory solution of some problem. Such conflict solution may call for overcoming major or minor differences of views between delegations. In the absence of a compromise resolution there might have been no action whatsoever or at most a decision taken by a severely split vote, which usually has an unfavourable effect on the execution of whatever was thus adopted. In the order of increasing personal involvement the following categories of presidential assistance to the solution of conflicts can be distinguished:

a. *Chairman permits time for informal negotiations*

Soon after an agenda item has been debated in a conference meeting, it may become apparent that time is needed for informal conversations. The chairman will then be asked to start a meeting later than scheduled, or even to cancel it. This request will normally be granted. The chairman may, as a form of mild pressure towards expediting things, inquire how much time will be needed to come to a conclusion. It may be a question of days rather than hours. Delegates not participating in the talks tend to show some impatience and this may affect the chairman himself. Yet, if there is a chance of reaching a compromise solution on some important issue, he will permit the talks to go on. Of course, the conference can take up other agenda items while informal talks on the disputed question are continuing. As sometimes happens in the Main Committees of the General Assembly, in particular towards the end of the session, there may even be several informal negotiating groups meeting simultaneously.

In the arrangements now described the chairman's role does not go beyond adapting the conference schedule to the needs of negotiating parties, who themselves decide on all other details. Thus, if the negotiating is to be done on behalf of two large groups of countries, each group appoints its own negotiators.

The negotiations during the 1957 and 1958 sessions of the General Assembly on the establishment of the U.N. Special Fund were marked by prolonged negotiations in informal groups.[17]

b. *The chairman actively promotes informal negotiations, but does not participate himself*

In contrast to the situation just described it happens that for some reason the two sides disputing a question are reluctant to take the initiative to meet. The chairman, after having talked informally to the opposing delegations to make sure that a suggestion coming from him will not run into serious opposition, can help by proposing to the conference that informal negotiations should start promptly. Two variations occur: either the chairman does not appoint specifically named countries or he does mention names of countries. In the latter case, which is the less frequent, he will have consulted the principal delegations involved as to which countries to name.

At the beginning of the fifteenth session of the ECE Committee on the Development of Trade (October 1966) it became apparent that on the question of recommendations on so-called East-West trade (a problem that had been before the committee for several years) neither side was ready to take the initiative of proposing a compromise text or even of meeting informally. The chairman of the Committee then proposed in plenary session that an informal group of delegates representing opposing points of view (which were known from previous sessions and from a discussion in the committee) should meet informally as soon as possible. Informal encounters then took place but failed to produce a compromise solution.

c. *The chairman promotes informal negotiations and takes part in them himself*

A third form of involvement of the chairman is when he actively participates in informal negotiations, trying to bring opposing sides together. A variety of forms exists: the chairman may preside over meetings of the informal group, but not himself attempt to do the job of drafting a compromise text, or he may preside, and suggest on his own initiative a wording intended to be the compromise on the entire question or on some key paragraph. Another possibility is that the chairman not only presides at informal negotiating group sessions, but is specially requested by delegates to produce a compromise text. If a compromise is reached it may be just acceptable without any great enthusiasm. The normal practice of submitting a joint draft resolution of the countries who previously had sponsored separate drafts, may then be abandoned. Instead, the chairman will be asked to present the compromise text in his own name. This is what happened, for example, during the fifth session of the Trade and Development Board (Geneva, 1967) when after prolonged disagreements on the general nature and the details of the agenda for the second session of the U.N. Conference on Trade and Development (New Delhi, 1968), the President submitted, after lengthy informal consultations with members of the Board, his personal evaluation of the salient "points of crystallization" with respect to the tasks on which the second UNCTAD Conference should concentrate. The President's summary was accepted by the spokesmen for the various groups "as a valuable guide to the work of the Conference" and was incorporated in the draft provisional agenda, which was subsequently unanimously adopted.[18]

The following example from the twelfth session of the General Assembly (1957) is, one may surmise, a combination of presidential involvement in behind-the-scenes negotiation, and a request from the parties concerned to present the compromise in the president's name. Consideration of the Algerian question in the Political Committee had produced an exact tie: thirty-seven to thirty-seven, with eight abstentions. Four days before the end of the Assembly the question was due to come up in plenary session. "The ill-informed shuddered at the thought of the whole debate being gone through again, with no better prospect of agreement on anything. But the well-informed winked. Sir Leslie Munro of New Zealand, the Assembly President, wasted no time that morning. Without inviting anybody to speak, he produced, like a rabbit from a hat, a draft resolution—a carefully phrased compromise text— which until that moment had not seen the light of day. It was carried by eighty votes to none, without debate, there and then".[19]

d. *Exploratory mediation*

Another special situation arises when countries disagreeing on an important question feel that a multilateral encounter will be unproductive, but that exploratory bilateral talks between each of them and the chairman may give some result. An example of this was provided by a meeting of an UNCTAD working party on cocoa (Geneva, March 1966): the president was requested by all delegations to investigate bilaterally in confidential talks with each delegation the views of each government on the thorny question of the price or price range to be inserted in an international commodity agreement on cocoa, due to be negotiated later that year. There was a general feeling that it would be unproductive to have the price question discussed in the committee itself or even in an informal group, since this might easily have led to a major clash. The bilateral talks between the chairman and each of the delegations gave the chairman an insight into how far governments differed or agreed on the price question. The result was not published but was sufficiently encouraging to permit the president to report that views on the price problem, although differing as between governments, were not so far apart as to impede the calling of the International Cocoa Conference, which was held later in 1966.

VI. SECRETARIATS AND CONFERENCE DIPLOMACY

1. *Introduction*

In conferences which are completely *ad hoc,* unrelated to an existing international organization, the role of the secretariat is usually limited to providing essential conference services. Sometimes, however, a specially recruited secretariat plays an important substantive role. Thus, the staff of scientists recruited to prepare and help run the U.N. Conference on the Application of Science and Technology (Geneva, 1963) had an important influence on the conference: it gave help in the screening of papers submitted to the conference, wrote summaries and assisted the various panels into which the conference was split up.

In conferences belonging to the meeting cycle of an international organization, the secretariat not only provides the essential conference services but also, usually, plays an important role in relation to the substantive agenda of the conferences. A more or less considerable part of that agenda will deal with activities of the organization with which the secretariat is directly concerned.

Sometimes the secretariat is empowered, by tradition or under the rules of procedure, to adjust the timing of conferences. Myrdal noted in this connection: "Even the more formal of these functions and powers of the Secretariat, e.g. to call, or to call off, meetings when the Secretariat has been given such power . . . do have material importance for the work in the organization".[1] One example is the General Agreement on Tariffs and Trade where the executive head has by tradition been a major decision-maker in regard to the date of meetings. This tradition could not have been maintained had there not been full confidence that the Secretariat would observe the principle of objectively correct action in the general interest of all members rather than in the particular interest of any one State or group of States.

A distinction must be made between the head of the secretariat, often referred to as the "executive head" and the rest of the secretariat. In some cases the executive head is active and the secretariat more passively inclined, or vice versa. By and large, however, it can be said that the position of the secretariat in general is strongly influenced by that of its executive head, more than the other way round. This assumes that the secretariat meets certain minimum requirements as to numbers and quality, for even the best executive head finds himself crippled by lack of assistance.

With the exception of studies on the Secretary-General of the United Nations most studies on the secretariats of international organizations deal with them as part of a description of these organizations themselves.[2] From the point of view of conference diplomacy we are interested in pinning down the role of the secretariat in the achievement of objectives of international conferences. There are of course general external circumstances which are of essential importance to the success or failure of conferences and which thereby indirectly determine the role of the secretariat: the general political climate, the world (or regional or national) economic situation, the accumulated record and experience of the organization, etc. There are also, however, specific factors directly affecting the role of the secretariat, and in particular of its head. The principal factors are:

(*a*) the statutory role of the executive head and of the secretariat. The constitution and other basic instruments of an organization indicate the powers or functions of the executive head, his rights to take initiatives and his duties vis-à-vis the organization and the membership. Alternatively, the constitution may be silent on the powers of the secretariat. In certain extreme cases there is no constitution and therefore limitations on the role of the executive head will follow from any decisions of the governing bodies and from gradually developed habits.

(*b*) The personality of the executive head. He may be a man of action exploiting every possibility for new initiatives and for strengthening his own position and that of the secretariat, or he may be more inclined to be an "administrator" in the strict sense of the word.

(*c*) The degree of confidence which member states have in the executive head and his secretariat. Such confidence is determined by a combination of influences: the character and objectives of the organization served by the executive head, the position taken on various issues by the governments, whether the executive head was appointed with the full cooperation of the governments from which confidence is expected, and, finally, whether there is a good personal relationship between the executive head and high level officials of member governments.

It can be argued that the confluence of these three factors determines what might be called the "intensity" of secretariat activity, which can be defined as the combined quantity and quality of new secretariat activities, undertaken either on the initiative of the secretariat itself or of governments.

The following table gives, purely illustratively, some combinations of the three factors mentioned, (columns A, B and C) and the possibly resulting secretariat intensity (column D):

Illustration II. **Secretariat Intensity**

A Statutory Position of executive head	B Personality of executive head	C Confidence in secretariat	D Secretariat intensity
(1) strong	active	great	high
(2) weak	active	great	high
(3) weak	active	average	medium
(4) weak	passive	small	low

Obviously these combinations are arbitrarily chosen and the resulting secretariat intensity could well be different from what has been indicated in column D. The reason why we speculate, at the end of line (2), on a resultant high secretariat intensity is that an active executive head can exploit many situations precisely because his basic constitution does not contain any inhibiting stipulations.

The rest of this chapter will serve to provide the background for the analytic frame given here. In section 2 possible variations in the statutory position of the head of the secretariat are discussed. In section 3 the main variations in personality types of the head of the secretariat are examined. In sections 4 and 5 there is a discussion of the "filling of the vacuum", the adroit application of secretariat activity in situations where governments or other organizations have not yet pre-empted the field. Section 4 is concentrated on the secretariat role in political conflicts; section 5 reviews the ways in which a secretariat can develop the activities of its organization.

Not only is every secretariat of an international organization or conference different from every other secretariat, but the same secretariat may change in character over a period of time, even under the same executive head. The careful conference diplomat will see to it that he knows before or at the beginning of a conference the position and any expected new initiatives of the secretariat.

2. *The constitutional position of the executive head*

If the constitution lays down in general or specific terms what the executive head's powers are, it is possible for him to take initiatives.

The most conspicuous example of this is the authority conferred (by art. 99 of the U.N. Charter) on the Secretary-General to bring to the attention of the Security Council any matter which in his opinion may threaten the maintenance of international peace and security. Used a number of times, art. 99 has probably also had the effect of provoking governments involved in a dispute to bring it before the Security Council rather than to wait to be called to appear before the Council as a result of action by the Secretary-General under art. 99. The Secretary-General of the United Nations has at times made use of this authority, or on other occasions made it clear that he would have done so had the question not been brought before the Security Council by a government.[3]

In economic questions the United Nations Charter does not specifically allocate tasks to the Secretary-General as one of the organs of the United Nations, but stipulates what the Organization shall do to promote international economic and social cooperation (chapter IX of the U.N. Charter). It states that the Economic and Social Council is responsible for the discharge of the functions of the Organization set forth in that chapter. This deficiency of the Charter is, however, compensated for by the Rules of Procedure of the Economic and Social Council which provide that the Secretary-General can propose items to be included in the provisional agenda for each session (rule 10) and that the Secretary-General "shall be responsible for keeping the members of the Council informed of any questions which may be brought before it for consideration" (rule 30). The combination of these two rules together with the right of the Secretary-General to make oral or written statements to the Economic and Social Council obviously give the Secretary-General considerable leeway to take the lead in bringing questions before it.

In some organizations responsibilities of an executive character are shared by the president and the head of the secretariat. This, for example, is the case in the World Meteorological Organization, which has a President to whom the Secretary-General is subordinated for certain functions.

In the constitutions of most specialized agencies one also finds an allocation of certain powers to the executive head. Art. 8 of the Constitution of the International Labour Organization simply states that the Director-General, "subject to the instructions of the Governing Body, shall be responsible for the efficient conduct of the International Labour Office and for such other duties as may be assigned to him". The Constitution of the ILO contains a number of information-transmitting tasks for the Director-General and a general directive to the Office to prepare the documents on the various items of the agenda for the meetings of the conference. These in themselves may of course be important. But such a normal right as that of submitting the draft budget and programme is not explicitly provided for in the ILO Constitution. This omission is to be explained by the fact that the ILO Constitution was inspired by the League of Nations Covenant, both drafted in the context of the Versailles Treaty negotiations. Under the League system ILO expenditures were part of the League of Nations budget. The budget submission right of the Director-General of ILO has in the meantime come to exist through requests from the Governing Body.

The Constitution of the World Health Organization explicitly provides (art. 34), that the Director-General "shall prepare and submit annually to the Board the financial statements and budget estimates of the Organization". There can be no doubt that the right to submit budgets and programmes constitutes an important basis on which executive heads can prepare their own initiatives.

Sometimes, within one organization one can detect two different types of secretariat. An example is the European Economic Community. On the one hand the Commission, with its supranational functions, including the right to make proposals and its various managerial tasks, has such an active role that on purpose it has not been given the name of Secretariat. On the other hand the Secretariat of the Council of Ministers is a traditional secretariat in the sense of an office preparing meetings and documentation for the Council of Ministers.

The Statute of the International Atomic Energy Agency provides, apart from a Director-General and his staff, for a separate "staff of inspectors", who have specified responsibilities in regard to the so-called safeguards applicable to Agency projects. These inspectors have rights vis-à-vis the Agency and vis-à-vis the governments concerned (art. 12, B and C, of the IAEA Statute). The Director-General must transmit reports of the inspectors on "non-compliance" to the Board of Governors. He has no discretion to hold up or modify such reports.

There are organizations whose executive head functions without a permanent statute, provided by a constitution. For example, the General Agreement on Tariffs and Trade grew gradually into an organization. Yet its executive head continued to function under the briefest possible provision of the rules of procedure for sessions of the Contracting Parties of GATT, stating that "the usual duties of a secretariat shall . . . be performed by the Executive Secretary . . . on a reimbursable basis". The absence of a more elaborate statutory provision has not prevented the executive head of GATT from playing a leading role in the work of GATT (cf. chapter XI).

3. *The personality of the head of the secretariat: Secretary or General?*[4]

Despite the risk of generalizing dangerously, one can roughly divide the secretariats and their heads into two broad categories: those who emphasize the administrative side of their function, faithfully executing whatever tasks may have been assigned to them, and those who, in addition to their administrative function, look for new initiatives and try to promote the adoption by governments of these initiatives. This difference was noticeable in the cases of the first Secretary-General of the League of Nations (Sir Eric Drummond) and the first Director-General of the International Labour Office (Albert Thomas). It was described in these terms:

"As to the manner of proceeding along the path, Drummond and Albert Thomas ... developed such contrasting patterns of operation as to present their descendants of the United Nations generation with a clear awareness of the fundamental alternatives. Drummond, a British civil servant by temperament and conviction as well as experience, established the prototype of an efficient and unobtrusive administrative direction, while Thomas, an irrepressible veteran of French politics and labor activity, created the pattern of articulate and dynamic leadership in matters of policy. The categories which they established will dominate the concept of secretary-generalship for generations to come".[5]

It should be added that, as Hammarskjöld has pointed out, Drummond himself can be credited with the building up of a truly international secretariat, both in its composition and its responsibilities, in spite of silence on this point of the League of Nations Covenant.[6] Before the existence of the League, staffs were seconded from national governments to international organizations, a practice which, although it has not disappeared, has in most organizations been replaced by the building up of a permanent staff, whose careers are wholly or mostly in the service of international organizations.

It is no exaggeration to say that the role of secretariats in conference diplomacy is gradually increasing. This is not the place to analyse the reasons, but it is important to note the fact. Occasionally this development is commented upon by a delegate, as the following observation of a committee rapporteur during the 13th UNESCO conference (1964) illustrates:

"It has sometimes seemed to me that, with the formidable growth of these organizations, their functions, budgets and administrative machineries, the power and the voice of Member States have become weaker in relation to that of the central administration, or, if the word is permitted, of the international bureaucracy; and this is simply because of the growing complexity of the issues which often makes it difficult to follow them in sufficient detail. This growth of the power of bureaucracy would, in fact, seem to correspond with the general pattern of development of power structures. . .".[7]

4. *Filling the vacuum: political conflicts*

During Dag Hammarskjöld's term of office as Secretary-General of the United Nations, a new concept of the role of the executive head of an intergovernmental organization came into being. Hammarskjöld noted that in some cases "the political organs stated their objectives and the measures to be taken in reasonably specific terms, leaving only a narrow area for executive discretion. But in other cases—and these generally involved the most controversial situations—the Secretary-General was confronted with mandates of a highly general character, expressing the bare minimum of agreement attainable in the organs".[8] In such situations, there existed a 'vacuum' and the Secretary-General was, in Hammarskjöld's view, the logical organ to fill this vacuum. Suez, Lebanon, Jordan, the Congo were some of the political conflicts where such a vacuum of decision-making was glaringly apparent.

On his re-election to a second term as Secretary-General, Hammarskjöld expounded the "vacuum filling concept" as follows:

"I do not believe that the Secretary-General should be asked to act, by the Member States, if no guidance for his action is to be found either in the Charter or in the decisions of the main organs of the United Nations; within the limits thus set, however, I believe it to be his duty to use his office and, indeed, the machinery of the Organization to its utmost capacity and to the full extent permitted at each stage by practical circumstances.

On the other hand, I believe that it is in keeping with the philosophy of the Charter that the Secretary-General should be expected to act also without such guidance, should this appear to him necessary in order to help in filling any vacuum that may appear in the systems which the Charter and traditional diplomacy provide for the safeguarding of peace and security".[9]

In his lecture "The International Civil Servant in Law and in Fact" [10] Hammarskjöld elaborated his belief that "the independence and international character of the Secretariat required not only resistance to national pressures in matters of personnel, but also . . . the independent implementation of controversial political decisions in a manner fully consistent with the exclusively international responsibility of the Secretary-General". Therefore the absence of a decision by a responsible organ on specific courses of action was for Hammarskjöld insufficient reason not to take action, even though "this course of . . . non-action may be tempting; it enables him to avoid criticism by refusing to act until other political organs resolve the dilemma". But Hammarskjöld rejected such a refuge and firmly believed that "the Secretary-General remains under the obligation to carry out the policies as adopted by the organs; the essential requirement is that he does this on the basis of his exclusively international responsibility and not in the interest of any particular State or groups of States". He believed that it was possible to resolve controversial questions on a truly international basis without obtaining the formal decision of the organs. This is not the place to offer, with the benefit of hindsight, comments on Hammarskjöld's vacuum theory as applied for example in the Congo. What is relevant to the study of conference diplomacy is that in a situation of international conflict appropriate and constructive action by the head of an international secretariat may take place in the absence of action by governments or serve as a trigger to prod governments into doing what is necessary. The alert conference diplomat will weigh the pro's and contra's of such action by a secretariat. If he does not like it, he will have to get a majority for some alternative action that he does want; he will only be successful if the action he has in mind has more appeal for this majority than the action contemplated by the secretariat. Such weighing of pro's and contra's can only take place if the proposed secretariat action is made known in advance. Sometimes secretariat action will assume the character of accomplished fact, a real "filling of a vacuum".

5. *Filling the vacuum: activities of organizations*

A considerable part of conference diplomacy has to do with authorizing and—once authorized—overseeing the various activities of intergovernmental organizations. Secretariats are naturally keen to expand their activities.

When they see a "vacuum" in international activities, inside the scope of their organization, they see a field or subject for action and will do something to fill it. Many new activities are prepared by studies carried out by the secretariat, by outside experts or by some group of mixed composition.

Indeed, most international organizations in the United Nations system spend a considerable amount of their resources on studies of various kinds. It frequently happens that a secretariat proposes new studies, usually of course with the explicit or implicit idea that this will lead later to some kind of international action under the auspices of the organization. In his "Introduction to the Annual Report of the Secretary-General on the Work of the Organization, 16 June 1965-15 June 1966" U Thant pointed out that "no organ of the United Nations has ever carried out a comprehensive study of the consequences of the invention of nuclear weapons. ... Their destructive power, their quantities in stockpile, the manner of their use, and the amount of human and material resources devoted to their manufacture and potential delivery have expanded far beyond the comprehension of most people and, I suspect, of many Governments". U Thant therefore concluded that "the time has come for an appropriate body of the United Nations to explore and weigh the impact and implications of all aspects of nuclear weapons, including problems of a military, political, economic and social nature relating to the manufacture, acquisition, deployment and development of these weapons and their possible use".[11]

This initiative resulted in the adoption of G.A. resolution 2162A (XXI) which requested the Secretary-General to prepare—with the assistance of qualified consultant experts—a report on "the effects of the possible use of nuclear weapons and on the acquisition and further development of these weapons".

In 1950 Trygve Lie, then Secretary-General of the United Nations, decided, partly in order not to allow "the United Nations to wither on the vine" and partly to prepare "in every possible way for an ultimate peaceful settlement of the cold war as the alternative to a Third World War", to submit first to the governments of the Big Powers and later to the United Nations General Assembly a "Memorandum of Points for Consideration in the Development of a Twenty-Year Program for Achieving Peace Through the United Nations". After a fairly sympathetic reception in Washington, London and Paris and a more reserved reaction in Moscow the General Assembly adopted a resolution commending the Secretary-General for his initiative and requesting the appropriate organs of the United Nations to give consideration to it.[12]

In the above examples the head of the secretariat has made certain proposals publicly. Another possibility is that not the head, but some official of the secretariat proposes an idea for a study or a new organizational activity to a delegation member whom he knows and trusts, hoping that the delegate will make the idea his own and get his delegation's approval to pursue it actively. The conference diplomat thus approached will wish to make certain that the idea in question is not the private hobby of the particular secretariat member, but does indeed reflect a wide segment of secretariat opinion, preferably also that of the secretariat's top leadership. If that is not the case, the conference diplomat who adopts such an idea exposes himself to the risk of running into counter-action not just by delegates but also by opposing sides within the secretariat. Cox had drawn attention to the existence of "competing poles of authority within staffs" and to the fact that internal opposition (to the executive head) "will be fortified by the ability of the top officials concerned to activate a group of the organization's constituents to put pressure on the executive head".[13]

In certain international organizations traditions have come to prevail which imply a considerable role for the secretariat in the creation of new activities. Thus, Broches related that when the establishment of two new affiliates, the International Finance Corporation and the International Development Association, was under consideration, "instead of calling diplomatic conferences to consider the creation of the new institutions and the constituent instruments which were to govern them, it was the Executive Directors of the Bank who undertook the task of formulating charters for the new institutions and presenting them to member governments for signature." The same procedure was applied in relation to the Bank's newest affiliate, the International Center for Settlement of Investment Disputes, which "will make available facilities to which Contracting States and foreign investors which are nationals of other Contracting States have access on a voluntary basis for the settlement of investment disputes between them in accordance with rules" laid down in the Convention establishing the Center. The idea of this Center started with an initiative from the President of the IBRD (who is the head of the staff, as it is called, of the Bank), to undertake a study of measures to improve the international investment climate. A draft of the Convention on the Settlement of Investment Disputes was subsequently discussed by the Executive Directors, who, although representing governments, are at the same time international civil servants. It was then brought before a series of regional meetings in Santiago de Chile, Geneva and Bangkok attended by governmental experts. "The experts attending did so in a personal capacity, but most of the experts were in fact high officials of their respective countries so that we obtained a good insight in national governmental attitudes as well as a wealth of information on national policies and laws with respect to foreign investment. We received many suggestions for changes or improvement of the text. The four meetings dealt with the same text, but at each succeeding meeting I summarized the comments made at the earlier meetings and rather lengthy summary records of the four meetings were circulated to all participants. I think it is fair to characterize the regional meetings as a most worthwhile two-way educational exercise. Having presided over all four meetings, I can testify to the constructive spirit in which the experts set about their task, including not a few who had serious reservations or objections to the basic principle of international adjudication of investment disputes".[14]

After further consideration by the Executive Directors, the Governors of all member countries at the 19th annual meeting in Tokyo (September 1964) instructed the Executive Directors to formulate a convention and to submit it to member governments. The Executive Directors created a legal committee, to which 61 countries appointed representatives, with special rules of procedure "which envisaged that the Committee would try to reach a consensus on every issue, and giving the Chairman the right to refer disputed points to the Executive Directors for decision. No provision was made for formal voting. This flexible system was successful beyond expectation. Without any real debate we quickly reached agreement in the Legal Committee. Where differences arose we would first try to reconcile them. Failing reconciliation, the Chair would take the sense of the meeting and would regard the issue settled by the majority (on a one country, one vote, basis) unless the issue was regarded as a major one in the opinion of those in the minority. In that event further attempts at reconciliation would be undertaken and the issue would be regarded as settled if a substantial majority was obtained". The voting method just described deviates from the weighted voting formula normally applied in IBRD meetings.

The example serves to demonstrate that constructive results can be achieved by the combination of appropriate secretariat action, flexible non-voting decision-making procedures adopted by governments and the determination to arrive at a specific objective.

VII. DELEGATIONS AND PERMANENT MISSIONS; THEIR GENERAL CHARACTERISTICS

1. *What is a delegation?*

Delegations and delegates constitute—in most cases—the principal participants in conference diplomacy. A delegation can consist of only one person or it can be very large, and have, for example, 61 members, as was the case for the largest delegation (that of the Soviet Union), at the first U.N. Conference on Trade and Development (Geneva, 1964).

Delegations to most conferences of the United Nations system are composed as follows: a head of delegation usually called, in conformity with the relevant rules of procedure, a representative, one or more alternate representatives, one of whom could be indicated as the "deputy head of delegation", one or more advisers or experts.

Under the rules of the U.N. General Assembly there can be at most five representatives and five alternate representatives, and "as many advisers, technical advisers, experts and persons of similar status as may be required by the delegation" (rule 25 of the Rules of Procedure of the U.N. General Assembly). In ECOSOC there is one representative, who may be accompanied by such alternate representatives and advisers as may be required" (rule 18). Somewhat similar provisions exist in most of the specialized agencies, with certain interesting variations, limiting the freedom with which member countries can designate delegates, either as to their number or as to the professional background which they are supposed to have. The most important special case is that of the ILO. Its Constitution stipulates that each member country shall be represented at the annual General Conference by four representatives, of whom two shall be government delegates, the two others to represent the employers and the workpeople (art. 3 of the ILO Constitution). The non-governmental delegates and their advisers must be chosen "in agreement with the industrial organizations, ... which are most representative of employers or workpeople" (art. 3, par. 5 of the Constitution). The ILO Constitution also specifies that the number of advisers accompanying each delegate shall not exceed two for each item on the agenda of the meeting and that when questions affecting women are to be considered, at least one of the advisers should be a woman. In the WHO annual Assembly the (maximum three) delegates "should be chosen from among persons most qualified by their technical competence in the field of health, preferably representing the national health administration of the Member" (art. 11 of the WHO Constitution). The WMO goes further: its constitution stipulates that the "principal delegate" should be the director of the meteorological service. On the other hand the UNESCO Constitution only demands that representatives should be selected in consultation with the national UNESCO Commission, if it exists.

The differing designations [1] encountered in various conferences could for the sake of clarity be replaced by a single designation, as for instance: Representative(s), Alternate Representative(s) and Advisers. The distinction between advisers, experts and "persons of similar status" as made in the General Assembly rules, has in practice been abandoned by many delegations. A few governments, for example the Soviet Union, designate some delegation members as advisers and others as experts.

While fairly large delegations are sent to periodic plenary conferences of the large organizations, the numerous smaller meetings are usually attended by delegations consisting of one, two or three persons. The numerous meetings of subcommittees and working groups of the regional economic commissions of the United Nations, the various types of "governing body" organs, the so-called functional commissions of the Economic and Social Council (which deal with such subjects as Human Rights, Social Development, Statistics, Population Questions), subcommittees of the specialized agencies, all these are normally attended by fairly small delegations.

2. *The composition of delegations: (a) credentials* [2]

The rules for the issuance of credentials are by now more or less standardized: the Head of State, or the Minister of Foreign Affairs or, exceptionally, another minister, issues credentials of delegations. In most conferences, credentials are verified by a special Committee on Credentials. In some this verification is done by the officers of the committee or conference, i.e. by the chairman, vice-chairman and rapporteur. Credentials must be correct in two ways: the delegates must conform to any requirements set by the constitution or rules in question; and they must be issued by the proper authority in the proper form. Normally, the report of a credentials committee is short, and simply states that credentials have been found in good order. Occasionally it is criticized from the floor, even though in many conferences it is not voted upon but only "noted". In view of the ILO rule that the employer and worker delegates to ILO conferences must be chosen from among representative organizations, the credentials of certain employer and worker delegates have been at times challenged by other delegations. In U.N. conferences, the credentials of the Republic of China (Taiwan) delegates are regularly challenged by delegations from countries which feel that delegates from the People's Republic of China should occupy the seat of China.

At conferences where an international treaty is negotiated the head of the delegation (if desired also other members of the delegation) must be given "full powers", which the International Law Commission has defined as "a document emanating from the competent authority of a State designating a person to represent the State for negotiating, adopting or authenticating the text of a treaty, for expressing the consent of the State to be bound by a treaty or for accomplishing any other act with respect to a treaty". A treaty itself is defined as "an international agreement concluded between States in written form and governed by international law, whether embodied in a single instrument or in two or more related instruments and whatever its particular designation".[3] On purpose the ILC has used the term "treaty" as a generic term covering all forms of international agreement between states.

3. *The composition of delegations: (b) nationality*

Normally a delegation is composed of persons having the nationality of the country represented by the delegation, or, in the case of experts acting in their own capacity, having the nationality of the country which has nominated them. Various exceptions do, however, occur.

Firstly, it can happen that a delegation includes citizens of another country or persons having double nationality, perhaps because the country cannot make available enough people for a large delegation. The persons thus included in the delegation of country X are not identifiable as citizens of country Y. They are indicated with diplomatic or *ad hoc* titles, such as alternate representative, or special adviser.

The second possibility is that a country, for manpower reasons or under some reciprocal arrangement, accredits somebody from another country with which is has close relations, and openly indicates that the delegate is a citizen from the other country. This procedure was used when Belgium, a member of the U.N. Scientific Committee on the Effects of Atomic Radiation, accredited a Dutch professor of physics as its representative. The arrangement has apparently worked out satisfactorily, because it was continued for several years.

The third situation is where a country includes in a delegation nationals from friendly countries with which it has close ties, not so much because of manpower shortage reasons but because of the increasing difficulty in getting elected to committees and councils with a restricted membership. In recent years organs with a restricted membership have not been enlarged in any ratio commensurate with the great increase in total membership of most organizations.

In many conferences of the U.N. system several agenda items are only indirectly related to the national interest of delegations, and result in studies, which are supposed to be useful to the world community. This means that it is less urgent to be a member of such an organ for reasons of immediate national interest. Prestige may of course still be a motive to seek membership. The confluence of limited direct national interest and the increasing difficulty of getting elected to committees or councils with a restricted membership has encouraged arrangements whereby, although nominally only one country is a member of an organ, its delegation includes citizens from other countries. At the 36th to 41st sessions of the Economic and Social Council (1964-1966) the delegation of Luxemburg included a number of advisers from Belgium and the Netherlands. The Swedish delegation to the 41st session of ECOSOC included as special advisers nationals from Denmark, Finland and Norway. The Economic and Social Council is difficult to get elected to and concentrates on tasks where each nation serves mankind in general or large groups, such as the underdeveloped part of the world, rather than its own direct interests. It is therefore logical that the experiment of *de facto* joint delegations should have found application in ECOSOC. Larger recourse to the practice of joint delegations may have a mitigating influence on the fierceness of some election struggles.

The fourth possibility is that countries have a joint delegation because they are united in a treaty or economic union, and the subject on which they are negotiating is one which requires joint representation as a result of that treaty, or as a result of an understanding otherwise reached. In the sphere of trade negotiations a well-known example is that of the joint Benelux (Belgium, Netherlands, Luxemburg) delegations which since 1948 have been negotiating trade agreements with other countries. In the multilateral sphere the joint European Economic Community delegation participating in the Kennedy round of trade negotiations, carried out from 1964 to 1967 under the auspices of the General Agreement on Tariffs and Trade, is an example. The Nordic countries also negotiated in the last phase of the Kennedy round (from December 1, 1966 to June 30, 1967) with a joint delegation. The negotiating techniques of the Kennedy Round are reverted to in Chapter XI.

4. *The composition of delegations: (c) diplomats, pseudo-diplomats, experts, public or parliamentary members; summit diplomacy*

In bilateral diplomacy negotiations are in principle carried out by professional diplomats, i.e. ambassadors and their collaborators in permanent diplomatic missions, or by Foreign Ministers and their collaborators. Even so, bilateral diplomacy of an *ad hoc* character carried out by all sorts of persons who cannot be called foreign policy or diplomatic specialists has become a near-normal feature of contemporary international relations.[4]

In conference diplomacy one can discover a range of possibilities: delegations exclusively composed of professional diplomats, delegations composed of a mixture of professional diplomats and others, delegations in which there are no professional diplomats but only specialists in certain fields. C. Labeyrie-Ménahem has created the term "para-diplomates" which could be anglicized as "pseudo-diplomats".[5] They are the people who for various reasons find themselves involved in an international negotiation, which even though, or perhaps because, it is limited to a specific subject, may be of considerable importance. Examples abound. In Geneva, under auspices of the Economic Commission for Europe, experts meet in subcommittees or working parties to discuss and negotiate on such diverse subjects as international standards for various fruits and vegetables, or international safety provisions for motor vehicles, or regulations for the registration of inland vessels. In some cases formal international agreements, to be signed, accepted and ratified, are thus negotiated. In others, voluntary standards are drawn up to which each country can accede as it wishes.

The following possibilities of delegation composition can be distinguished:

a. *The leadership of the delegation is in the hands of foreign policy specialists (defined as either professional diplomats or Foreign Office personnel); the delegation has several members with other affiliations*

Such a mixed composition is typical of the average delegation to the annual sessions of the General Assembly. The head of the delegation for most countries is either the Foreign Minister (by whatever name, for instance Secretary of State), or the Permanent Representative to the United Nations, or, exceptionally, another Minister. Some countries will make their Permanent Representative head of the delegation, with a footnote to the delegation list indicating that the Foreign Minister is *ex officio* head of the delegation for the duration of his presence at the Assembly session. Senior members of the Permanent Mission or of the Foreign Office are made representatives or alternate representatives. In some cases, members of parliament will also be made representative or alternate representative. Persons representing various walks of life (e.g. trade unions, women's organizations) may also be on the delegation. For example, at the twentieth session ot fhe U.N. General Assembly the ten representatives and alternate representatives of the Netherlands delegation consisted of the Minister of Foreign Affairs, the State Secretary of Foreign Affairs, the Permanent Representative to the U.N., a representative of Surinam (self-governing part of the Kingdom of the Netherlands situated in the Western Hemisphere), four members of the Netherlands Parliament, one professor of international law, and one ambassador (Permanent Representative to the International Atomic Energy Agency). Under advisers were listed 11 names, those of 7 members of the Permanent Mission in New York, two senior officials of the Ministry of Foreign Affairs, one representative of a women's organization and one representative of a trade union organization. The United States delegation to the General Assembly regularly includes four members of Congress (two from the Republican and two from the Democratic Party).

Delegations to *ad hoc* conferences with a diplomatic character, for example the conference held in Vienna in 1961 which drew up a new convention on diplomatic relations, will be headed by professional foreign affairs specialists, or by international law experts.

b. *Leadership is in the hands of a minister or policy official not connected with the Ministry for Foreign Affairs; the delegation consists mostly of personnel pertaining to the government department of the head of delegation*

This happens frequently in general conferences or other meetings of the specialized agencies. We have already seen that the WHO constitution prescribes that the leaders of delegations to the annual World Health Assembly should be persons responsible for public health. In the case of the International Labour Conferences heads of delegation are usually Ministers of Labour or Social Affairs. The foreign affairs specialists will generally give advice on any political matter that may come up, such as objections to the presence of certain states in a conference or the wish to have certain non-members present.

In recent years the activities of the various U.N. specialized agencies and of the U.N. have become increasingly intertwined: on the one hand there are more and more joint activities of several organizations and on the other hand different but related aspects of one and the same question are dealt with in different organizations. This has posed the problems of avoiding duplication of activities and of coordination between the activities of the various agencies and programmes. The foreign affairs specialists or sometimes officials from finance ministries will look after any coordination aspects that may come up in specialized agency meetings. For delegations of mixed composition, the drafting of precise instructions is of considerable importance in order to avoid conflicting views within the delegation between people belonging to different departments. The draft instructions should have been discussed beforehand in the capital of the country, so as to harmonize any diverging views between, say, the Ministry of Foreign Affairs, the Ministry of Finance and the department with substantive responsibility for the matters to be discussed at the conference.

c. *No foreign policy personnel involved; the delegation is composed wholly of specialists from certain government departments*

This category comprises the numerous conferences held at a place where there is no permanent mission (otherwise a member of that mission could be on the delegation). It also includes highly technical meetings where the need to have a foreign policy specialist on the delegation is usually not felt by those who appoint the delegation. Yet, some of these technical meetings engage in the drafting of international agreements although not always in perfect legal form. Standard setting and regulation-drafting committees under the ECE, the FAO, the ITU etc. are a case in point. It is important that the treaty or legal division of the Ministry of Foreign Affairs should be consulted before the conference, so that no errors are made in the tricky field of the legal aspects of international agreements. This will prevent what has occasionally occurred: a government is committed without really knowing about it. Therefore, in this case too the prior writting of instructions or of a so-called position paper is important.

Delegations in this category and also in the one mentioned under (b) sometimes comprise persons representing private business interests. For example, many delegations to UNCTAD conferences on cocoa and on lead and zinc included business representatives as advisers. While serving on a delegation a businessman just like any other delegation member comes under the instructions given to the delegation, and he is therefore not supposed to express possible deviating views to other delegations.

d. *The specialist attending a group of experts or rapporteurs in his individual capacity*

This category is distinguished from the previous ones in that the expert or 'special rapporteur' is not under formal government instructions. But actually he may have oral or unofficial instructions, in particular if, as frequently happens, he has been nominated by his government (instead of having been freely selected by the secretariat) to serve on a particular expert group. For example a group could be charged with drafting the terms of reference of a mandate for a new research institute. The expert, who is called by the Secretary-General of the sponsoring organization to give advice on this, is assumed to have a 'positive' attitude towards the tasks of the new institute, or otherwise he would not have been invited. Occasionally the experts start "from scratch" and some of them submit papers at the beginning of their session. However, the expert will often find that the secretariat has already drafted an outline of what he and his colleagues-experts are supposed to do. He is expected to give his blessing to it, perhaps after minor or sometimes major modifications. His position is comparable to the well-known case of the international technical assistance expert who is called to a less-developed country to find that the particular country knows very well what it has to do but needs the respected endorsement of the foreign specialist in order to obtain external assistance or public acceptance of a project.

e. *Summit diplomacy* [6]

Occasionally delegations are led by a head of state or a head of government, if only for part of a conference. Experience shows that the actual decisions of an intergovernmental conference are usually not affected by the presence of such personalities. However, the process of arriving at decisions may be slowed down, because the heads of government or of state may make longer speeches, or because normal meetings are adjourned. Alternatively it may be speeded up, namely if on some knotty problem a head of state or of government can take an immediate decision. This latter possibility is, however, rather exceptional, because in many countries the head of state has only ceremonial functions, while heads of government, even if they have special powers, will usually not be in a position to take decisions beyond the instructions given previously to the delegation.

5. *Permanent missions and permanent delegations*

Permanent missions, sometimes called permanent delegations, are in relation to conference diplomacy what normal diplomatic missions (embassies and legations) are in connection with bilateral diplomacy. Neither the League of Nations Covenant, nor the United Nations Charter, nor the Rome Treaty on the European Economic Community provide for permanent representatives or missions or delegations. Yet, since the Second World War permanent missions to various international organizations have attained considerable importance. In the case of the League of Nations, where the permanent delegation system originated, it is not supposed to have been significant.[7] On the other hand, in the case of the U.N., the EEC, the Organization for Economic Co-operation and Development, the Council of Europe and NATO, permanent missions or delegations constitute an essential part of the decision-making process.

As the name indicates, permanent missions or delegations are physically located at the headquarters site of the organization to which they are accredited. Each permanent representative is accredited to one or more organizations. In *New York* all U.N. member countries maintain permanent missions, headed by a Permanent Representative, who usually has the rank of Ambassador. He is accredited to the United Nations and, like a chief of mission in a bilateral post, begins his activity by handing a letter containing his credentials to the Secretary-General of the United Nations. Contrary to standard practice in bilateral diplomacy, there is no question of obtaining prior agreement, so-called "agrément", for a new Permanent Representative. Nor can he be called "persona non grata" by the Secretary-General; he or his collaborators can, however, be expelled by the government of the host country if he is accused of having engaged in espionage or similar activities.

In *Geneva* many, but not all member countries of the U.N. have permanent missions. In September 1967 there were 76 permanent representatives (a few of them are not actually at Geneva, but ambassadors in Bern, Paris or Brussels, and also accredited to Geneva). The situation in Geneva is more complex than in New York or elsewhere, because of the large number of intergovernmental organizations established there. Some permanent representatives are accredited to all organizations, some are accredited to selected organizations. A few organizations do not have local permanent representatives formally accredited (example: CERN, European Organization for Nuclear Research), although they maintain informal contact. The reason appears to be that they do not wish to have any interference with their direct contacts with government departments in the capitals. Even the organizations to which permanent representatives are accredited frequently like to maintain—formally or informally (through personal letters)—direct links with government departments in the capitals.

In Geneva the United Nations system in the narrow sense comprises the Office of the United Nations (formerly called the European Office of the United Nations), headed by a Director-General. In this Office are a number of U.N. bureaux, including four semi-autonomous U.N. organizations:

—the UNCTAD, U.N. Conference on Trade and Development, a permanent organization, within the U.N., for trade and development, headed by a Secretary-General;

—the Office of the U.N. High Commissioner for Refugees;

—the Economic Commission for Europe, the secretariat of which is headed by an Executive Secretary;

—the International Narcotics Control Board (which as from 1968 is the successor organ to the Permanent Central Opium Board and the Drug Supervisory Body).

Accreditation to the Office of the U.N. in Geneva takes care of accreditation to all these organizations, although some governments write separate letters of introduction to some of the executive heads mentioned, a procedure specially justified if they consider the organization of particular importance to them. The Geneva list of permanent missions lists one "Permanent Representative to UNCTAD", who is in fact his country's Ambassador in Brussels. In some permanent missions in Geneva one finds specific persons listed as "Permanent Representative to GATT".

There are four U.N. specialized agencies in Geneva to which separate accreditation is necessary: the International Labour Organization (the secretariat of which is called the International Labour Office), the World Health Organization, the International Telecommunication Union, the World Meteorological Organization. Then there are intergovernmental organizations which are not U.N. specialized agencies: EFTA (European Free Trade Association), GATT (General Agreement on Tariffs and Trade), the Intergovernmental Committee for European Migration (ICEM), the World Intellectual Property Organization (successor as from 1968 to BIRPI (Bureaux Internationaux Réunis pour la Propriété Intellectuelle)), the European Organization for Nuclear Research (CERN). The International Red Cross Committee (CICR, Comité International de la Croix-Rouge), although its activities are wholly international, is a Swiss organization; some governments deal with it through their permanent representatives and others through their consulates in Geneva or their embassies in Bern.

Some missions incorporate in their list the names of people who are in Geneva for some lengthy, yet temporary, conference, such as the GATT Trade Negotiations Conference or the Eighteen-Nation Disarmament Conference. Thus one found in the (July/August 1966) list for the United States one Ambassador, Head of the Permanent Mission and Permanent Representative, one Minister who is the Deputy Permanent Representative, one Ambassador for Trade Negotiations, and one Ambassador without special designation but of whom it was known that he dealt exclusively with the Eighteen-Nation Disarmament Committee. Some countries which are not members of the U.N. have observer missions. In New York the Federal Republic of Germany and Switzerland have a "Permanent Observer to the United Nations". In Geneva the title of the corresponding official is "Permanent Observer to the Office of the United Nations and Permanent Representative to the International Institutions in Geneva", because Switzerland and the Federal Republic of Germany are full members of certain specialized agencies and other intergovernmental organizations. Most permanent representatives in Geneva are listed as "Permanent Representative to the Office of the United Nations and other international organizations at Geneva". There is no complete uniformity.

In *Vienna,* seat of the International Atomic Energy Agency and of UNIDO, many member states have Permanent Representatives. Some of them are at the same time the Ambassadors to Austria and others are especially designated. Liaison with FAO and UNESCO is maintained by many governments through specialized diplomats in the embassies in Rome and Paris respectively.

A peculiar situation exists in relation to the World Meteorological Organization. Contrary to other organizations, its Constitution provides for "Permanent Representatives". These are the directors of the meteorological services who are expected to act on technical matters between sessions of the WMO Congress which is held only once every four years. Since most of the diplomatic representatives in Geneva are also accredited to the WMO, that organization has two sets of Permanent Representatives.

A relatively new development is the nomination of permanent representatives of international organizations (usually called, however, head of the liaison office, or chief of the permanent mission), residing in cities where their organization is frequently called upon to be represented in some capacity at international conferences. Thus several of the specialized agencies maintain "liaison offices" at U.N. headquarters in New York. In Geneva the IMF has a liaison office and the EEC a permanent mission.

The functions of permanent missions can be described as follows:

a. *General liaison with the secretariat of the organization to which they are accredited*

The permanent missions keep themselves posted on the current state of secretariat activities and of any new initiatives being developed in the secretariat. The missions transmit documents and reports to their capital and receive from the Ministry of Foreign Affairs or from other departments information and answers to questionnaires or official notes circulated by the secretariats of the organization. This function is sometimes called the "post-office" function of permanent missions. It is nonetheless important to the smooth functioning of organizations, although several organizations also maintain an intensive direct correspondence with member governments. The custom has developed that, generally speaking, permanent missions receive copies of such correspondence. The more specialized an organization is, the more direct contact it has with government departments in the capital. However, some countries maintain specialized attachés for such organizations as the ILO, the WHO, the WMO and the ITU. In that case these attachés and hence the permanent missions have intensive direct contacts. The permanent missions also serve as intermediaries for the preparation of visits of secretariat officials to their capital, or by officials of their own governments to a secretariat.

b. *Preparation and follow-up of conferences*

The agenda, arrangement of business and working methods of conferences, both the periodically recurring ones and *ad hoc* conferences, are discussed between the permanent missions and the secretariats, on various levels, depending on the importance of the question. Similarly, once a conference is over, and the question of how various decisions will be implemented arises, interested governments will discuss this with the secretariat through their permanent missions.

c. *Participation in conferences*

The Permanent Representative and his collaborators will participate in the meetings and conferences of the organization(s) they are accredited to. How and in what way depends on the sort of meeting, on the use the Government wishes to make of its permanent mission, on the size of the permanent mission in relation to the number of meetings simultaneously to be served, etc. It is important to realize that once the Permanent Representative or one of his collaborators becomes the head or member of a delegation to a conference, his activities are formally no different from those of other members of the delegation. In other words, he loses so to say his characteristic of a permanent mission member. But he loses it only in form, not in substance: the fact of the matter is that the permanent mission members, through year-long work in connection with the organization to which they are accredited, constitute a nucleus in the conferences of the organization which they attend as delegates. They are often the "work-horses" of conferences. At the General Assembly, for example, permanent mission members will sit constantly at meetings of the seven committees into which the General Assembly splits up, take care of most of the liaison and lobbying work with other delegations, prepare speeches in linguistically and substantively correct form for delegates from the capital who are their superiors in status or rank, but who, perhaps because they are for the first time at the conference, are not sufficiently familiar with the work to "swim alone".

The continuous presence in such places as New York and Geneva of the permanent missions, which the late Dag Hammerskjöld called "a continuous diplomatic conference",[8] has had a number of effects. For one thing, the group system is losing some of its sharp characteristics because in between conferences members of different groups, or leading members of groups, can maintain informal contact, learn to know each other's points of view better, and—generally speaking— help to prepare encounters between the groups during the conference. Friendship, contact, and communication in general may have been favourably affected through the continuous "social inter-action" [9] between permanent mission members.

The existence of a permanent mission can also lead to possible unfavourable effects. The first is that governments, confronted as frequently happens with a shortage of qualified personnel, will tend to use permanent mission members for assignments where a real expert is needed and so lower the standard of the meeting. An example is provided by some of the functional commissions operating under the general aegis of the Economic and Social Council, to which certain countries have at times delegated non-specialized permanent mission personnel.

In Geneva a member of a permanent mission may find himself in the morning serving as political adviser to a technical delegation to a conference of the ITU, in the afternoon attending a coordination meeting of the group of countries to which his government belongs on the forthcoming meeting of the UNCTAD Committee on Shipping, the next morning represent his country in a meeting on East-West trade of a committee of the ECE and the following afternoon keep in touch with a meeting of the Eighteen-Nation Disarmament Committee. This jumping from one subject to another of permanent mission members may be more pronounced in Geneva, with its diversity in organizations.

The ideal solution is that general and specialized expertise should be present at all meetings where this is necessary. This can be achieved, either by making the permanent mission member "representative" and attaching to him a technical adviser, who in most cases will have come from the capital, or making the technical man the "representative" and attaching the permanent mission member to him as alternate or adviser.

Another possible disadvantage suspected by some observers [10] is that some permanent mission members or heads of mission will strive to obtain chairmanships or other positions as officer of a committee, in the belief that this increases their standing or their chances of advancement in their own service. The more committees there are, the more places of chairman etc. are to be filled, and, hence, permanent mission members might be biased towards the creation of additional international bodies. The impression of this writer is that permanent missions have become so fully occupied that they have become a negligible factor as a special pressure group towards the creation of new bodies. Such pressures, if they exist, are more likely to come from secretariats and governments.

There is a third negative aspect of permanent missions, which should be mentioned. This is the phenomenon that might be called "reverse diplomacy". A permanent mission head or member, in particular if his posting extends over a long period, may become so identified with the hopes and frustrations of the organizations he is accredited to, that he pleads their cause (often their secretariat's cause) vis-à-vis his own government. This may mean that he is becoming a less effective spokesman for his government regarding requests or complaints which it may have. The same phenomenon is well known in bilateral diplomacy.

6. *The internal organization and working methods of delegations*

Assuming that the delegation is sensibly composed with general political, diplomatic and specialized knowledge represented in a balanced way, efficiency can be easily achieved. In this context "efficiency" is used in its narrower sense, i.e. limited to the delegation's working methods. This is of course quite different from "efficiency" as applied to success in the conference's final results, which depends on a great many factors partly beyond an individual delegation's control.

The following arrangements will greatly enhance delegation efficiency:

a. *A good relationship between the head of the delegation and the delegation members including a sensible distribution of work*

The head of the delegation will see to it not only that the delegation performs its task in conformity with its instructions, but also that the delegation can work as a team. The allocation of specific tasks is done right at the beginning or even before the conference starts. This distribution of work should leave no ambiguities, because if there is overlapping or lack of clarity in the work distribution, some friction between delegation members is inevitable.

Furthermore, unnecessarily frequent delegation meetings combined with the fact that delegation members see each other all day long (also at breakfast and in the evening, if they are housed in the same hotel) can obviously cause colleagues to get on each other's nerves, and produce a kind of "delegation claustrophobia".

The head of the delegation is expected to make decisions on questionable points, unless, of course, he decides that the matter must be referred back to the government at home. Like the chairman of a conference, the head of a delegation should be fair and rapid in ruling on questions submitted to him. A considerable part of this process of head-of-delegation-decision-making will take place at the delegation meeting.

b. *The delegation meeting*

It is common practice, even for small delegations of two or three persons, to have regular delegation meetings. How often? This cannot be stated in general. At U.N. General Assembly sessions some delegations meet every morning (if only briefly), others three times a week, others again twice a week. The delegation meeting will serve mainly the following purposes:

(*i*) the exchange of information on events of the previous day(s);

(*ii*) to discuss the tactical behaviour of the delegation in the coming days on specific points, including votes to be cast, and to arrive at specific conclusions, either by agreement in the delegation as a whole or by a decision of the delegation head;

(*iii*) there will be cases where a decision as mentioned under (*ii*) is not possible, either because the delegation's instructions are incomplete, or lacking, or because the delegation feels that in the light of developments at the conference modified instructions are necessary. In the latter case proposals from the delegation may have the practical effect of producing changes in the policy of the government in the capital;

(*iv*) sometimes subjects come up which are not directly the object of action at the conference. This, for example, happens when a delegation member suggests some new initiative to be taken at a future session of the same body or a modification of an existing government policy. If the delegation in its majority or as a whole is sympathetic towards the new initiative and this delegation position is reported to the capital, the new idea may be included in the government's instructions for a later conference. Thus a delegation meeting may become the point where a new government policy or initiative was first discussed;

(*v*) the delegation meeting will also serve to review the allocation of specific tasks, including the question of who will make a certain speech or statement, for the coming days. Occasionally, the text of major statements, or the main points of such statements, are discussed in the delegation meeting.

The usefulness of keeping a record of delegation meetings must be decided for each conference. In certain cases government departments at home will wish to see minutes kept, giving them a summary of developments at the conference.

c. *Reporting*

As part of the allocation of tasks, it must be clearly indicated who is in charge of drafting reports to the government at home. Usually this will correspond with the allocation of items of the agenda to delegation members. The reports go out under the responsibility of the head of delegation. He must decide whether he wants to see all reports personally before they are dispatched, or whether he delegates this approval in whole or in part to one or more members of the delegation.

The report will go out by mail, telegram or telex. In the latter two cases the choice is between an "open" or a coded telegram, a choice dictated by the status of the question discussed. For example, if the report contains not only a summary of what happened in the public meeting, but also an account of informal lobby discussions with named delegations, and perhaps ends with a request for instructions, the cable or telex is normally coded.

At large conferences, such as the U.N. General Assembly, some delegations develop a system requiring each delegation member who attends a formal meeting (if two or more attend the same meeting, it will have to be clear who has this task) to write a daily brief report, which will be typed or stencilled. A copy will be sent to the government; in important cases its contents will be incorporated in a telegraphed report. These daily summaries become precious material for those in charge of making the final report of the delegation on the whole conference.

d. *The allocation of tasks*

As was stressed all tasks must be specifically assigned at the outset of the conference, including reporting. In a conference like the U.N. General Assembly there will be one delegation member for each of the main committees, usually somebody from the permanent mission or from the Foreign Affairs Ministry, whose special task it is to follow "his" committee very closely. He also serves as the clearing point for draft resolutions and other material relating to that particular committee and will be in charge of drafting the relevant part of the final delegation report. In U.S. State Department terminology he is called the delegation's "executive officer" for a particular committee. Also, large delegations will have a delegation secretary (sometimes—in important conferences—called secretary-general) who supervises the administrative side of delegation activities and assists the delegation chairman in maintaining the smooth functioning of the delegation.

It is important for each member of the delegation to receive the task for which he is best suited. In particular, those who engage in "lobby talks" and negotiations should be carefully chosen. Relations with the press should be entrusted to one member of the delegation, preferably the press attaché of the permanent mission.

VIII. CONFERENCE DIPLOMATS—REQUIREMENTS AND CHARACTERISTICS

1. *The relevancy of traditional qualifications to conference diplomats*

Books on diplomacy often describe fundamental qualifications required of diplomats. We shall discuss some of them in the light of conference diplomacy, adding a few aptitudes specifically needed in this kind of diplomacy. The order in which they appear is not related to the value attached to each of the character traits discussed.

Diplomacy has changed in the course of time and so, presumably, have the requirements to be met by the "ideal diplomatist". In the sixteenth century the general opinion was that "an ambassador should be a trained theologian, should be well versed in Aristotle and Plato, and should be able at a moment's notice to solve the most abstruse problems in correct dialectical form: he should also be expert in mathematics, architecture, music, physics and civil and canon law. He should speak and write Latin fluently and must also be proficient in Greek, Spanish, French, German and Turkish. While being a trained classical scholar, a historian, a geographer and an expert in military science, he must also have a cultured taste for poetry. And above all he must be of excellent family, rich, and endowed with a fine physical presence".

In the seventeenth century this had already become more subtly qualified. Abraham de Wicquefort talks about three required qualifications for those sent on an embassy: birth, studies and experience. For him the right birth is determined not by belonging to the nobility, but by "natural excellence and the force of genius", to which he added that "most Grands Seigneurs are more qualified for an embassy of ceremony than for negotiations".[1]

At the beginning of the eighteenth century the Abbé Duguet in his "Institution of a Prince or Treaty on the Qualities, Virtues and Duties of a Sovereign" counsels that an ambassador "must be very wise, moderate, secret, attentive, well versed in history, especially of his country and of the country to which he is sent; knowledgeable in good manners in general, and particularly in the rules of the court where he resides; full of dignity, but an enemy of false glory. . .".

a. *Truthfulness and honesty*

Ever since de Callières in his "How to Negotiate with Sovereigns" urged envoys "not to tell lies", truthfulness has been mentioned foremost as a requirement for the serious diplomat.

The conference diplomat exposes himself dangerously if he wilfully commits misrepresentations or avoidable errors, because these are likely to be discovered sooner or later by his fellow delegates. He may be confronted with his mistake in a speech by another delegate, or he may be approached in an informal way. In both cases he will be challenged about the truthfulness of what he said. The conference diplomat will therefore be careful to make sure that the facts he mentions in official sessions, in informal speeches or in private conversations can be upheld. On the other hand, the trouble is that "truth" in many cases is not a single unique thing. As soon as matters of policy are discussed, truth may be one thing to some, and something else again to others.

One can speak of dishonesty in conference diplomacy in cases where a government subscribes to a compromise solution knowing that later it is deliberately going to give a completely different interpretation from that agreed at the time of adoption of the compromise. On the other hand, there is no dishonesty if both before and after a compromise decision is taken, opposing parties know that the text will lend itself to differing interpretations. The preferable course of action will be to put these differing interpretations on record, possibly in an "explanation of vote". This is what happened upon adoption of resolution 1219 (XII) of the General Assembly on the U.N. Special Fund, when India argued that the new Fund was a step on the way to a large Capital Development Fund, while the United States said that the Special Fund stood entirely by itself.[2]

The following are some of the data which frequently cross the path of the conference diplomat and for which truthfulness and accuracy are important:

(1) legal and historical references: the conference diplomat will frequently wish to quote from existing treaties, agreements, resolutions, or to refer to historical precedents or situations. In doing so he must make sure not only that his quotations and references are correct, but also that he has not—intentionally or inadvertently—left out a reference to a relevant text which his opponents might cite in criticism of his proposal or argument;

(2) statistics: in principle statistics are an easy category of facts on the argument that "figures do not lie". In practice difficulties often arise, because of ambiguities and divergencies surrounding so many statistical data. Sometimes these result from differing definitions. This

was the case with statistics on the flow of financial assistance to less-developed countries, for which the U.N. and the OECD gave different figures, because they used different methods or definitions. More difficult is the absence or unreliability of statistical data on certain phenomena or for certain countries;

(3) references to the amount of support for a proposal. Whether one mentions countries by name or not, the conference diplomat must be sure that publicly or privately expressed indications of support correspond with the approximate actual situation. This may be particularly important in election campaigns. Country A may be tempted to get support for its candidate with statements that such and such other countries have already agreed to vote for him, and will country X please join the numerous supporters. If country X checks and finds that some alleged supporters are in fact not, or not yet, supporting the candidate, confidence in country A and its candidate can be shattered.

b. *Precision*

"The great high-roads of history are strewn with little shrines of peace which have either been left unfinished, or have collapsed when completed, for the sole reason that their foundations were built on the sands of some verbal misconception".[3]

This comment by Nicolson on accuracy as a requirement for diplomats takes on a somewhat different complexion in conference diplomacy. Ambiguity and vagueness are probably as frequent in conference diplomacy as precision and single-minded clarity. The reason is that efforts towards compromises often result in texts that lend themselves to differing, even opposing interpretations. The first resolution (of July 14, 1960) adopted by the U.N. Security Council on the U.N. role in the Congo was vague in the sense that it could be interpreted to mean either a minimal role for the U.N. or a large role. The dynamic interpretation given by the then Secretary-General of the U.N., Dag Hammarskjöld, on the basis of requests from the Government of the Republic of the Congo, led to large-scale activities of the U.N. in the Congo. Efforts to define in detail what the role of the United Nations was to have been would no doubt have run into serious difficulties with one or the other of the veto-holding members of the Security Council. Deliberate vagueness was the only way out. Similar examples in both political and economic fields abound in the United Nations, and, although to a lesser extent, in the specialized agencies.

c. *Calm and good temper*

Diplomats are supposed not to betray their emotions. De Callières pointed out that those who are of an unequal temper and not master of their passions are more suitable for warfare than for negotiation. And Cambon observed, "the passions of the crowd are alien to the diplomat who maintains a surprisingly reserved attitude".[4]

Calm is certainly an indispensable qualification for the conference diplomat. The tumult of certain conference debates, with procedural interventions following each other in quick succession, or the bitter attacks to which even an innocent delegation may in an exceptional situation be exposed, require a full command of one's temper.

If there does not appear to be much difference between "calm" and "good temper" in this context, they may be compared to strategy and tactics. "Calm", in the sense of avoiding emotional involvement which could prejudice the course of negotiations, is strategy. "Good temper" is tactics, a question of style and manners which must be present in every diplomat's mind, all the more when he is dealing with the harassing facts of large-scale conference life. Losing one's temper in a conference can be particularly embarrassing, with large numbers of delegates as witnesses. The delegate who loses his temper may get the reputation of being invariably hot-tempered. He will have considerable difficulty in getting rid of such a "label".

On the other hand, exaggerated placidity, like a constantly applied "stiff upper lip" attitude, will provoke its own kind of irritation in international conferences. The conference diplomat who behaves in this way may soon be considered "cold" and uninterested in the important objectives pursued by the conference, and therefore runs the risk of being written off as not worth the trouble of approaching.

d. *Patience, modesty and zeal*

Patience and modesty have been advocated by practically all writers on the requirements for diplomats. Modesty has been equated with the avoidance of vanity.

The conference diplomat is probably even more than the conventional diplomat required to exercise patience. Initiatives which his government has instructed him to put forward in a conference may not prove realizable in the first conference where they are launched. Chances for adoption may be better one or two years later, when the idea has "ripened" and the initiating government has done some quiet spadework in the intervals between conferences to propagate its ideas. Patience in a deeper sense is a superior sense of timing: to know how and when to act and when to keep quiet.

Nicolson warned that "the dangers of vanity in a negotiator can scarcely be exaggerated. It tempts him to disregard the advice or opinions of those who may have had longer experience of a country, or of a problem, than he possesses himself. It renders him vulnerable to the flattery or the attacks of those with whom he is negotiating. It encourages him to take too personal a view of the nature and purposes of his functions and in extreme cases to prefer a brilliant but undesirable triumph to some unostentatious but more prudent compromise. It leads him to boast of his victories and thereby to incur the hatred of those whom he has vanquished. It may prevent him, at some crucial moment, from confessing to his government that his predictions or his information were incorrect. It prompts him to incur or to provoke unnecessary friction over matters which are of purely social importance." [5]

As a result of greater publicity and the inclination "to play to the gallery" the cult of vanity, of "false glory", is probably even more tempting in conference diplomacy than in traditional diplomacy. A modest conference diplomat finds that politeness abounds and that he may be abundantly praised for a speech which he himself considers only average. A variety of reasons, some of them tactical, may cause such praise. One of them may be the desire of another delegation to win over to its cause or point of view the delegation to which the speaker belongs. If the press, radio or television gives some attention to a speech, the speaker may become even more flattered.

However, modesty need not and should not prevent the right kind of zeal which I would define as "enthusiastic diligency". Talleyrand's famous advice "Surtout pas trop de zèle", must not be interpreted too limitatively. The successful conference diplomat will adapt his actions to a given situation, avoiding both the label of being lazy and that of being overzealous. He can and should take initiatives both within his own delegation and in the conference. In some cases taking an initiative means long preparation and getting clearance from one's superiors. In other situations, such as a procedural debate where points of order are raised, a delegate can take initiatives using his own immediate judgement.

e. *Adaptability*

De Callières pointed out that most men are more interested in what they want to say than in what others tell them; his advice was that one of the most necessary requirements for a negotiator (the term diplomat did not yet exist) was to be able to listen with attention and reflection. This is indeed the clue to true adaptability; to be able to take in what the other person is arguing. Placing oneself in the position of one's conversational partner is of considerable assistance in achieving such mental absorption.

The conference milieu poses its own peculiar requirements of adaptability. The conference diplomat may have to work on more than one problem and in more than one spot at the same time. He must be able to jump from one problem to another with great speed and mental efficiency. Also, he will often be in a situation of talking to or negotiating not with one person, but with a group. Adaptability then implies the capacity of judging the psychological climate and the overall views of the group.

f. *Loyalty*

Loyalty in traditional diplomacy means loyalty to one's own government and sovereign, and, in a different way, to the government of accreditation. The prolonged stationing of a conference diplomat in a post may affect his loyalty (usually without his actually realizing it) by an enhanced attachment to the work of the organization with which the conference diplomat deals, a situation of "reverse diplomacy" (see p. 126). However, the inverse may also happen: the conference diplomat gets "fed up" with the organization(s) he has dealt with for such a long time. In either case his judgement is necessarily affected, and his value to his government lessened.

The conference diplomat's loyalty may be put to the test if he is elected to the post of chairman or some other office of a committee or conference. Normally his government will have desired or allowed his election. As a presiding officer the conference diplomat is temporarily taken out of his delegation; he owes his primary loyalty to the conference as a whole. This can put him into conflict with his own government and delegation. He may for example "lean over backwards" before ruling in favour of his own delegation which has made a point of order. His delegation will naturally take this amiss. Conversely, his attitude can tend to favour the group of countries to which his own government belongs. Others will not like that. He may be drawn into mediating in a conflict with which his government would prefer him to have nothing to do. These are some of the possible risks inherent in conference diplomacy.

A discussion of the requirements of diplomacy should stress some qualifications specifically needed by conference diplomats:

g. *Physical and mental endurance*

The long working hours resulting not only from conference meetings, but also because of delegation meetings, time needed to prepare telegrams, social functions, concentrated work on different problems, all demand extreme endurance, both physical and mental, from the conference diplomat.

h. *Speed*

The conference diplomat must be able to work fast. Telegrams reporting on some new development or asking for instructions cannot be leisurely drafted and redrafted. The predominance of oral communication requires fast thinking and clear formulation, which—from the point of view of time available—contrasts with the leisurely time-consuming attention which even today is applied in bilateral diplomacy to most notes exchanged between embassies and Foreign Offices.

i. *Linguistic versatility*

As will be discussed in chapter X, the conference diplomat often has to communicate in a language not his own. Even if one of the conference languages is his mother tongue, it is essential that he can participate in conversations in one of the other languages.

j. *Courage*

The conference diplomat must not be afraid to make a speech or take some decision. He may not have time to consult his head of delegation on how to vote on some important resolution or amendment, and must then have the courage to come to his own decision.

2. *Characteristics of conference diplomats*

We have referred above to the need for adaptability. The best way to adapt oneself to the conference milieu is to have a thorough knowledge of the subjects coming up at the conference and to be as familiar as possible with the documentation and with the points of view of other delegations. But the individual peculiarities of other delegates are also important. An early recognition of these traits as they appear in conferences will help one to react most effectively. The following brief and too superficial sketches of conference delegate types are offered in order to assist the process of early recognition.

a. *The silent*

The silent delegate may be a newcomer, who feels his way around. Or he may be an old-timer who has learnt through experience that speeches are rarely effective. It is possible that the delegate who is silent in meetings is quite active in the lobby. He can therefore well be at the same time a lobbyist.

b. *The lobbyist*

The term is here used in the sense of a person active in the lobby or whatever facilities may be near the conference room (not in the sense of a person or representative of a pressure group coming from the outside and trying to influence the proceedings). Since the lobbyist tries to do most of his business outside the conference room, some other member of his delegation must be in the committee chair.

c. *The orator*

In at least one respect the opposite of the lobbyist, he never misses a chance to make a speech or statement before as large an audience as possible. If he is also a good speaker, his major speeches will be a delight to listen to. But in the midst of what has been called "rhetoric plethora" his speeches must be far above the average if they are to continue to attract attention. The story has been told that one United Nations delegate accidentally picked up the speech another delegate had just made, "and found it marginally annotated almost like a musical score with one passage heavily marked: Weak point. Shout".[6]

d. *The procedural specialist*

Normally not very conspicuous in his conference behaviour, he becomes an active participant when a procedural debate breaks out. Fully acquainted with the rules, he knows how and when to make a point of order. He delights in such debates, and is frequently informally consulted on procedural points by other delegates.

e. *Old- versus new-timers*

There are, of course, real old "old-timers". At the time that this is written, they would be (in U.N. meetings) those who attended League of Nations meetings. In spite of its lack of success, the time of the League fills those who personally witnessed its meetings with nostalgia.

"The veteran of Geneva who participates in the hurly-burly of United Nations, New York, must often be tempted to exclaim, 'the League was never like this!' ".[7] Also, in conferences of the International Labour Organization, founded in 1919, a number of real old-timers can be found.

However, in the average conference of the United Nations or the specialized agencies it is another type of old-timer that one encounters more often: the delegate who has been at that particular type of meeting several times, who knows the organization inside out and can predict "which way the cookies crumble". Newcomers are expected to behave respectfully vis-à-vis such old-timers. A revolt of the newcomers against the old hands can therefore only be successful if the newcomers know exactly what they are doing and are numerous enough to be able to hint at the use they can make of their majority vote if they so wish. The advent of so many newly independent nations with attitudes which are often at variance with those of the "old" nations, is often accompanied by the same psychological relations as exist between "new" and "old" delegates.

3. *Professional background and conference diplomacy*

Is there an ideal academic or professional background for conference diplomacy? The answer is that no single type of academic training automatically produces conference diplomats, just as little as it produces conventional diplomats. A few observations on the relation between specific types of training or background and conference diplomacy can be made:

a. *The lawyer*

Many diplomats have had legal training. There is no doubt that sound legal training is valuable in conference diplomacy. Conference diplomacy means a constant exposure to legal texts. The lawyer is supposed to be capable of detecting subtle differences between one wording and another. He is supposed to be able to have a facility for drafting. The lawyer brings, however, both the assets and the liabilities from his training to a conference: he may have a tendency to place too much value on formal and legal considerations. His general training should make it possible to grasp without difficulty the substance of a subject, whether economic, political or anything else. His legal training may be so different from that of other delegates with a legal background whom he meets at the conference, that he must beware of the difficulties this could cause. The difference between the Anglo-Saxon and Latin legal systems comes to mind in this context.

b. *The economist*

Economists, in particular if they have made economic policy their speciality, are accustomed to analysing various possible solutions of a problem on the basis of a single set of data. Conference diplomacy very often also entails choosing one solution out of different conceivable ones for a given problem. The economist with experience in methods of problem-solving has a definite advantage in conference diplomacy.

Statistics of all kinds and budgets for organizations are normal material put before conference delegates. The economist is expected to have a good command of this kind of documentation and to be able to recognize quickly any fallacies or discrepancies.

On the negative side the economist may have a lack of feeling for political and legal problems. He may tend to overemphasize the substantive, economic aspects of a problem. Such an attitude tends to underestimate the degree to which political elements get intertwined with the various substantive aspects of a problem.

c. *The political scientist*

Political science as a separate modern discipline is relatively new. Hence the number of academic graduates in political science in the diplomatic profession is still small, in particular in Europe. In so far as academic training in political science imparts to future conference diplomats essential elements of law, economics and politics (in particular a knowledge of various political systems and conflict-solving methods), it could constitute the ideal training for the conference diplomat. The danger is, however, that conference diplomats thus trained have had too little of each of these disciplines. Intelligent people will always be able to overcome any such deficiency (the same is true for the lawyer who is deficient in economics, for the economist who does not know enough law).

The practice found in many secondary schools and universities of organizing "model general assemblies" is certainly good. One may expect that the next generation of conference delegates will thus have been better trained than previous generations.

d. *The historian*

History is certainly useful as a professional background to conference diplomacy. Many problems coming before international conferences have a long history. In the case of territorial conflicts this history may be one of centuries. With more ease than those with different backgrounds the historian will be able to put problems in their proper perspective, although here again a narrow historical approach, like a purely legalistic or economic one, will run its head into the brick wall of present-day political factors.

e. *The parliamentarian*

Conference diplomacy overlaps to a considerable extent with what has been called parliamentary diplomacy. Not unnaturally, one might ask to what extent national parliamentary experience is useful in conference diplomacy. The national parliamentarian is used to making public appearances in an important forum, and he is presumably also accustomed to finding solutions, often in the form of compromises, for difficult problems. Such experiences are valuable in conference diplomacy.

Parliamentarians, when members of their national delegations to large international conferences, usually adapt quickly to the typical international conference milieu in which they find themselves. Even so, the parliamentarian cannot dispense with the expert knowledge really needed to do a first class job in the conference which he attends. If he does not have that expert knowledge himself he will have to rely on other members of the delegation.

IX. GROUPS IN CONFERENCE DIPLOMACY

1. *Introduction and definitions*

It is well-known that groups of delegations undertake common functions in the conference framework. Many recent studies of groups concentrate on the degree of continuing voting coherence of the members of various groups.[1] However, there are constant shifts in the alignments of nations in conference diplomacy. Bailey's statement "The outstanding fact about the way States associate in the General Assembly is the tendency of Member States to affiliate differently for different purposes" [2] is applicable to most intergovernmental conferences. In other words, "there are divisions . . . between the various regional areas . . . between developed and underdeveloped countries, between agricultural and industrial countries, between exporting and importing countries, between donors and receivers of economic aid, between totalitarian and democratic countries and a whole host of other divisions".[3] The word "bloc", seen in this context of shifting alignments, is not a useful concept. Hovet defines a bloc as "a group of states which meets regularly in caucus and the members of which are bound in their votes in the General Assembly by the caucus decision".[4] Even the Soviet bloc, often cited as a typical example, has over the years become less homogeneous. The single notion of "group" appears therefore more logical than the somewhat artificial distinction between group and bloc.

Whether one likes them or not, blocs and groups will no doubt remain an essential feature of conference diplomacy. Group meetings have become a wholly normal occurrence during international conferences. In conferences such as those of UNCTAD one finds them scheduled in the daily bulletin on a par with the official sessions. In some organizations groups have had recognized status for a long time, for example in the ILO, where the tripartite structure has caused the governments', employers' and workers' groups to meet separately.

The average conference diplomat will have to live in and with groups. The more he knows about the methods, prejudices and opinions of various groups and blocs the easier it will be for him to determine the right attitudes.

In this chapter we shall first indicate, in section 2, the main groups which can be recognized in contemporary international conferences. In section 3 there is an analysis of the main functions which the groups perform. In section 4 we take a brief look at what sort of relations are important in connection with the phenomenon of groups. In section 5 some observations are made on the effect of groups on the negotiating process.

2. *Types of groups*

Although the function of any group at a specific conference is more important than its formal existence, a number of groups are so well-known that they must be mentioned. They can be divided into:

(*a*) Regional groups
(*b*) Political groups
(*c*) Groups resulting from intergovernmental economic treaties
(*d*) Groups based on a common level of economic development or some other common interest.

a. *Regional groups*

Some well-known examples are:
African group
Asian group
Latin American "caucus"
Nordic countries (Denmark, Finland, Iceland, Norway, Sweden)
Soviet Union and its allied Eastern European countries
Western European group

In their straight geographical sense these groups have two main reasons for existing: to exchange information (which, however, tends more and more to take place in one of the economic or political groupings mentioned below) and to agree on candidates for elections in cases where geographical criteria are important. The presidency of each General Assembly session and that of the plenary conference of most specialized agencies rotates among the various regions, principally Asia, Africa, the Western Hemisphere and Europe. Similar to, but not quite identical with these regional groups are those formed because, according to a constitution or resolution, they are expected to nominate a given number of candidates for certain posts. (See p. 146.)

The Western European group and the Latin American "caucus", as it is called, are among the oldest on the international conference scene. Some of these groups meet regularly, especially just before and during major conferences like the U.N. General Assembly, others meet as the need arises.

b. *Political groups*

Examples are:
Arab League
Commonwealth
NATO
Non-aligned Nations
Organization of American States
Warsaw Pact
Western European Union

The Commonwealth grouping has become, in most conferences, a very loose one. It includes highly developed, less-developed and very underdeveloped countries. Politically, many of its members consider themselves "non-aligned". Indeed, the non-aligned countries, stressing the fact that they do not belong to any political alliance and adopting an attitude of "positive neutrality", have in many conferences become an identifiable group. Its exact composition and activities appear to vary from conference to conference. Formal Conferences of the Non-Aligned Nations were held in Belgrade (1961) and Cairo (1964).[5] The NATO countries may be assumed to consult on certain U.N. matters in their regular meetings. By and large there is little evidence that–with the possible exception of the Warsaw Pact and the Arab League— formal political groupings as such play an active role in conference diplomacy.

c. *Groups based on formal international economic agreements*

Benelux
EEC (European Economic Community)
EFTA (European Free Trade Association)
OECD (all Western European countries, plus Greece, Turkey, the
    United States, Canada, Japan)

The countries belonging to these groups have group meetings more or less often and try to coordinate their interests whenever this appears necessary. In some conferences, for example those of the GATT, the European Economic Community countries, with their common external customs tariff, frequently operate as a unit, with a single spokesman, except for matters which clearly fall within the sphere of each Member State. The steady growth of the EEC, which is to be completed by 1970, implies a gradual transfer of national tasks and responsibilities to the Community, represented by the European Commission or by a delegation composed of officials of the Member States and of the Commission.[6]

d. *Groupings based on a common level of economic development or some other common interest*

Prior to the first UNCTAD Conference (Geneva, 1964) the less-developed countries first consulted each other in a conference held at Cairo, which led to a joint declaration and common positions. At "UNCTAD I" these countries established a well organized, streamlined set-up known at that time as "the group of 75", and later, with the addition of some more countries as "the group of 77". During the conference the group held meetings, not only at the head of delegation level, but also for each of the six commissions into which the conference had split up. The efficiency of their cooperation, in spite of known differences of views, impressed everybody. The "75" were able to develop common points of view on most issues, and defended these positions with vigour and intelligence.

After the first UNCTAD Conference the "77" continued to make use of their coordination machinery. In Geneva, headquarters of the UNCTAD Secretariat, they took up the practice of meeting once a week or more often, as necessary. On the UNCTAD Board of 55 members, 31 out of the "77" are members. The "77" also coordinated their positions in regard to other conferences (for example in GATT), formed a coordinating committee to prepare for the Second UNCTAD Conference (New Delhi, February/March 1968), and held a conference in Algiers (October 1967) for the same purpose. In the Second (Economic and Financial) Committee of the General Assembly the "77" sometimes operated as a homogeneous bloc.

At the same UNCTAD Conference of 1964 the developed market economy countries also aimed at coordinating their positions. Their group, called group B, consisted of the OECD countries plus Australia and New Zealand, and several smaller states (San Marino, Liechtenstein) and the Holy See, all of which were represented at the UNCTAD Conference.

By and large the groupings emerging from the first UNCTAD conference were the less-developed countries of the world on the one hand and the developed countries on the other, the latter being subdivided into a large number of market economy countries and a smaller number of state trading countries.

In conferences with specific objectives *ad hoc* groupings, or coalitions, derived from common interests, usually emerge quite naturally. In chapter XI this will be illustrated with the alignments that arose in trade and disarmament negotiations. In commodity conferences, where the aim is to arrive at price stabilization agreements, it is normal to find countries that are major exporters of a commodity, and therefore interested in a relatively high price, grouped together, confronting countries that are major importers, and anxious to have stable supplies at prices that are not too high.

In conferences of the ECE it is customary for the market economy countries of Western Europe to take coordinated positions on many questions, as do the centrally planned states of Eastern Europe. The Western and the Eastern countries of the ECE each have regular "caucus" meetings in Geneva throughout the year.[7]

A recent group based on common interests is that consisting of about ten governments of developed countries, all contributors of more than 1% to the budgets of the United Nations and the specialized agencies, who meet once a year in order, as stated in the press release issued after the fourth such meeting in 1967, "to review the programs and budgets of the specialized agencies and to examine possible improvements in their operations so as to enhance the effectiveness of their contribution to world economic and social development and to facilitate international support for their work".

A well-known case of an *ad hoc* group is the alignment which a common language sometimes brings about. When documents are not available in French, the French language countries protest *en bloc* about this lapsus. In the UNCTAD Shipping Committee the major shipping countries have formed a fairly homogeneous group.

3. *Functions of groups*

The functions performed by groups can be distinguished—in ascending order of commitment of the members—in the following way:

a. *To exchange information on all or part of the agenda of a conference, either in advance or during a conference*

For example, the seven members of the Western European Union (Belgium, France, Italy, Luxemburg, Netherlands, Federal Republic of Germany, United Kingdom) meet before every U.N. General Assembly and Economic and Social Council session to go over the agenda, without specifically developing common positions to be taken at these conferences.

b. *To develop common general positions on important agenda items, without definite voting commitment*

In this case, there is not only an exchange of information but also an effort to arrive at approximately identical positions for all delegations participating in group meetings. The OECD members, expanded by certain non-members, endeavour as the so-called group B (see p. 144) to coordinate their positions on various issues and agenda items in UNCTAD Conferences.

c. *To develop common positions on certain agenda items or initiatives with agreement on how to vote*

Efforts to find not only common positions, but also agreements on how to vote, can and do occur in almost every group. They occur systematically in groups of nations bound together by a treaty requiring common points of view on certain questions, as is the case for the member countries of the European Economic Community.

More and more in conferences one can encounter examples of geographical, political or *ad hoc* groups deciding to vote in a certain way on at least one proposal, on a certain amendment, or on an expected procedural move. Explicit coordination of voting behaviour is increasing, while in the past a tacit, or at most an improvised, understanding arrived at just before voting led to voting alignments.

d. *To agree on candidates to be put forward by the group or on a common vote for candidates from outside the group*

This is one of the functions where development of a common point of view has meaning only if there is also agreement on how to vote. This may be for a single agreed slate of candidates of the grouping itself as well as for some combination out of a number of competing candidates of other groups. In connection with such election agreements there may be a joint plan of campaign for or against certain candidates.

The formation of groups specifically designed to put forward candidates for certain positions has been pushed by the increasing habit for some basic decision to allocate the number of seats going to certain groups. For instance, according to General Assembly resolution 1990 (XVIII), which superseded resolution 1192 (XII), seventeen vice-presidents of the General Assembly are to be elected on the basis of the following pattern:

7 from Asian and African States
1 from an Eastern European State

3 from Latin American States

2 from Western European and other States

5 from the permanent members of the Security Council.

This adds up to 18; the solution is that the area from which the President comes, loses one vice-presidency.

Resolution 1995 (XIX) of the General Assembly establishing UNCTAD provides that the 55 members of the UNCTAD Board, the permanent organ, shall be elected by the conference (the plenary organ), as follows:

22 from 61 states listed in part A of the Annex to the resolution, all economically less-developed countries;

18 from 29 states listed in part B, which are by and large the economically developed countries (including, however, some developing countries in Europe, e.g. Cyprus, Greece, Portugal, and Spain, but not Yugoslavia, which is included in the previous group;

9 from 22 countries listed in part C, which are the Western Hemisphere countries, except Canada and the United States, both included in group B;

6 from 9 states listed in part D, which are the Eastern European countries.

Theoretically, the UNCTAD conference could freely elect countries out of these four groups. In practice the groups nominate their candidates, on the basis of consultations within each group, and under a gentlemen's arrangement each group accepts the candidates nominated by the other.

In the case of UNCTAD the groups mentioned in the resolution for election purposes represent in fact the main economic systems concerned with UNCTAD questions. The main function of groups A, B, C and D, as they have come to be called, is to develop common positions on agenda items. On the other hand at General Assembly sessions the nomination of candidates for vice-president has remained the main function of the "Western European and other" group, which grew out of resolution 1192 (XII). Efforts to have this group also discuss other questions have apparently not given results. Certain political questions before the General Assembly are reviewed in what is called the Western group, which also includes Japan and the United States. Economic questions are examined in a group corresponding to group B of the UNCTAD system.

e. *To agree on a common spokesman, and on the contents of the statement to be delivered*

As discussed in chapter II a group of sponsors of a draft resolution usually agrees on a common spokesman to introduce its text in the meeting. Furthermore, any of the groups we have discussed above may in a particular situation decide on a common spokesman. The formalization of groups in the UNCTAD has led to statements in UNCTAD organs made on behalf of "all less-developed countries" or on behalf of "group B countries". At the end of the Kennedy Round of trade negotiations a group of less-developed countries presented a statement through a common spokesman. Such group declarations have substantive contents in contrast to the traditionally innocuous joint common statement in the form of expressions of thanks delivered at the end of a conference.

f. *To undertake joint action for or against a certain proposal*

Although linked to functions b and c, such a "lobbying" function can be separate. A common position and an agreement on voting do not necessarily entail joint lobbying. Conversely, a joint lobbying campaign obviously requires an agreed position on the proposal or issue behind it.

Concluding observation

These distinctions are not rigid. It frequently happens that groups existing for a certain reason or with a previously declared objective, will on occasion, when faced with a particular situation or problem, carry out a different function than the one for which they were originally formed. For example, a group formed only to exchange information may be pushed by a specific problem to decide on a common voting position.

4. *Groups and the negotiating process in conference diplomacy*

a. *Relations between various groups, and of groups with the president*

In a large conference the official or unofficial leaders of the various groups may wish to meet each other to explore positions, and possibly initiate a process of negotiation. At the first UNCTAD conference the leaders of the various groups met regularly with the President. In the 1964-67 GATT Trade Conference known as the Kennedy Round the representatives of some groups and some of the most important countries met, under the presidency of the Director-General of GATT, as an informal steering committee, dealing both with substantive and procedural questions (cf. Chapter XI).

b. *Relations between members of a group and the group*

To the extent that it has become customary in a conference for initiatives to emanate from groups, the individual delegation must consider carefully whether, within the group to which it belongs, it wishes to put forward some proposal, initiative or suggestion, in order to gain group endorsement. If there is a "group within the group" to which the delegation belongs, it will try to get prior support for its ideas from such a subgroup. If a delegation wants to "go it alone", without group endorsement, it must have mapped out a strategy to gain support from other groups, or from some *ad hoc* combination of delegations.

c. *Relations between groups and the secretariat*

If close relations exist between one group and the secretariat, this can provide a fertile terrain for cooperation: plans prepared in the secretariat are taken over by delegations who are members of a group and presented (as their own or as a secretariat idea) in a group meeting. If such a situation exists, groups that do not have close relations with the secretariat will clearly try to improve them. They will otherwise find themselves confronted with proposals which take them by surprise and some of which they may not like. In any conference where the secretariat plays an active role, early contact between the various groups and the secretariat is essential.

5. *The effect of groups on the negotiating process*

It is hazardous to generalize on the advantages and disadvantages of groups for the effective conduct of conference diplomacy, since each conference presents its own "make-up" of groups. In analysing the behaviour of each group in a specific conference, one can come to a conclusion as to its effect on the outcome of the conference. However, it is possible to identify some effects which, with hesitation, can be called positive or negative. This hesitation arises from the consideration that for some the mere existence of the group system is more important than some of these so-called negative effects, which are therefore regarded as being negligible. Others would argue that what will be called hereafter greater inflexibility in the negotiating process is favourable because it reflects greater unity and strength of weak countries and therefore is desirable.

As regards the positive side of the group system one can agree with Hovet's general conclusion that "... as the United Nations has become enlarged both in its membership and in terms of the variety of interests represented in that membership, the bloc and group arrangements have become a necessity for effective negotiation. In any case, it is clear that participation in a caucusing group is advantageous to a member state, and participation in several caucus groups even more advantageous. It provides an opportunity to create a combined voting power which can be a critical factor in negotiating with other groups ... Participation in caucusing groups can open avenues for a variety of diplomatic techniques. A group caucus pursuing a common point of view can cast its members in different roles in order to explore possible areas of negotiation. A group caucus can benefit from collective interpretations of factors present in other groups, a procedure which can often indicate subtleties of cohesion and division that are pertinent to working out acceptable compromises." [8]

This comment appears applicable not only to the United Nations, but to conferences of all organizations with large and increasing membership. Specifically, the positive effect of the group system would be a gain in conference efficiency, especially if negotiating procedures between groups become an established routine, and communications between groups are made easier by the existence of such procedures. Moreover, in so far as statements by group spokesmen replace a large number of individual speeches, time may be saved.

On the negative side it has become apparent, that the "willingness to seek areas of acceptable compromise" expected by Hovet may be absent, and, indeed, have been replaced by a sort of group inflexibility which makes the negotiation of compromise agreements more difficult.

This is likely to occur where a "demand-offer" type of conflict arises: a group of countries presents maximum demands to another group which tends to respond with minimum offers. During the first UNCTAD conference the experience was that within the group of "77" there was a tendency for countries which might possibly have been willing to accept moderate compromise positions to align themselves out of group solidarity with more extreme demands advanced by certain countries and then adopted by the group as a whole. The Western market economy countries, the principal group confronting the "77", underwent a similar process, but in the opposite direction: countries that normally might be expected to take the lead in negotiating for compromise solutions, accepted joint positions of the group. These positions resulted in minimal offers to the less-developed countries. It was difficult to obtain modification of the less-developed countries' and Western group positions, once established and publicly expressed in conference sessions. Thus, the pattern that emerged from the first UNCTAD conference was that maximum demands came into head-on collision with minimum offers.

This had a delaying effect on the usual search by any large conference to find constructive middle ground. Only towards the end of the conference a number of small conciliation bodies was able to arrive at last minute compromise texts on a number of important issues.[9]

A specially delicate problem may be posed by the relations between the secretariats of the organizations and different groups. In UNCTAD the various groups lead a semi-formal existence because they emerged as an outgrowth of the lists of states annexed to resolution 1995 for election purposes. As a result the Secretariat does not have to have scruples about having close contacts with the groups. Similarly, in the ILO with the constitutionally recognized existence of three groups (governments, employers, workers), around which the entire structure of the ILO revolves, relations between the groups and the Secretariat are governed by standard procedures. Of course every secretariat must see to it that it treats all groups on a basis of equality.

In other organizations, where the groups lead a more informal life, the situation may be different. At the 20th World Health Assembly (Geneva, 1967) delegations disagreed on the magnitude of the 1969 budget of the WHO. After lengthy corridor discussions and a relatively brief debate in the Committee on Programme and Budget this committee adopted, by a split vote, a resolution recommending to the Director-General that "as a general orientation in preparing his proposed programme and budget estimates for 1969 he should, taking account of the views expressed by delegations during the discussions at the Twentieth World Health Assembly, propose an increase in the programme such as will give a budget increase of an order or magnitude of about 7 per cent, giving a total of approximately $ 60.000.000, provided that no unusual and unforeseen developments occur which would result in additional resources being required by the organization". In plenary session an amendment was presented to replace the percentage of 7 by 9, and subsequently adopted (again with a split vote). The brief debate in plenary session showed that, by and large, less-developed countries were in favour of the amendment and the consequent additional increase in WHO activities, while developed countries opposed it. There is, however, no explicit mention of any group points of view, or of negotiation between groups, or between groups and the secretariat. Yet the Director-General, shortly before the vote, made a statement which included the following references to groups: ". . . I do not believe that, in the democratic system that should exist in this organization, there is any problem of confrontation of different groups. I think it is quite clear that countries have differing needs, and any delegate has the right to ask for what he believes the Organization should do . . . I should like to say that yesterday I was extremely unhappy at giving the impression to the Assembly that I was working with groups in order to save the situation. I have to say to the Assembly that if I have dealt with any group, it was not with one of the groups mentioned yesterday in the Committee on Programme and Budget. And I can guarantee the Assembly that, from now on, the only groups that I am prepared to deal with are the regional committees of the Organization, which represent the real structure of this Organization." (WHO document A20/VR/13 of May 26, 1967).

In the absence of a published record of Committee on Programme and Budget sessions, the groups to which the Director-General alluded cannot be identified. The interesting thing is that he specifically expressed his aversion to working with informal groups, and went on record that henceforward he would only have contacts with the formal groups recognized in the WHO, namely the regional committees.

In conclusion, it must be stressed that the group system is in constant evolution. The UNCTAD group negotiating procedures have evolved in the direction of greater flexibility since the first UNCTAD Conference. This flexibility is probably the combined result of certain divided points of view within the groups and of their increased awareness that rigid group positions do not lead to constructive results.

X. TACTICS, INSTRUCTIONS, SPEECHES, AND CONCILIATION IN CONFERENCE DIPLOMACY

1. *Tactics in conference diplomacy*

The use of threats, warnings, promises, and other tactical moves occur in conference diplomacy as much as in traditional diplomacy.[1]

In conference diplomacy the interplay of delegations and the secretariat, and, whenever he assumes an active role, the chairman, produces a larger number of combinations and permutations of the use of various tactical devices than are available in bilateral diplomacy. The situation is different for those who want to get a proposal adopted from that of delegations who merely wish to oppose others' proposals.

a. *Tactics to get a proposal adopted*

A delegation wishing to get a proposal adopted can choose from an arsenal of tactical devices, including threats, warnings, bluffs and inducements. Essentially, however, it must convince the required majority of participants including, if advisable, the secretariat that adoption of the proposal then and there at the particular conference is desirable. A delegation that wishes to oppose a proposal has a larger choice of tactical weapons available because it can aim not only at outright defeat, but also at deferment of a decision until a later conference. Usually it is easier to preach procrastination than action where the waverers are concerned. Thus, against the single objective: adoption, pursued by proponents of a proposal, opponents can choose from two alternative objectives: *defeat* or *deferment*. This situation militates against a single delegation or a small number of delegations seeking to have a proposal adopted. In practice this disadvantage is mitigated by the fact that in the United Nations and the specialized agencies initiatives often emanate from an established or an *ad hoc* group comprising a large number of countries. On issues such as the economic development of less-developed countries or colonial questions large numbers of countries come forward with draft resolutions. Powerful countries, if they cannot immediately line up a sufficient number of smaller countries to support a proposal, can exert various kinds of pressure. Small countries must use persuasion to get a sufficient number of allies, except in a very few cases where they can also exercise some sort of pressure.

Whether to aim at a group of formal sponsors or to sponsor a draft resolution alone is a tactical decision of considerable importance. In certain cases a delegation may prefer to sponsor a draft resolution alone, keeping full freedom of action. More normally a group of sponsors will be constituted. The criteria for the choice of the group of sponsors will depend on the subject of the proposal. Usually, some sort of geographic distribution is aimed at: at least one country from each area of the world. In questions related to the economic development of less-developed countries there may be an effort to compose the sponsor group of both developed and less-developed countries, or, alternatively, a group of less-developed countries may not wish to have indusized countries as co-sponsors.

The following methods are all a combination of some sort of pressure and persuasion:

(1) *Intellectual arguments.* A great many initiatives and proposals are adopted mainly on their intellectual strength. The proponents demonstrate that the proposal is coming at the right time and place. In this case no threats, pressures or rewards are necessary to obtain wide support. Most secretariat proposals for new initiatives (studies, action, or whatever it may be) are backed up with intellectual arguments. Delegations putting forward secretariat proposals as their own can and will use intellectual arguments. The satisfaction of getting adopted what it sees as right, plus possibly a certain amount of prestige, are the main recompense for a delegation relying exclusively on intellectual arguments in defence of its proposal (cf. chapter IV, p. 76-78).

(2) *Promises.* A delegation may get one or more other delegations on its side by promising something. The "something" could be support for some initiative or desire of the other delegation. The promise can be economic or financial: a large or rich country may hold out a promise of financial or economic aid to a smaller or weaker country in exchange for a pledge of support. The delegation confronted with such an economic or financial pledge will have to decide whether it is in its national interest to abandon its initial opposition.

The promise could also be political, for example backing in some issue or dispute where the country is claimant or defendant. In some cases a pledge for mutual support is made. Such a pledge is usually on unrelated issues of considerable, and roughly equal, importance. A delegation which has a proposal on problem X, in which it has a direct stake of its own, obtains support from delegation B, which has a direct stake in problem Y, and vice versa.

In election campaigns, if two delegations are each trying to get some elected position in either the same organization or conference, or in two different organizations or conferences (provided of course they are members of both), they can pledge mutual help.

The exchange of roughly equivalent support pledges is often referred to as "log-rolling", a term derived from the method of transporting logs of timber on North American rivers.

(3) *Over-asking or under-offering.* In bilateral negotiations it is well known that the party which has certain demands will over-ask, in the hope that its opponent will finally agree to an offer which corresponds with what is really wanted. Similarly, the party that has something to offer will often start offering less than what it is willing to settle for in the end.

In multilateral negotiations, the same phenomenon is frequently observed. It can be encountered in negotiations between groups at a conference. It sometimes takes the form of deliberately including in the text of a proposal language known to be unacceptable to others, with the intention of exploiting the subsequent deletion of the incriminated words as a concession. Such "over-asking" may be compared with "under-offering", i.e. a deliberate decision to omit certain words or paragraphs from a text in order to accede later to a request for their inclusion. In that way a mere gesture can be made to look like a real concession.

b. *Threats and warnings*

In bilateral diplomacy the effect of any threat or warning is limited to the negotiating partner to whom such a tactical move is addressed. Unless the threat or warning gets publicity (sometimes intentionally, in the hope of mobilizing public opinion and thus putting pressure on the negotiating partner), it remains within the private realm of a confidential negotiation. With the argument of "changed circumstances", withdrawal of the warning or threat, or simply not putting it into effect, remain entirely possible. In bilateral diplomacy threats may take the form of an ultimatum: unless before a certain date B offers some concession, A will withdraw from the negotiation. The date may be moved several times.

In conference diplomacy threats and warnings take on a different appearance because, even if they are expressed informally in a confidential negotiation, they inevitably become known to several countries and may even be addressed to the conference as a whole.

The withdrawal-of-negotiation type of ultimatum may seem unfair for use in conference diplomacy because delegations, by the nature of their agreement to participate in the conference, are supposed to sit a conference out until its official closure. What might be called "sub-ultimatums", threats to cease participating in the discussion of a certain issue rather than leaving the conference entirely, do occur in conference diplomacy: 'If before date X we cannot reach agreement on this draft resolution my delegation will cease to take part in any effort to reach a compromise'. In this vein quite a few warnings have been expressed, mostly in informal negotiating groups.

What warnings and threats are most frequently encountered in conference diplomacy? The following are some fairly typical examples:

(1) *Warning that a country's delegation, while remaining in the conference, will not participate in the discussion of a certain agenda item, nor in any voting on draft decisions on the item.* The Union of South Africa made such a warning and then carried it out in the U.N. General Assembly when the question of apartheid was dealt with at various sessions. Such a warning remains without practical effect, in the sense that it does not modify the position of other delegations. Therefore, it is, if carried out, mostly an expression of displeasure and irritation that presumably has the desired effect on domestic public or parliamentary opinion.

(2) *Threat that a delegation will leave the conference.* The effective carrying out of this threat may damage the country that leaves a conference more than it hurts others, unless the walkout has financial consequences for the organization the conference deals with. When the delegation of the Soviet Union left the Security Council at the beginning of 1950, stating that it would not return as long as the seat of China was not occupied by the representatives of the People's Republic of China, the main result was to avoid casting an otherwise probable veto on the decision (June 1950) to have the United Nations intervene in the Korean conflict. At the beginning of August, 1950, the Soviet Union returned to the Council.

A fairly common phenomenon (around 1967) has become the temporary walkout by groups of delegations when the floor is taken by a speaker from a government with which they not only have no diplomatic relations but of whose policies they are extremely critical. Such a walkout is, like non-participation in the discussion, a demonstration of extreme displeasure; it does not, in itself, affect the decision-making process.

(3) *Threat of non-participation in new activity.* Quite frequently a delegation will warn the other participants in a conference that if a certain draft resolution is adopted it will not take part in the new organization or activity contained in that resolution. This, for example, has been the attitude of the United States government vis-à-vis plans to create a large United Nations Fund to finance capital investments in less-developed countries. Such a fund, referred to as SUNFED (Special United Nations Fund for Economic Development) in the 1950's and now called U.N. Capital Development Fund, was after years of deliberations established at the 21st session of the General Assembly (Resolution 2186 (XXI)).

(4) *Threat of non-support.* Threats can take the form of the exact reverse of the mutual support pledge described earlier: delegation A, confronted with a negative attitude of delegation B on problem X, on which delegation A wants some action, announces to delegation B that in that case delegation A will oppose a proposal by delegation B on problem Y. Negotiations may, before the moment of decision, transform such a situation into one of a mutual pledge for support.

(5) *Threat of withdrawal of assistance.* Similarly, instead of a promise of financial assistance a large country may threaten a smaller country with the withdrawal of financial or economic aid.

Where are threats and promises made? The conference itself is the obvious arena for producing many promises, threats and warnings. To the extent that these have a bilateral character (support on some issue, withdrawal of support, promise or threat of withdrawal of financial aid), diplomatic channels will be used by the government making the threat, warning or promise. This will be done either by calling in the ambassador of the country it wants to influence, or by having its own diplomatic representatives make a démarche in the capitals concerned.

c. *Other tactics for opposing a proposal*

The delegation that wants to oppose a proposal can have recourse, apart from the described efforts to persuade others to cast a negative vote (or to abstain), to a variety of devices:

(1) A competing draft resolution can be introduced in such a way that the sponsors of the first resolution are forced to negotiate some compromise. The sponsor(s) of the competing resolution can then start delaying tactics by raising successive difficulties in the negotiations. In the end they can either accept a compromise which in essence means defeat for

the sponsors of the original resolution or try to have the two drafts sent on to next year's conference or to a higher body.

An example of the latter situation is furnished by the October 1966 session of the Committee on the Development of Trade of the Economic Commission for Europe which had before it two competing draft resolutions, respectively by Belgium and Sweden and by Czechoslovakia and Hungary, with recommendations concerning trade relations between countries with different economic systems in Eastern and Western Europe. It would have been difficult in any case to negotiate a compromise merging these two draft resolutions. This became virtually impossible when a third draft resolution was submitted by the Soviet Union. The result was that all three draft resolutions were transmitted to the parent body, the ECE plenary session held in April 1967, which succeeded in adopting a single draft not based on the three previous texts. This feat was achieved by leaving out the more controversial points and limiting the text to generalities and to the establishment of a group of governmental experts to study the matter further.

(2) The argument that no financial and human resources are available for a proposed activity. The strength of such an argument will increase or diminish in the light of the position which the secretariat may be willing to take, either publicly in a statement, or privately in lobby conversations. The position of the secretariat becomes pivotal if its view is one of two extremes: that the new activity can be entirely done with existing funds and manpower, or that no money or people whatsoever are available.

(3) Another argument often advanced against a proposal for a new activity is that other organizations are effectively dealing with the question.

(4) A separate argument frequently heard is "time is not ripe", either in general or specifically, because a proposal must wait for the results of some other activity or study.

(5) Procedural motions can be used to obtain deferment of the consideration of a proposal. It is recalled (cf. p. 51) that the following motions have precedence over all other proposals and in the following order:
(*a*) to suspend the meeting
(*b*) to adjourn the meeting
(*c*) to adjourn the debate on the item under discussion
(*d*) for the closure of the debate on the item under discussion.

Of these motions the first three have a delaying effect. However, motions to suspend or adjourn a meeting are quite often made by the sponsors of a proposal, in order to consult each other or with a view to negotiate with others. A motion for the closure of the debate is usually made by those who want to press for a vote in favour of a proposal. Occasionally it is used by opponents of a proposal, who feel that more debate may weaken their ranks.

Some tactical arguments and devices resemble well-known games or plays:

"Black Peter": I do not like this proposal, but I tell people I support it, expecting that country X which is against it will be left with the stigma of having been responsible for its rejection.

"Hide and Seek": My arguments are hidden beneath a mass of rhetoric and of largely irrelevant considerations. If you search carefully you may dig up some of them, but it won't change things.

"Ping-Pong": In Organization B: We must not do this in this organization. It is probably outside its terms of reference. Besides, organizations X, Y and Z are working on it. Similar argument repeated in X, Y and Z. The same game can be played between the various organs of the same organization, or between a committee and its subcommittees.

"Hurdles": New hurdles are erected when one or more have been taken. They may be financial, or a reference to one's parliament, or . . .

"Poker": I hide my hand, I have lots of trumps, but I do not show anything.

"Waiting for Godot": We must wait till the time is ripe.

d. *Lobbies, social functions and the exercise of persuasion*[2]

Most efforts by delegations to persuade other delegations take place in conversations in the lobby or lounge near the conference room. Other such efforts are made in group meetings. Some group meetings are held in the lobby or delegates' lounge, with delegates huddling together, others are held in conference rooms, occasionally with interpretation provided by the conference secretariat or by a friendly organization. Quite often group meetings take place in a delegation office. The "business luncheon" has become customary at many conferences. Small luncheons provide an opportunity to discuss some issues quietly, and, if desired to examine some document or other paper. The same useful function can be fulfilled by small dinner parties. Large cocktail parties or receptions can be used to transmit pieces of paper with draft resolutions; they are also useful to get or give information. They are obviously not the place to discuss any issue or problem in depth.

All social functions may help in obtaining compromise solutions. Some conferences (e.g. WHO meetings, the Executive Committee of the U.N. High Commisioner for Refugees) have the habit of a coffee break in the

morning and a tea pause in the afternoon. If there happens to be a difficult situation in the meeting, the astute chairman can have such interruptions start a little earlier and in any case they can be used for purposes
of reconciliation.

Many, if not most, cocktail parties, receptions, luncheons or dinners
during conferences are not given for negotiating purposes, but for reasons
of national or personal ostentation. A special case is the reception or
luncheon or dinner given to support an election campaign. This is a fairly
normal practice. A few words spoken at the beginning or end of the
luncheon or dinner, alluding in not too direct terms to the known interest of the host delegation in being elected to some organ or post, may
have the desired effect and help to find a few useful votes.

2. *Instructions*

"Special written instructions are indispensable". This dictum by Satow [3]
can be considered applicable to conference diplomacy, although not always followed. In practice, there are considerable differences in the
amount and nature of instructions which delegations receive. Especially
in general, mostly deliberative conferences many delegations arrive
without written or oral instructions or with instructions on only a few
items. No reliable data are available on this score. The absence of instructions appears to indicate either a certain lack of interest of the
government concerned, or the fact that it has full confidence in the experience, knowledge and good sense of its delegation.

Some of the different types of instructions are the following:

a. *Everything dealt with in detail*

This is confined to questions of paramount importance to the instruct-
ing government, for example, a political conflict in which it is involved,
or some international treaty to be negotiated to which it attaches great
importance. If the delegation wants to deviate from the prescribed line,
it must ask for specific authorization.

In the hypothetical case of a conflict beween country A and country
B over the sovereignty of territory X lying between these two countries,
a detailed instruction to the delegation of A might be along the following lines:

'The delegation will oppose any moves by the delegation of B or by
those who support its position that might be prejudicial to our rightful
claims to territory X. The delegation must therefore oppose all draft
resolutions that may appear to give any validity to the claim of B. It

must endeavour to get a majority for our claim to X. If this is not possible, it can, as a maximum, accept an appeal by the conference to A and B to aim at a peaceful conclusion of the conflict. In carrying out this instruction the delegation should keep in close touch with the delegations of . . . who support our point of view. It must report daily on the evolution of the situation, so that, if and when necessary, new instructions can be given.'

In practice, such a detailed instruction would include various contingent possibilities, on the lines of chess moves.

b. *General position outlined*

This is the sort of instruction where certain limits within which the delegation can operate are outlined, while tactical and other details are left to the delegation itself. For example, on the level of the budget of an organization, the instruction might read:

'The delegation can agree with a budget level between 18 and 20 million dollars. It should oppose increases above 20 million dollars and can agree to cuts bringing the level below 18 million dollars only if a large majority of member countries agrees to such cuts.'

In this category fall the so-called "position papers" which are the preferred method for writing instructions (for each agenda item or issue) of some countries.

c. *Position related to that of other countries*

In many conferences the delegation of country A is instructed to align itself with the position either of a group to which it belongs or to that of specifically named countries, perhaps one of the big powers. If the delegation feels that such alignment leads to positions incompatible with general or specific policies of its government, it will ask for modified instructions. Similarly, a delegation will generally not like an isolated position, and in that case also ask for new instructions.

Concluding observations

In all situations a delegation will not only look at the written letter of its instructions. It must understand the spirit in which they are written. The positions taken by the government in the past, which may not be identical to that described in the instruction, must be remembered.

The relation of the head of delegation or the negotiator to the sources of instruction can be highly important: if the head of delegation is very close to these sources and has their full confidence, his instructions will tend to be somewhat more widely formulated than if the delegate is not personally known to those who draw up the instruction. This is not important for the numerous more or less routine items which fill conference agendas, but it can make quite a difference in a case, such as the sovereignty conflict of our example, where the country is directly involved in an important question, or in disputes where the country is not directly involved, yet is able and eager to play a mediating role. Lall has given the following example:

"When V.K. Krishna Menon developed and introduced at the Seventh Session of the General Assembly the resolution on the Korean situation containing substantive proposals relating to the then unsolved problem of prisoners of war he held no position in the Indian Cabinet; yet he formulated a delicate negotiating arrangement which eventually came to be adopted, and made possible a cease-fire in Korea. He did this without specific instructions on matters of detail from the Government of India. He was able to act as the did because he understood and was attuned to the thinking of Prime Minister Nehru on such matters."[4]

3. *Communications and speeches*

a. *The significance of effective communication*

It is an elementary truth that the success of any diplomatic act will be directly dependent on the degree of effectiveness in establishing communications with the other party. In bilateral diplomacy there is only one party with which one communicates. In conference diplomacy one communicates with all other participants including the secretariat. The mere multiplication of the number of recipients of "messages" renders the establishment of effective communications much more difficult in conference diplomacy than in traditional bilateral diplomacy. In conference diplomacy some sort of average has to be struck, in such a way that the conference diplomat's message reaches all or a maximum number of conference participants. The result may well be that the contents of a statement to be delivered in a formal meeting thus becomes too simple and unintelligent for some, too difficult or complicated for others. Hence, in most situations it is necessary to supplement formal statements with other forms of communication such as personal conversations and informal explanatory memoranda. Indeed, it is not always sufficiently realized that although speeches and statements are an important element in conference diplomacy communications, they are by no means the only one. Visual expressions, maintaining silence when challenged, informal conversations in lobbies, in delegation offices, at luncheons, dinners and cocktail parties, informal group meetings, delegation press releases, all these may be as important a channel of communication as the conference statement, pronounced in plenary or committee session.

Effective communication means making one's thoughts understood by others and understanding oneself other participants' thoughts and ideas. Three potential stumbling blocks for effective communications in conference diplomacy must be distinguished:

—*linguistic difficulties:* delegates and secretariat members must not run into serious language difficulties in talking to each other. In the formal meetings interpretation will remove many of these difficulties. However, since most of the decision-making process takes place in informal meetings without interpretation services, it is clear that a minimum of verbal understanding is indispensable to achieve communication in the linguistic sense.

—*intellectual short-circuits:* there must be an ability to grasp what the other is saying. Most arguments in international conferences center on the relative advantages or disadvantages of specific courses of action. Delegates will explain these advantages or disadvantages. It is necessary that their reasoning can be understood and followed by other delegates.

—*conceptual roadblocks:* in different parts of the world different value systems exist: basic standards and norms are not the same, so that a word may have a different significance for different people. For example, "to some compromise signifies a legitimate effort to reach an agreement by mutual concessions, to others it may imply an immoral or cynical sacrifice of principle".[5] In some conferences or negotiations the Latin tendency to define everything in considerable detail clashes with Anglo-Saxon pragmatism, with its preference for leaving things vague, for "muddling through". To establish communications in the conceptual sense, conference diplomats will see to it that their proposals, and the arguments to defend these proposals are presented in such a way that they are receivable in the communications sense by those to whom they are addressed.

It is bad enough if there is a lack of communication on one of these three scores. It is worse, when such lack of communication remains hidden under the veil of pretended understanding. Delegate A has made a proposal, first in a statement, then in private conversations in the lobby. Delegate B is nodding gravely, similar reactions come from delegates C, D, and E. The delegate reports to his superiors that the four countries to whose representatives he has spoken, are in full agreement with his proposal. Later, perhaps just before or at the time of voting, the sobering truth becomes clear: the consent that delegate A believed he had acquired has either vanished or never existed. Of course, in our hypothetical example there is no proof whether the dissenting position was due to "misunderstanding" caused by a gap in linguistic, intellectual or conceptual communication, or by genuine disagreement, perhaps because the superiors of delegates B, C and D overruled their men's point of view, and the latter found it embarrassing to inform delegate A of this disagreement.

Practically every conference has working languages, in one of which statements must be made. In contemporary conferences, these are always English and French, and very often Russian and Spanish. In most contemporary conferences there is simultaneous interpretation. In the U.N. Security Council there is both simultaneous and consecutive interpretation. The latter method has the advantage of giving additional time for consultation among delegates. Probably, consecutive interpretation leads to less misunderstanding, also because many delegates can first listen to the original speech and then to the translation. In some conferences it is habitually permitted, especially to heads of state or government ministers, to speak one's own language, provided the delegation has made available in advance to the interpreters the full translation into one of the working languages. It is evident that those who are permitted to speak their mother tongue are placed in an advantageous position compared to those who are not. The result is that a great many speeches are made in a rather unimaginative "conference English" or "conference French", abounding with clichés, notably the use of certain adjectives, such as: constructive, progressive, forward-looking, positive, negative, important. The jocular suggestion, sometimes heard, that all delegates should be obliged to speak another language than their own, in order to put everybody on the same footing, would presumably make things worse, since even more delegates would have to speak in a foreign language. While the language advantage or disadvantage is not so serious for statements prepared at leisure, and then read, it can become acute when an impromptu intervention suddenly becomes necessary, and a delegate may be groping for the right words (sometimes a delegate sitting close to him will whisper the appropriate expression).

b. *Types of speeches in conference diplomacy*

The following categories of conference statements can be distinguished:

General debate statements. These are statements covering all or most of the conference agenda in a single speech. The annual general debate at the U.N. General Assembly and the general debate at the annual International Labour Conference are typical examples. The general debate statement often goes beyond the subjects covered by the conference agenda. A delegate will use the occasion to expose his government's policy or viewpoint on important questions even if they are not on the agenda. An example is furnished by the numerous references in general debate statements during the 21st and 22nd sessions (1966 and 1967) of the General Assembly to the war in Viet-Nam, even though that conflict did not constitute an agenda item. The general debate statement of the average delegate will not attract more than routine attention in the conference, unless it contains drastically new proposals or a fundamentally changed position on some issue on which the attitude of the speaker's country is important in terms of decisions to be taken by the conference. The general debate may also be used to attract attention in the speaker's country.

General statements on specific agenda items. Although this may sound like a contradiction in terms, general statements on specific agenda items are quite common. Some agenda items are so wide in themselves ("Review of the world economic situation", often an Economic and Social Council agenda item, is an example), that they lead to speeches which are hardly distinguishable from "general debate" statements. On the other hand on a specific and complicated question the "keynote" speech by a delegation which has made a special study of the subject will be helpful. Often a representative of the Secretariat will make an explanatory statement, especially if there is a secretariat report.

Statements to introduce a draft proposal. Such statements, often made on behalf of all delegations who are sponsors of a draft resolution, are intended to convince the conference to adopt the proposal. They are, therefore, drafted with great care. Unless the proposal consists of a single paragraph, comments on the more important paragraphs of the preamble and of the operative part will be given. Similarly, replies by the sponsor(s) on the acceptability of amendments must be clear. An ambiguous comment by the sponsor on the acceptability of an amendment will lead to misunderstandings; it will very likely be interpreted as acceptance rather than rejection. Informal contacts in or outside the conference room may serve to clarify the situation, unless the sponsors of the proposal consciously desire an ambiguous situation to persist for some time.

Statements commenting on proposals by others. The preceding comments apply: clarity is generally desirable. If the delegation making the comment desires some modification of the draft resolution tabled by other delegations, it may be useful to include the specific words of the amendment in the statement. Alternatively, the delegation may state the general nature of the modifications it wishes and propose informal contacts with the sponsors in order to negotiate an agreed text.

Statements on points of order and procedural motions. They are supposed to be brief, and either ask for a ruling by the chairman (point of order) or make a procedural proposal. In both cases the appropriate rule from the rules of procedure should be invoked (cf. chapter III, p. 50-52). A statement under the "right of reply" should limit itself to a rebuttal of something that was specifically addressed to the delegate, his government or his country.

Statements in explanation of vote. The rules of procedure of most organizations and conferences explicitly or tacitly permit explanations of vote either before or after voting. The significance is that these statements are permitted even though the debate on the agenda item or on the resolution to be voted upon has been closed. In practice, many statements "in explanation of my delegation's vote" do much more than that. This may occasionally lead to a remark by the chairman, asking the speaker to limit himself to the explanation of his vote.

The following are some of the more frequent reasons for an explanation of vote:

(*a*) the delegation has voted differently from what it has itself indicated during the earlier debate. Perhaps last-minute instructions from its capital have modified an earlier delegation stand. This indeed is a quite legitimate reason to explain a vote.

(*b*) the delegation believes that its earlier statements have not made its position quite clear. The explanation of vote gives a last opportunity to do so.

(*c*) The delegation has not taken the floor earlier, for whatever reason. At the last moment it has decided, perhaps after having received its instructions only at a late stage, how to vote. The explanation of vote is the only way, the debate on the agenda item having been closed, to put its views before the meeting. Whether the summary record will actually summarize those views depends on whether the conference in question has the habit of merely recording: "The following delegations made a statement in explanation of their vote: . . ." or whether such statements are summarized one by one.

(*d*) The delegation has voted in favour of a draft resolution, but wants to reserve the position of its government as to the legal effects. Although such explanations are superfluous in most conferences of the U.N. system, because most resolutions are mere recommendations, they are quite customary. The same is often done for the financial implications, again—in most cases—unnecessarily, because either every member country, however it voted, is subjected to the financial consequences of the decision for the budget of the organization (on the assumption that the budget is assessed according to a predetermined scale) or the resolution requires voluntary contributions. In the latter case every country remains wholly free in its decision whether, and how much, to contribute.

c. *Length of speeches*

The rules of procedure of many conferences provide for a possible limitation of the time allowed to each speaker or of the number of times a speaker is allowed to speak on each question (e.g. rules 74 and 115 of the General Assembly). In practice, such limitation remains exceptional, and appeals by the chairman calling for brevity followed by voluntary selfrestraint of speakers are the main method applied. However, in the ILO General Conferences the rules of procedure provide for a mandatory 15 minute limit, which is strictly enforced.

It is not possible to state generally what length of a statement is the most desirable. Some sort of happy medium between the Scylla of the extremely brief statement, so concise and not preceded by some introductory remarks that it fails to receive the attention the speaker had hoped for, and the Charybdis of the long, drawn-out, repetitious and therefore tedious speech, read in a monotonous voice from a prepared text, is usually possible.

d. *Conference diplomatic language*

The traditional diplomatic language of notes and letters between the ambassador and the country to which he is accredited has found its more or less natural evolution into something that might be called "conference diplomatic language".

While clarity and straightforwardness are always considered the ideal for conference speakers, in practice a host of manners of speech has become more or less normal in conferences of the U.N. organizations. Experienced delegates immediately recognize the significance of any of the following stereotype phrases. With the reservation that their exact meaning will always depend on the context in which they have been used, some of the phrases frequently used, with their possible meaning are presented in Illustration III.

Illustration III. **Conference Diplomatic Language**

Phrase	*Possible meaning*
My delegation has the greatest sympathy for the proposal made by the distinguished delegate of . . . However, it wishes to point out . . .	The proposal of delegation . . . is not wholly without sense, but we disagree for the following reasons . . .
My delegation is not able to support this draft resolution.	My delegation will either abstain or vote against this draft resolution, but it has not made up its mind as between these two possibilities.
I agree with the distinguished delegate of . . . that in principle speedy action is necessary on this question, but . . .	I am not in favour of speedy action.
The proposal is very interesting, but we must avoid duplication of activities with certain other organizations.	The proposal does not belong in this organization.
While I have deep respect for the distinguished delegate of . . ., who has stated his views with intelligence and conviction, I must point out that . . .	I do not agree with the delegate of . . .
I conclude that our exchange of views has been extremely useful, even though we have not reached agreement.	Disagreement is what I wanted, and therefore the debate has been useful for my purpose.

4. *Conciliation*

Every conference is in its own way an effort towards conciliation of potentially or actually divergent points of view of governments. The United Nations itself is supposed to be (art. 1 of the Charter) "a center for harmonizing the actions of nations".

Conciliation in the legal sense differs somewhat from that normal in conference diplomacy. A well known legal definition of conciliation is "the process of settling a dispute by referring it to a commission of persons whose task it is to elucidate the facts and (usually after hearing the parties and endeavouring to bring them to an agreement) to make a report containing proposals for a settlement, but which does not have the binding character of an award or judgement".[6] In conference diplomacy conciliation is mostly an implicit process, hardly distinguishable from the processes of negotiation leading to consensus.

Legally there are a number of examples of formal conciliation procedures applicable to conference diplomacy, including those foreseen in chapter VI of the U.N. Charter on the pacific settlement of disputes and possible use of the U.N. Panels for Inquiry and Conciliation created by the General Assembly in 1949. Each Member State was asked to designate up to five persons "who by reason of their training, experience, character and standing were deemed to be well fitted to serve as members of commissions of inquiry and conciliation". Although lists with the names of such persons have been regularly circulated among Member States, by 1967 no panel had ever been constituted.

Certain international agreements have their own conciliation procedures. The General Agreement on Tariffs and Trade has from time to time set up panels of experts to facilitate the solution of trade conflicts such as those that would result from claims by one contracting party of "nullification or impairment" (heading of article XXIII of the GATT) of concessions granted by another contracting party in earlier tariff negotiations. In the GATT the panel procedure has also been used as an improvisation, without reference to an article of the Agreement. This was notably the case during the so-called "chicken war" between the United States and the EEC: The United States had objected to certain import fees, resulting from the new agricultural policy of the EEC, imposed by the Federal Republic of Germany on imports of poultry. These fees were contrary to a tariff concession by Germany in an earlier round of tariff negotiations. After the EEC had conceded the right of the United States to increase certain duties in retaliation, a dispute arose over the value of U.S. poultry exports affected. This value had to be related to exports in a base period and had to take into account the effect of quantitative restrictions in Germany which had artificially limited the volume of poultry imports. The U.S. and the EEC then requested the Council of GATT to constitute an impartial panel to render an advisory opinion on the value of United States poultry exports affected by the new fees, as of September 1, 1960. The panel was promptly constituted, with the Executive Secretary of GATT as Chairman. After a few months the panel delivered its verdict: a value of

$ 26 million, which was considerably less than the amount the United States had put forward and more than that which had been conceded by the EEC. Both parties accepted the advisory opinion, and the United States put into effect duty increases covering approximately $26 million worth of exports of the EEC to the United States. This example of conciliation by voluntary arbitration [7] can be considered to have been facilitated by the flexibility and speed typical of the GATT conference system.

In 1966 the Contracting Parties of GATT approved a decision to facilitate conciliation procedures for conflicts between less-developed and highly developed countries. The objective was to speed up the conciliation process in cases of complaints from less-developed countries against developed countries.

The normal conferences and meetings of the United Nations and the specialized agencies do not have special conciliation procedures. It is tacitly assumed that somehow an effort will be made to reconcile opposing points of view, through one of the informal processes which we have described. An exception is the conciliation procedure provided for in considerable detail in resolution 1995 (XIX) of the General Assembly, on the establishment of the United Nations Conference on Trade and Development as an organ of the General Assembly. It became a separate but not an "independent" organization, as would have been the case if a specialized agency had been created.

Paragraph 5 of resolution 1995 sets forth procedures "designed to provide a process of conciliation to take place before voting and to provide an adequate basis for the adoption of recommendations with regard to proposals of a specific nature for actions substantially affecting the economic or financial interests of particular countries". The essence of the procedure is that in carefully outlined cases a certain minimum number of members (ten for proposals before the Conference, five for proposals before the Board, and three for proposals before a Committee) may request postponement of the voting, if necessary to the next session, during which time a conciliation committee is to endeavour to reach agreement. The conciliation procedure applies to proposals for specific action affecting the economic or financial interests of particular countries in such fields as economic plans or programmes, trade, monetary or economic assistance policies, or proposals affecting rights or obligations under international agreements or treaties. On the other hand it does not apply to procedural matters or to proposals for studies or to recommendations and declarations of a general character not calling for specific action.

An UNCTAD Conciliation Committee is to be appointed by the President of the Conference or the Chairman of the Board, must be small in size, and include countries specially interested in the matter with respect to which conciliation is initiated. The members must be selected on an equitable geographical basis. The Conciliation Committee must endeavour to reach agreement during the same session of the Conference, the Board or the Committee during which it was established. If this is not possible, it must report to the next session of the Board or the Conference, whichever is earlier. Within the Conciliation Committee there is no voting. The Conciliation Committee must utilize the good offices of the Secretary-General of UNCTAD "as fully as practicable". If the Conciliation Committee is unable to reach agreement, the Board or the Conference can recommend a further period of conciliation. It is implicit, however, that if there is a majority which does not wish to continue the conciliation process, a vote on the disputed proposal can be imposed by that majority.

Because the UNCTAD conciliation procedures have not been used (by 1967), it is difficult to assess their significance. It must be assumed that they have had some value as a "stick behind the door". While the UNCTAD Conference of 1964 saw a lot of voting, most decisions of the UNCTAD Board and the three principal committees (Commodities, Manufactured Products, Finance and Invisibles) have been achieved as a consensus arrived at through negotiation, so that voting has become more and more exceptional.

A system of institutionalized conciliation after the UNCTAD pattern may, in the words of Schachter, "be one of the more promising proposals for bridging the gap between majority voting and minority power".[8]

XI. CASE STUDIES IN CONFERENCE DIPLOMACY: TRADE, DISARMAMENT, AID TO A LESS-DEVELOPED COUNTRY

In the previous chapter an effort has been made to analyse conference diplomacy with examples derived for the greater part from the United Nations and the specialized agencies. This chapter presents two case studies of negotiating conferences, on trade and disarmament respectively, and one brief description of an unusual intergovernmental conference organized by a single government. Thus it is hoped to complete the picture given by the analysis and the examples in the earlier chapters. The analysis of disarmament negotiations (section 1) and of trade negotiations (section 2) includes brief—too brief for experts—summaries of developments since the Second World War. There then follows—the main objective of this chapter—a comparison (section 3) of disarmament and trade negotiations, in which an effort is made to stress several conference diplomacy elements (role of chairman, of secretariat, of groups of countries, of publicity and privacy) encountered in previous chapters. The final section describes an intergovernmental conference held in Amsterdam (February, 1967) on the subject of the economic and financial situation in Indonesia, and shows that conference diplomacy techniques, if rightly applied, can assist in making a conference organized by a single country a success.

1. *Disarmament negotiations*

Since the Second World War [1] with the advent of nuclear weapons, disarmament and arms control negotiations have covered a wide range of questions, including:

(*a*) general and complete disarmament, linked with the question of the establishment of an "International Disarmament Organization";

(*b*) limitations on the use, spread or production of nuclear weapons, for example:

—nuclear weapons tests in the atmosphere, in outer space and under water

—underground nuclear tests

—non-proliferation of nuclear weapons

—denuclearization of certain areas, for example Latin America

—freezing of the production of so-called "strategic nuclear vehicles", i.e. means of transmission or transport of nuclear weapons
—the destruction of certain weapons, i.e. bomber aircraft
—the banning of nuclear weapons from outer space;
(c) Miscellaneous measures related to disarmament or to the avoidance of war:
—measures to avoid war by accident, by miscalculation and surprise attack, including the Agreement on a Direct Communications Link between the Soviet Union and the United States
—reduction in military budgets
—declaration against war propaganda
—non-aggression pacts between regional defense organizations, i.e. between NATO and the Warsaw Pact
—banning of nuclear weapons from outer space.

The subjects mentioned under (b) and (c) are usually grouped together under the heading "collateral disarmament measures" as distinguished from general and complete disarmament.

After the Second World War disarmament negotiations were first conducted in the United Nations Atomic Energy Commission (established by resolution 1 of the first session of the General Assembly in 1946), consisting of the Security Council members plus Canada, when not a member of the Council, and the U.N. Commission for Conventional Armaments (established by the Security Council in 1947), the membership of which was identical to that of the Security Council. Both were succeeded in 1952 by the U.N. Disarmament Commission created by the General Assembly as an organ of the Security Council. The membership of the new Commission was again that of the Security Council plus Canada. This Commission at the suggestion of the General Assembly, established a five-member subcommittee, consisting of Canada, France, the Soviet Union, the United Kingdom and the United States. The subcommittee, which started its work in 1954, was unable to come to any agreed recommendations. Both the Western countries and the Soviet Union made fundamental revisions of their policies in the period 1953-1958. President Eisenhower, in his famous United Nations address (December 8, 1953), proposed an international "atoms for peace" programme, which was to result in the creation (1956) of the International Atomic Energy Agency. This address also paved the way for the new United States policy of promoting "partial immediately realizable measures" rather than insisting on general and complete disarmament.

The 1955 summit conference of the Heads of State of France, the Soviet Union, the United Kingdom and the United States confirmed this new trend; President Eisenhower proposed as a "confidence-building" proposal his "Open Skies" plan (submitting military establishments to aerial inspection) and Premier Bulganin proposed a ground control system regarding dangerous concentrations of military land forces or of air or naval forces.

The U.N. Disarmament Commission adjourned in 1957. It was enlarged in 1957 to fourteen members and in 1958 again to include all United Nations member states. It met in 1959, 1960 and 1965. Through its Subcommittee of five members it set the scene for some important developments, such as the Conference of Experts in 1958, which came in the wake of the General Assembly of 1957, often called the "Disarmament General Assembly", because it discussed at great length disarmament issues, and—in resolution 1148 (XII)—had urged all states concerned to reach a comprehensive disarmament agreement. At the Conference of Experts Western (British, French, Canadian and American) and Eastern (Soviet Russian and other) scientists explored various scientific aspects of an agreement on the cessation of testing nuclear bombs, including the question of verification of the observance of an agreed cessation of testing. A separate Conference of Experts for the Study of Possible Measures Which Might Be Helpful in Preventing Surprise Attack met in Geneva in July and August 1958. That year also saw the beginning of the Conference on Discontinuance of Nuclear Weapons Tests which was to go or until January 1962, without achieving agreed results. In 1959 after more than two years of negotiations between the principal powers, agreement was reached by the Foreign Ministers of the United States, the Soviet Union and France, confirmed by the Disarmament Commission and the General Assembly, to set up a Ten Nation Disarmament Commission, consisting of Canada, France, Italy, the United Kingdom and the United States on the Western side and Bulgaria, Czechoslovakia, Poland, Romania and the Soviet Union on the Eastern side. This Commission met only briefly; in the summer of 1960 the five Communist countries withdrew, a reflection of the deteriorating political climate. In 1961 the Soviet Union and the United States were able to agree on a joint statement of agreed principles as a basis for future multilateral negotiations on disarmament and on the establishment of a new Eighteen-Nation Disarmament Committee. The composition of this committee was subsequently approved by the U.N. General Assembly (resolution 1722 (XVI)). The ENDC, as it is usually called, consists of the ten countries that had constituted the 10-nation committee plus Brazil, Burma, Ethiopia, India, Mexico, Nigeria, Sweden and the United Arab Republic. The ENDC has become the principal forum for disarmament and arms control negotiations and met for the first time on March 14, 1962. It has been meeting continuously since, with occasional interruptions for longer or shorter periods, in particular during sessions of the U.N. General Assembly. France, although a member, has not attended any ENDC sessions. The principal results so far (1967) are usually considered to have been:

—the Treaty Banning Nuclear Weapon Tests in the Atmosphere, in Outer Space and Under Water, usually referred to as the Partial Test Ban Treaty, signed at Moscow on August 5, 1963

—the Memorandum of Understanding between the United States and the U.S.S.R. Regarding the Establishment of a Direct Communications Link, signed at Geneva on June 20, 1963

—the draft Treaty on the Non-Proliferation of Nuclear Arms.

The commitment not to place in orbit nuclear weapons, in the Treaty on Principles Governing the Activities of States in the Exploration and Use of Outer Space, including the Moon and other Celestial Bodies, can be put on the credit side of ENDC, which as early as 1962 after a Canadian initiative, discussed the principle underlying this commitment. The final phase of negotiations on the Test Ban Treaty took place in Moscow between the United States, the United Kingdom and the Soviet Union, although there seems no doubt "that the treaty could not have been so quickly agreed upon in Moscow without the previous years of intensive discussions in Geneva in which they had explored every alleyway, every avenue and every consideration and thus knew the exact dimensions and impact of every proposal, so they could understand exactly what they were doing".[2]

The direct communications link, often referred to as the "hot-line" between the Soviet Union and the United States was negotiated in Geneva by the Soviet and United States delegations to the ENDC and was discussed in ENDC in general terms as one of several suggested measures to reduce the risk of war.

The ENDC was meant to be a negotiating committee. This is visible from General Assembly Resolution 1660 (XVI) which urged the Soviet Union and the United States to reach agreement on the composition of a negotiating body which both they and the rest of the world could regard as satisfactory, and from General Assembly Resolution 1722 (XVI) which requested the Committee to "undertake negotiations with a view of reaching, on the basis of the joint statement of agreed principles . . ., agreement on general and complete disarmament under effective international control". Later resolutions of the General Assembly repeated this request; some of them urged the ENDC to give special attention either to collateral measures in general, or to specific ones, namely the discontinuance of nuclear weapons tests and the prevention of the spread of nuclear weapons. The ENDC decided at an early stage that concurrently with the elaboration of agreement on general and complete disarmament, it would give attention to various proposals for lessening international tension, consolidating confidence among States and facilitating general and complete disarmament. Thus the old conflict as to which should have priority, general disarmament or partial measures, had been solved, at least procedurally. In practice, the ENDC gradually devoted more and more time and attention to the various partial, so-called collateral measures.

The ENDC has several distinctive characteristics:

(*i*) Although not established as a United Nations organ, it maintains close links with the United Nations. It accepts requests on the orientation of its work from the General Assembly and reports every year to the General Assembly.

(*ii*) It has provided the framework within which the principal powers concerned, namely the Soviet Union and the United States, negotiate in the direct sense of the word, a great deal of it at the site of the ENDC Conference, Geneva. These powers are under pressure to report the results of their negotiations as soon as possible to ENDC meetings. For most of the smaller powers the ENDC has become a deliberative forum, where they can put forward their comments, ideas and proposals. The eight non-aligned nations have from time to time put forward common proposals or memoranda, or have tried to do so. This involved some negotiating among the members of the group of non-aligned countries.

(*iii*) The ENDC has neither fixed permanent terms of reference nor written rules of procedure. The terms of reference can be said to be based on the agreement reached between the co-chairmen and on the requests emanating from the General Assembly. Although occasionally there are in ENDC meetings references to its procedures, one will look in vain for a document containing the "rules of procedure".

(*iv*) The ENDC functions under the leadership of two co-chairmen, the United States and the Soviet-Union. The co-chairmen are not presidents of the meetings, but constitute a powerful steering committee. As soon and as long as the two superpowers whose representatives constitute this steering committee are in agreement, they exercise a preponderant influence on the ENDC. The subjects to be discussed (a formal numbered agenda does not exist), the frequency of the meetings, the dates of convening and of adjournment and, most important, the sort of recommendations arrived at in the Committee, all are strongly influenced by the two co-chairmen, if, as and when they are in agreement.

(*v*) Completely separated from the function of co-chairmen is that of the presiding officer. Each ENDC meeting (the meetings have so far usually been held twice a week, on Tuesday morning and Thursday morning) is presided over by a different ENDC member; the rotation is in the alphabetical order of the names of the member states in English.

(*vi*) While the outside appearance of the ENDC is that of a deliberative body, its decisions and agreements are arrived at through a process of negotiation, with a view to reaching a consensus. Thus far, no vote has ever taken place in the ENDC.

2. *Multilateral trade negotiations*

This section concentrates on the trade negotiating framework as it has developed in GATT, leaving aside trade negotiations in various regional organizations, such as OECD, EEC, EFTA, LAFTA, etc. . The GATT is a multilateral trade agreement which was drafted (in 1947) simultaneously with the Charter for a permanent International Trade Organization, adopted at Havana in 1948. The ITO was conceived as a specialized agency of the United Nations. However, as a result of opposition of the United States Congress, the ITO Charter was not ratified by the United States and therefore not by most other governments. Thus the GATT, originally intended as a temporary arrangement pending the entry into force of the Havana Charter, has been since 1948 the only multilateral instrument which lays down rules of conduct for trade, and which has been accepted by a high proportion of the trading nations.

The GATT has become the most important framework within which multilateral trade negotiations have taken place since the Second World War. These negotiations have all had as background the three fundamental principles of GATT, which its Secretariat has summarized as follows:

"The first principle is that trade should be conducted on the basis of non-discrimination. In particular, all contracting parties are bound by the most-favoured-nation clause in the application of import and export duties and charges and in their administration.

The second general principle is that protection shall be afforded to domestic industries exclusively through the customs tariff and not through other commercial measures. Thus the use of import quotas as a means of protection is prohibited. Import quotas may be used for certain other purposes—notably to redress a country's balance of payments—but the circumstances in which they may be used are very carefully defined, and there are elaborate procedures for consultations so as to ensure that quotas comply with the conditions laid down and to minimize any damage to the trade of other countries.

The third principle, inherent throughout the Agreement, is the concept of consultation aimed at avoiding damage to the trading interests of contracting parties".[3]

From 1947, when the "first round" of trade negotiations took place in Geneva, until and including the so-called Dillon Round of 1960/61 the negotiations dealt predominantly with customs tariffs.

In the period 1947-1961 there were five multilateral tariff negotiating conferences under GATT auspices, three in Geneva (1947, 1956, 1960-61), one in Annecy (1949) and one in Torquay (1950-1951). These five tariff conferences in fact consisted of a large number of simultaneously conducted bilateral negotiations, the results of which were "multilateralized" in the final phase of each conference. The negotiating procedure may be summarized as follows: At a date several weeks or months prior to the beginning of negotiations the participating governments sent to each other "request lists", mostly related to tariff positions in which the requesting country was the "principal supplier" or at least had an important interest vis-à-vis the country to which the request was made.

At an agreed date, each government participating in the negotiation deposited "offer lists" indicating for each tariff position (or part of a tariff position, called "ex item" in the GATT jargon) the concession it was prepared to make: a reduction to a stated level or by an indicated percentage, or the consolidation, called "binding", of the existing level.

Both the request and the offer lists were kept secret. The offer lists were circulated by the Secretariat to all participants. After a time lapse for the study of the offer lists, negotiations began by pairs of countries on the items for which they were principal supplier to each other. There were usually two phases in these talks: the first one consisted of elucidation and information, where countries would explain in reply to questions why a certain offer was limited to what it was, or why certain items had been excluded from offers completely. In 1956 this was done for the first time in a multilateral forum: delegations had to explain and defend their total offer lists. The second phase was that of negotiation. Each delegation would endeavour to find a method of demonstrating equilibrium or lack of it between concessions offered and to be obtained. A favoured device was to calculate the amount of trade covered by potential concessions. In the later phases of the bilateral negotiations there were numerous contacts between delegations on tariff positions which had not been the subject of direct negotiations between them in the earlier phase (because on these positions they were not principal supplier to one another). These contacts constituted the main conference aspect of the tariff negotiations "old style"; if delegation A had been engaged in a bilateral talk with delegation B, the concluding phase of that negotiation made it essential that it also contacted other delegations to find out what it might expect on items in which it was not the principal supplier. As the bilateral talks were completed, the results were circulated to the other participating countries. There was then a last negotiating phase where those who felt that they were not getting their *quid pro quo* would seek additional concessions or would announce withdrawals of concessions provisionally offered. Such withdrawals might set off a chain reaction of withdrawals by other countries. Finally schedules were drawn up, which contained the concessions given by each participating country—as a result of the operation of the most-favoured-nation clause—to all contracting parties of the GATT. The schedules were annexed to a protocol signed at the end of each tariff conference. The emphasis on bilateral negotiations, the secrecy surrounding them, and the absence of texts to be agreed upon by all participating nations (except for non-controversial phrases in the final protocol) explain the absence or nearly so of some of the usual conference phenomena, such as mediation or conciliation by the president or by the secretariat.

In the course of the period 1947 to 1961 it became clear that the established method of product-by-product negotiations between each importing country and its principal suppliers was producing decreasingly significant results. The United States "reciprocal trade agreements" legislation, especially the reduction in negotiating authority during the fifties, with limits to permitted maximum tariff reductions, contributed to this effect. Not only the United States, but also the other principal countries had decreased their tariffs in many cases to levels which they felt—rightly or wrongly—could hardly be further reduced. On the other hand the creation in Europe of the European Economic Community and the European Free Trade Association affected the value of concessions previously negotiated with countries outside these groupings. While the EFTA was a free trade area, with each country keeping its own external tariff, the EEC was a full customs union with its own common external tariff gradually replacing the separate tariffs of the six countries constituting the EEC.

Because Belgium, the Netherlands and Luxemburg had since January 1st 1948 a single tariff under the Benelux customs and economic union agreements, four customs tariffs (of Benelux, France, Federal Republic of Germany and Italy) were replaced by a single tariff. Even before 1961 the new EEC common tariff had already necessitated the renegotiation by the EEC of numerous previous concessions made by Benelux, France, the Federal Republic of Germany and Italy, compensation being given in cases where the new common tariff was higher than the rates as laid down in the schedules of the individual EEC member countries during the previous tariff rounds.

The need for a new approach was also felt because customs tariffs had become less and less significant for agricultural materials and products. The trade in these had been caught in an increasingly complicated network of quantitative restrictions and other measures to provide protection for and support of domestic production. Quantitative restrictions had also remained for a number of industrial products in spite of GATT's explicit provision to the contrary.

A step towards a new approach had already been contained in the offer, made by the EEC in the 1960/1961 tariff conference, the so-called "Dillon Round", to reduce its tariff "across-the-board", i.e. generally, by 20% on a basis of reciprocity.

The United States Government, under President Kennedy, took the lead in the new approach by enacting the Trade Expansion Act of 1962 which gave the Administration wide new powers to negotiate trade agreements, contrasting favourably with successive Reciprocal Trade Agreements Acts enacted since the depression years of the nineteen-thirties. The main features of what has come to be called the Kennedy Round were determined at a ministerial meeting of May 1963 at which it was agreed, (*i*) to hold comprehensive trade negotiations starting in 1964, with the widest possible participation, (*ii*) that the negotiations should cover all classes of products, including agricultural and primary products, and should deal with both tariff and non-tariff barriers, (*iii*) that the tariff negotiations should be based upon a plan of substantial linear, across-the-board tariff reductions, with a bare minimum of exceptions, (*iv*) that the trade negotiations should provide for acceptable conditions of access to world markets for agricultural products and (*v*) that every effort should be made to reduce barriers to exports of the less-developed countries. In May 1964 the Trade Negotiations Committee, which supervised the conduct of the Kennedy Round, met at ministerial level and formally opened the negotiating conference. As regards tariffs, 50 per cent was agreed as a working hypothesis for the general rate of linear reduction on industrial products. It was also decided that the exceptions to the 50 per cent reduction should only be those necessitated for reasons of overriding national interest and that such exceptions should be subject to confrontation and justification. Subsequently, in November 1964, countries which were participating on the basis of linear reduction tabled their exceptions lists.

As regards agriculture, it was agreed that the Kennedy Round should provide for acceptable conditions of access to world markets for agricultural products.

The Kennedy Round went on till late spring 1967, and, faced with the expiration on June 30, 1967 of the United States Government's authority to negotiate, finally delivered a "package" of achievements acceptable to all participants, even though less than what had originally been aimed at.[4]

The machinery of the Kennedy Round was more complex than that of the preceding tariff conferences. There was, as in the previous conferences, an overall Trade Negotiations Committee (its name significantly changed from the old-style Tariff Negotiations Committee), of which all countries participating in the negotiations were members. It met as needed during the entire Kennedy Round, mostly to approve a time-table or other procedural arrangements negotiated among the principal participants. For those agricultural commodities for which so-called "general arrangements" (international agreements dealing with prices, subsidies and conditions of access other than tariffs) were the aim, viz. cereals, dairy products and meat, special groups met, chaired either by the Director-General or one of his close collaborators. A Subcommittee of the Trade Negotiations Committee for Agricultural Products met infrequently. A Subcommittee for the Participation of Less-Developed Countries met several times to establish procedures for that participation and to review progress. A Subcommittee for Non-Tariff Barriers met rarely and did not achieve more than a provisional inventory of so-called non-tariff barriers. It created, however, an Anti-Dumping Group, a highly technical body which worked out a new "Anti-Dumping Code", uniform regulations on possible measures applicable in cases of dumping. For certain important industrial sectors (chemicals, pulp and paper, steel, cotton textiles) *ad hoc* groups of the principal trading countries met. There was also a group for tropical products, where the offers of the developed countries for these products were subjected to multilateral scrutiny and cross-examination. Almost all these committees and groups were chaired by the Director-General or by the Deputy Director-General or another high level official. All through the Kennedy Round there were numerous bilateral meetings, somewhat reminiscent of bilateral encounters under the old-style tariff negotiations, where lists of offers and exceptions to offers, and requests were subjected to scrutiny, to cross-examination and to efforts towards improvement.

The Kennedy Round has marked the introduction of a greater degree of multilateralism than hitherto known in trade negotiations. The "linear" approach, with—ideally—a generally agreed "across-the-board" tariff reduction, was supposed to make bilateral haggling on tariff cuts super-fluous. The negotiation of broad arrangements on cereals and other products was to be done in multilateral groups. The "linear cut" approach was, however, eroded in various ways. In the *first* place the principal partners, the EEC, Japan, the United Kingdom and the United States, attached exceptions lists to their offers, i.e. lists either totally excluding certain tariff positions from a reduction, or offering a reduction less than the provisionally agreed linear cut of 50%. These exceptions lists became the object of lengthy bilateral discussions and negotiations. Some of the exceptions were replaced by offers or improvements of partial offers, others were maintained. The United States had a number of exceptions prescribed by the Trade Expansion Act.

Secondly, the EEC made it clear that it felt that it could not reduce, by the general across-the-board linear cut, certain tariffs which were low compared with the high rates of other countries, especially the United States. Such large differences in tariffs were called "disparities".

The mandate of May 1964 had specified that in cases of tariff disparities which would be "meaningful in trade terms" "special rules of general and automatic application" would apply. However, the subsequent negotiations did not result in any such rules. One difficulty was that caused by the differences in tariff nomenclature between the United States and the EEC, as the result of which it was only towards the end of the negotiations that a clearer picture as to what were tariff disparities between these two negotiating partners was obtained. In general these were tariff positions covering an agreed minimum amount of trade and for which the United States rate of duty was at least double that of the EEC. A lengthy bilateral product-by-product negotiation then determined the degree of tariff reduction in each case.

The invoking of the "disparity rule" was, as Evans has shown,[5] an outgrowth of the traditional concept of reciprocity where each partner is only prepared to give as much in concessions as he receives: reductions in the tariffs of others must result in an increase in exports not less than the increase in imports from one's own tariff reductions. The general application of the "linear cut" would, in the view of the EEC and other participants, have led to a lack of reciprocity vis-à-vis the United States, of which certain tariff rates would have remained high even after the application of the full linear cut.

Thirdly the EEC did not want the linear cut applied to agricultural items falling under arrangements of the EEC Common Agricultural Policy. It was therefore agreed that the linear approach would not be applied to agricultural items. For these items selective offers were to be tabled before a certain date and bilateral talks became unavoidable. Only for cereals a real multilateral arrangement was negotiated in the Kennedy Round. Meat and dairy products, for which such arrangements had been contemplated, were, especially in the latter phases, included in bilateral talks. Moreover a basic disagreement stalemated the agricultural negotiations for a long time: the United States and certain other large exporters of agricultural materials wanted to negotiate on commitments by importing countries on access to their markets while the EEC wanted to concentrate on conditions of production, especially subsidies.

Thus in three important respects a wedge was driven into the true multilateralism of the new approach of the Kennedy Round: exceptions in general, invoking of "disparities", agricultural exceptions.

3. *A comparison of trade and disarmament negotiations*

A comparison between trade and disarmament negotiations can be made for:

- (*a*) general features
- (*b*) the role of the large powers
- (*c*) the role of the smaller powers
- (*d*) the role of United Nations organs and of the Secretariat
- (*e*) the timing and organization of the negotiations
- (*f*) the role of informal and formal groups
- (*g*) publicity and privacy
- (*h*) the influence of the private sector
- (*i*) the role of experts

a. *General features*

In trade and military disarmament conferences the decrease of levels of protection is a common objective. In the case of trade these levels of protection were mostly expressed as import duties and quantitative restrictions. In disarmament the goal of "general and complete disarmament" is supposed to be achieved by agreement on successive stages of gradually decreasing levels of armaments and various, some highly important collateral disarmament and arms control measures. The principles of "equilibrium of strength" and of "harmonization of levels of protection" are in both cases important. In military disarmament no country can afford to be less well protected—in relative terms and for certain powers, in particular the super-powers, in absolute terms— than other countries.

If the disarmament negotiators ever come to agree on gradually decreasing armaments, it is probable that countries with low levels of armaments will wish to disarm less than countries with high levels of armaments. Undoubtedly, the disarmament negotiations are dominated by the principle of "equilibrium of strength".[6]

If "equilibrium of strength" is the notion dominating disarmament negotiators, the corresponding concept for trade negotiators is "harmonization of levels of protection" which has recently come to the foreground. Trade negotiations always recognized the principle that the binding of a low duty is, in value, comparable to the decrease of a high duty. The application of this principle had led to some harmonization of tariff levels in as much as high duties came down considerably, while low duties were merely consolidated ("bound") or decreased by a small margin. The negotiations in the Kennedy Round have dealt with proposals, mainly from the EEC, that harmonization of levels of subsidy for agriculture should be internationally agreed, that new rules of conduct for international agricultural trade should be drafted and that industrial tariffs should be reduced in such a way that each negotiating partner would gradually move towards an agreed target rate.

The trouble with the harmonization idea, which grew out of the reciprocity concept (no true reciprocity without harmonization of tariff levels) is that it is based on the notion that imports are "bad" and exports are "good". A reduction in one's own level of protection against imports must be paid for with a reduction in somebody else's level of protection. However, in reality a reduction in levels of protection may be good for the importing country: fundamental economics teaches that such reduction may lead to a larger and cheaper volume of goods for consumers and may make industry or agriculture more efficient, because they have to face foreign competition.

Internationally agreed disarmament measures will lead to some monetary savings for the governments involved, and have great beneficial effects from lessened tensions and the improvement of prospects for peace. But the country that would concede more in disarmament concessions than its negotiating partners would expose itself to possible dangers. In multilateral trade negotiations there is a similarity: the country that would offer unduly large trade concessions in comparison with other countries might, if it has a sufficiently rich market, attract a large volume of imports (so-called "distortion of trade") and find its balance of payments endangered or certain industries damaged or wiped out (which may be good or bad economics, but certainly is bad politics).

b. *The role of the large powers*

The larger and the richer a country is, the more armaments it has and the bigger presumably is its stake in the consequences of disarmament (of itself and of other powers). This general rule, which also applies to smaller countries to the extent that they have a high level of armaments, has been strengthened by the advent of nuclear armaments with their extreme offensive and defensive possibilities. It is therefore not surprising that the nuclear powers, and in particular the two super-powers, are the focal and central point for disarmament negotiations. Two of the principal post-war results in nuclear arms control, viz. the Partial Test Ban Treaty and the progress towards a Non-Proliferation Treaty depended heavily on agreement on essential points between the two super-powers. The Test Ban Treaty was initially concluded between what the preamble of the Treaty calls the "Original Parties", viz. the United States, the United Kingdom and the Soviet Union. Simultaneously with its conclusion it was declared open for signature in Moscow, London and Washington to all States (article III of the Treaty). The latter formula has permitted signature by the German Democratic Republic in Moscow.

The preponderant position of the super-powers is reflected in the system of the two co-chairmen, the United States and the Soviet Union.

The institution of the co-chairmen has not only permitted the two biggest powers to discuss procedural matters (the ostensible motive for instituting co-chairmen) but also to negotiate substantive matters, even those not before the conference. The Direct Communications Link is one example of a question thus negotiated between the Soviet Union and the United States. It was subsequently discussed in ENDC meetings, but this might not have happened had it not been known that agreement between the two super-powers was forthcoming. This example also illustrates how a multilateral framework can provide the background for bilateral negotiations.

The achievement of agreement between the super-powers is not unrelated to the distribution of power. As Jacobson and Stein noted: "When the Moscow Treaty was signed, the relative position of the Soviet Union and the United States with respect to the development of nuclear weapons was very different from what it had been when the negotiations began in 1958. In 1958 the United States apparently held the technological lead with respect to all areas and levels of nuclear weapons development. By 1963 the Soviet Union had detonated larger weapons than the United States, and the test ban treaty would make it difficult, if not impossible, for the United States to develop weapons of such magnitude. In more general terms, the USSR appeared to have become technologically more advanced than the United States in the development of high-yield weapons; that is, weapons with a yield of 5 or 10 megatons or larger. The situation with respect to weapons with intermediate yield was indeterminate. The United States definitely held the lead in low-yield weapons; that is, weapons with a yield of less than one megaton. However, since continued underground testing was permitted under the treaty, and since weapons with such yields can be tested underground, presumably the Soviet Union could attempt to equal or surpass the United States level of achievement. This consideration might have made the treaty more attractive for the Soviet Union in 1963".[7] Thus in what has been called "the esoteric demi-monde of disarmament negotiations", "the realities of power politics, as distasteful and even offensive as they may be, cannot be ignored. . ." [8]

In trade negotiations the position is less clear-cut, in this respect, than in disarmament negotiations. The Soviet Union is not a member of GATT. The United States and the European Economic Community have sometimes been referred to as the two super-powers in the Kennedy Round. Other countries, however, played a role in the Kennedy Round which, although less decisive than that of the United States and the EEC, was quite essential to its successful conclusion. The institution of the co-chairmen, accepted without opposition in the ENDC, would not have contributed to the efficient management of the Kennedy Round negotiations, where the existence of two dominant economic powers already had the effect of irritating other participants who often had to submit to the lead given by the Big Two.

c. *The role of the smaller powers*

In the disarmament negotiations this role appears to consist of the following components. Firstly, the smaller powers, both in the General Assembly and in the ENDC, will endeavour to exercise moral pressure on the big powers to make headway towards disarmament. This moral pressure, significant as it may be, is usually difficult to measure. It was much in evidence during the negotiations on the Partial Test Ban Treaty.

Secondly, the smaller powers have endeavoured to promote compromises between the positions of the super-powers. In the ENDC the eight non-aligned countries have at various times submitted proposals designed to steer a middle way between the Soviet Union and the United States. A smaller country can also usefully propose a provisional measure. For example, when agreement on a non-proliferation treaty was not yet possible, Italy proposed a draft for a multilateral declaration on the non-acquisition of nuclear weapons (document ENDC/157), which was, however, not adopted. On the other hand the Canadian initiative on the non-orbiting of nuclear and other weapons (cf. p. 175) was successful.

U Thant described the eight non-aligned countries as having a "moderating and catalytic influence in helping to bridge the gap between extreme positions of either side." [9]

Thirdly, a smaller power, if endowed with advanced technological or scientific capabilities, may make intelligent proposals. Sweden is typical of this category. One of its contributions based on superior technical knowhow was that of September 2, 1965, tabled in the ENDC (document ENDC/154) for extended international cooperation in seismology for the purpose of detecting underground nuclear tests, the so-called "detection club".

Countries outside the ENDC have at times also exerted considerable influence on ENDC proceedings. For example, in connection with the non-proliferation treaty, the six countries bound by the EURATOM treaty could not automatically accept the provision that the control functions of EURATOM should be transferred to another agency, the International Atomic Energy Agency. The Federal Republic of Germany had a special position in this connection, partly as a member of EURA-TOM, partly as a country with an advanced stage of research on the peaceful application of atomic energy, and partly because, for the Soviet Union and others, it was essential that the Federal Republic of Germany would promptly accede to the treaty, once concluded.

The role of non-nuclear states in regard to the Partial Test Ban Treaty has been commented upon in these terms: "The proposition that other powers can affect the policies of the super-powers is implicit in what has already been said. The United Nations was one forum available to virtually all states during the test ban negotiations, and many of them sought to and did exercise influence through it. The Eighteen-Nation Disarmament Committee was a more effective instrument for those states which were members; there can be no doubt that both the USSR and the United States were more sensitive to pressures brought to bear and suggestions raised in this organ than in the more diffuse General Assembly. . . . It is further clear, though, that ultimately the super-powers, the USSR and the United States, or more accurately political configurations within them, determined whether or not there should be a nuclear test ban treaty. Other states and international organizations could influence the super-powers, and their internal political configurations, but they could not determine the course of events".[10]

In the Kennedy Round, the smaller powers had an important role to play due to the fact that in certain sectors some of these countries are of equal or greater importance than the United States or the EEC: Canada and the Scandinavian countries for paper and pulp, Australia, Argentina and Canada for wheat, Switzerland for watches and pharmaceutical products, New Zealand for dairy products, etc. These countries all did help determine the course of events. The less-developed countries as a group were often able to arrive at common positions which were defended with great persistence. This produced some concrete results.

d. *The role of United Nations organs and of the Secretariat*

Although the primary role in disarmament negotiations has been played by the big powers in direct dealings with each other, the function of United Nations organs, in particular the General Assembly, has been conspicuous. Article 11 of the United Nations Charter authorizes the General Assembly to consider "the principles governing disarmament and the regulation of armaments" on which the Assembly may make recommendations to member countries or to the Security Council. This the General Assembly has done at every session. The Security Council did not, except during the earliest period, develop substantial activity on disarmament, in spite of the specific mandate in art. 26 of the United Nations Charter, which states that it shall be responsible, with the assistance of the Military Staff Committee, for formulating plans for the establishment of a system for the regulation of armaments. Although the ENDC is not an Assembly Committee, as can also be seen from the fact that its documents do not contain the United Nations symbol, it can be said to work under General Assembly supervision. The continuous discussions in, and occasional exhortations from the General Assembly are a constant reminder to the big powers that disarmament is the business of all nations. The reports of the ENDC to the General Assembly are the basis for the annual review by the General Assembly of the ENDC's work in which all countries participate. Moreover, the resolutions adopted by the General Assembly become the terms of reference and lay down the general line.

What has been the role of the Secretariat in disarmament negotiations? One must distinguish between the role of the Secretary-General as one of the organs of the United Nations and that of the Secretariat. The successive Secretaries-General have at appropriate times given their views on disarmament questions, often in their annual report to the General Assembly, sometimes in press conferences or in speeches. It has also become customary at the opening of a new series of sessions of the ENDC for the Secretary-General of the United Nations to send a message. But in questions of disarmament the Secretary-General, so far as is known, has not become a mediator endeavouring to achieve compromise solutions between opposing sides. The reason that the Secretariat has not played a negotiating role of its own in matters of disarmament is undoubtedly that the governments, in particular those of the biggest powers, wanted to keep highly important, difficult and politically delicate matters of national security entirely in their own hands. For the same reason the ENDC has done without a rapporteur.[11]

As a servicing organ, the United Nations Secretariat fulfils a role in relation to the ENDC which is important in its own right. The ENDC meets in the United Nations Office in Geneva and relies wholly upon United Nations personnel for interpretation, translation of documents (English, French, Russian, Spanish are working languages), verbatim and summary records, etc. For this work the United Nations Secretariat enjoys the full confidence of all participants in the ENDC. Moreover the United Nations not only provides the meeting place and the technical facilities plus personnel, but the Secretary-General is represented at the ENDC by a Special Representative and a Deputy Special Representative. In the ENDC, the Secretariat, similarly to what one can observe in all organs of the United Nations, has become a continuous repository of knowledge regarding the procedure and practice of the ENDC and is always available to the delegations, in particular to smaller ones, as a reference source for substantive information as well.

In the trade negotiations the role of the Secretariat reflects the position of the GATT Secretariat in general. This Secretariat is legally that of the Interim Commission for the International Trade Organization, which was established in anticipation of the entry into force of the Havana Charter on the ITO. The secretariat continued as that of the General Agreement on Tariffs and Trade.[12]

During what one might call the bilateral phase of the tariff negotiations under GATT auspices (1947-1961), the role of the GATT Secretariat was necessarily somewhat limited, but included occasional help in mediating in bilateral disputes. The Director-General of GATT, Mr. E. Wyndham White, chaired the Tariff Negotiations Committees of the earlier rounds and the Trade Negotiations Committee which supervised the Kennedy Round. During the Kennedy Round with its many-sided disputes the role of the Secretariat became absolutely essential. The Director-General of GATT (*a*) continuously prodded governments to observe the necessary speed, (*b*) took an active hand in suggesting compromise formulas or texts for seemingly insuperable differences of position and (*c*) was able to propose towards the end of the negotiations a "package-deal" which proved acceptable to the governments concerned. It is generally agreed by all participants in the Kennedy Round that this "package" of compromise solutions, proposed in May 1967 by the Director-General of GATT on three or four key issues on which the principal negotiating parties in the Kennedy Round were at odds, made all the difference between success and failure of the Kennedy Round.

e. *Timing and organization of the negotiations*

The fundamental difference is that multilateral trade negotiations are still conducted as a series of separate, loosely connected conferences, each with its own set of issues and objectives, while the disarmament negotiations have proceeded since the establishment in 1962 of the ENDC in a single continuing conference. It has been argued that the existence of unalterable deadlines for each of the trade conferences has forced governments to take the necessary decisions. On the other hand the fixing of any specific deadlines in the disarmament talks has never proved to be effective and the practice was soon abandoned. All sorts of political and military considerations have led to delays in the highly sensitive disarmament talks. But in view of the vital security considerations involved in disarmament and the many national and regional governmental agencies that must be consulted before the taking of decisions at the highest levels of government, the fixing of deadlines in this field might only lead to embarrassment.

In the latest round of trade negotiations there was a definite time limit, namely June 30, 1967, which, although not explicitly agreed upon, was implicitly accepted by all participating countries. This date derived from the expiry of the United States Trade Expansion Act, which delegated negotiating authority to the President of the United States. The same act also had a number of restrictive provisions, for example prohibiting the reduction of certain tariffs.

Limited both as to time and substance, the negotiating authority of the United States Government in the Kennedy Round (even though much wider than that granted by previous trade agreements legislation) can be placed in juxtaposition with the limitations peculiar to the EEC. To understand the position of the EEC in the Kennedy Round of trade negotiations one must look at the structure of the Rome Treaty, at the various crises which the EEC went through during the Kennedy Round, i.e. in the period 1964-1967, and at the implications of the gradual building up of the Community in the direction of a full economic union. The Rome Treaty provides that tariff negotiations with third countries shall be conducted by the European Commission, in consultation with a special committee appointed by the Council of Ministers of the EEC and within the framework of directives issued by that Council. This Special Committee, usually called "Committee 111" after the number of the article in the Rome Treaty calling for its establishment, met frequently on two levels all through the Kennedy Round: that of its so-called titular members, namely high level commercial policy officials of the six member countries, and that of the alternate members. The Committee had a double function: it was the main channel through which the European Commission kept the Member States continuously informed of progress in the Kennedy Round and it elaborated new policy directives, called "mandates", for submission to the Council of Ministers. After approval by the Council these mandates became instructions to the European Commission, indicating the framework or limits within which it should negotiate. One of the problems of the European Commission, as negotiator for the EEC, was that these instructions left almost no lee-way to negotiate, in the sense of bargaining for more concessions from the negotiating partners by offering more concessions itself. Thus the Commission found itself in the position of having to go back to the Council of Ministers even for small modifications of its instructions. Since the Council normally did not meet more often that once a month, this alone caused delays. On top of this came the fact that the years of the Kennedy Round coincided with the years of formation of the common market, in particular the agricultural common market. As the EEC was negotiating on the basis of an integrated common market (for the industrial sector the common external EEC tariff was the basis of nego-tiation), it was necessary to know the common prices and other features of the Common Agricultural Policy in order to be able to give precise mandates to the European Commission. The elaboration of this policy led to occasional crises in the Community. The best known of these was the absence of France from most Community meetings during several months in the latter half of 1965, which caused delays in a number of Kennedy Round decisions to be taken by the EEC, in particular on the nature and extent of offers in the agricultural sector. The formation of the agricultural common market was carried out mostly by way of numer-ous community regulations for a series of commodities: cereals, dairy products, fats and oils, etc. Pending the elaboration of these regulations, the Council of Ministers found it difficult to establish clear directives to the Commission. Delays were again the result.

So far two organs involved in EEC decision-making for the Kennedy Round have been mentioned: the Council of Ministers and the Committee ex article 111 of the Rome Treaty. The third organ of considerable importance in general and to the Kennedy Round in particular was the Committee of Permanent Representatives of the Member States in Brus-sels. This committee which grew out of the Committee of Representa-tives (without the word "permanent") mentioned in article 151 of the Rome Treaty, has the task of reviewing all draft decisions to be submitted to the Council of Ministers. In practice many of the recommendations of the Committee ex art. 111 went unchanged to the Council of Ministers. However, in the later stages the Committee of Permanent Representatives worked on several difficult questions confronting the Community in these negotiations, and on some of them it made recommendations of its own to the Council of Ministers.[13]

The complex machinery which we have described, together with the for-mative problems of the common market and the political background causing delays in the decision-making machinery of the Community, can be considered to have been no less of an inhibiting factor than the legal limitations under which the United States negotiators operated. An additional reason for delay was the occasional disagreement of a Member State with some draft recommendation of the European Commission (usually first submitted to the Committee 111), causing it to ask at least for some delay in the proposed decision to be taken. In particular, "positive" decisions, designed to improve some offer of a concession, caused difficulties.

If after this analysis of the Kennedy Round one takes another look at the disarmament negotiations, it can be noted that the super-powers operate under few of the limitations of a legislative or operational character just described for the Kennedy Round. True, the United States atomic energy legislation has a series of specific requirements and prescriptions. There is, however, as far as is known, no pre-established legal requirement limiting the bargaining authority of the United States or the Soviet Union in disarmament and arms control talks. Obviously, any important achievement of these negotiations must be submitted to the parliaments. The 1963 Partial Test Ban Treaty went through lengthy hearings in the United States Congress before it was approved. Whatever constraints are important in the disarmament negotiations must be caused, one can conclude, by the basic interests of the super-powers, not by the effects of the structure of the negotiating machinery. In the Kennedy Round the legislative and operational difficulties described, although also presumably reflecting basic interests, became delaying factors in their own right.

f. *The role of informal and formal groups*

In trade negotiations as conducted in the Kennedy Round as well as in disarmament negotiations effected through the ENDC, many informal or semi-formal groups came into existence and produced a conference life cycle outside the formal meetings. The Kennedy Round was essentially a bargaining negotiation related to basic economic and commercial interests. In the Kennedy Round there were few discussions on texts: at the start on the general objectives and towards the end on multilateral agreements in their final phase of negotiation. Even in regard to these multilateral agreements the emphasis was heavily on bargaining on basic economic factors: the international reference price of wheat, the subsidy level for cereals or dairy products, guarantees by importers that there would be access for certain minimum quantities, the definition of surpluses and their treatment, the quantity of food aid to less-developed countries, the safeguard of the competitive power of the paper industry, and many others. This negotiation on basic economic questions promoted the establishment of informal groups identified with common viewpoints. Thus, in the committee endeavouring to hammer out an international agreement on cereals the principal exporters (Argentina, Australia, Canada and the United States) tabled joint proposals for the main outline of an agreement, and defended these proposals through common spokesmen. The importers of cereals consulted each other frequently, but did not similarly evolve into a grouping. The exporters' group, which had held meetings in Washington D.C., far from the official conference site (Geneva), in order to formulate its initial proposals, had great difficulty in developing or maintaining common viewpoints in the later stages of the negotiations. These difficulties led to delays because the exporting countries first had to negotiate with each other. Their situation became somewhat similar to that which prevailed within the EEC throughout the negotiations: there first had to be negotiations among the constituent states to develop common positions.

Another group which advanced from informal to formal status in the Kennedy Round was that of the Nordic countries: Denmark, Finland, Norway, Sweden. Originally negotiating separately in the Kennedy Round, they decided to constitute a single joint delegation for most questions (not for agricultural matters), headed by a high-level Swedish official. In the absence of a common external tariff there was no overriding need to have a single delegation. The main reason was to improve their bargaining position, inasmuch as the refusal by, say, the EEC, to meet the requests of one member country of the Nordic delegation, might provoke withdrawals of offers of all Nordic countries. The EFTA (European Free Trade Association) countries (consisting of the just mentioned Nordic countries plus the United Kingdom, Austria, Portugal and Switzerland) consulted occasionally on Kennedy Round questions, mostly in their regular Council meetings which were held weekly at the level of Permanent Representatives in Geneva and twice a year at ministerial level in Geneva or elsewhere.

The less-developed countries participating in the Kennedy Round discussed common problems in their group. These countries participated in the Kennedy Round under the so-called non-reciprocity principle: they were not expected to "pay" for the concessions they were going to receive. On the other hand they were asked to make offers for tariff reductions or other contributions to international trade, in particular with a view to benefiting other developing countries.

Two informal groups assumed the character of steering committees of the Kennedy Round. There was a group called "the big four", consisting of the United States, the EEC, the United Kingdom and Japan, which met periodically under the chairmanship of the Director-General of GATT (Mr. E. Wyndham-White) in his capacity of chairman of the formal Trade Negotiations Committee. The "group of four" solved procedural and timing problems among themselves, and prepared recommendations which were subsequently submitted by the chairman of the Trade Negotiations Committee to that committee. Some of these procedural questions were in fact matters of substance. For example, at one time one of the participants in the "group of four" suggested the setting up of a special group on sugar, similar to the already agreed groups on cereals, dairy products and meat. This proposal, innocent on the surface, was heavily resisted by another major participant, because the problems of sugar seemed to that participant unsolvable in the Kennedy Round, partly because one of the major sugar producers (Cuba) was not taking part in it. Towards the end of the Kennedy Round the group of four transformed itself into a larger group which often met at the level of the highest officials responsible for the negotiations in national capitals, these officials making frequent trips to Geneva. For other negotiating partners "Brussels" represented the six capitals, since M. Jean Rey (at that time a Member, since September 1967 the President of the European Commission) was the top negotiator for the EEC. This group consisted of the European Economic Community, Japan, the United Kingdom, the United States, the head of the Nordic Delegation, and —for certain questions—Switzerland, Australia and Canada. The group tried to deal with some major questions of substance, and was able to give the negotiations the much needed final push. This larger group too met under the chairmanship of the Director-General of GATT, mostly in his office, and at luncheons and dinners during their brief, usually one or two-day meetings.

Comparing the disarmament negotiations with the Kennedy Round, one finds a superficially simpler picture. The "steering committee" consists of the two co-chairmen of the ENDC, the United States and the Soviet Union. Although each of them held frequent consultations with other members of the ENDC, and particularly with its allies, there was not any larger central steering group for ENDC matters. The representative of the Secretary-General occasionally attended meetings of the two co-chairmen, in particular when the timing of meetings was discussed, but there was no question of his presiding over the two co-chairmen in any way comparable to the chairmanship of the Director-General of GATT over the steering committees of the Kennedy Round.

The membership of the ENDC split up into three clearly identifiable informal groups. The eight non-aligned member countries (Brazil, Burma, Ethiopia, India, Mexico, Nigeria, Sweden, and the United Arab Republic) held a group meeting once every week, or more often if required. In a sense they assumed the role of the "representatives of mankind": many of the questions discussed in the ENDC involved no direct national interests for them individually. At least this was the case for "general and complete disarmament" and for the negotiations which led to the treaty banning atmospheric atomic bomb tests. It is less true for the question of non-proliferation of atomic weapons, in which most of the eight had a more or less clearly identifiable national position. The remaining ten members of the ENDC were evenly divided between East and West. The five Eastern members, Bulgaria, Czechoslovakia, Poland, Romania, and the Soviet Union consulted together and usually took common points of view which followed the lead of the super-power among them, the Soviet Union. Similarly, the four Western members (Canada, Italy, the United Kingdom and the United States; France never took its seat) also consulted together in a group and were often in agreement with the United States. There were, however, notable exceptions, for example in the discussions on the non-proliferation treaty, when Italy expressed concern about the effects of this treaty on its peaceful nuclear industry and about possible interference with the work of EURATOM. It feared discrimination as compared with industries in the countries of the nuclear powers, to which the control clauses of the treaty would not apply. It is known that the Western countries met periodically, but not as the non-aligned countries on a fixed day every week. It may also be assumed that the Western members of ENDC consulted the other members of the North Atlantic Treaty Organization (NATO) on substantive questions. In ENDC the division into groups was mitigated by the continuous intensive contacts and private exchanges of views among ENDC members in each others' offices, at luncheons, dinners, and at receptions. This led to a sort of "club" atmosphere where confidences could be exchanged and new ideas aired and tested.

g. *Publicity and privacy*

Both in the Kennedy Round and in the ENDC the formal meetings were private. For the disarmament talks a verbatim record is kept, first circulated among the members of ENDC who can correct their statements within a certain period. This record is then issued in final form and—approximately two to three weeks after the day of the meeting— released for general public circulation. In this way the privacy of the ENDC meetings is maintained, yet everybody sincerely interested can study the "disarmament record".

In the Kennedy Round only a confidential summary record was issued after each meeting of the Trade Negotiations Committee. These records remained restricted. The numerous bilateral encounters between countries participating in the Kennedy Round took place without the presence of the Secretariat, and each side kept its own record. This was an extension of the traditional secrecy in tariff negotiations, where the smallest leak might have an effect on trade and where even after the completion of negotiations the publication of a record with certain detailed information on products could be unfair to private or national interests. The multilateral group meetings (cereals, dairy products, meat, anti-dumping group, etc.) kept no records. The secretariat would at times issue notes indicating the main issues to be resolved.

Both negotiations attracted lively interest from the press. In the ENDC the practice developed for delegations to give their statements to the press immediately after they were delivered. Statements were important in the ENDC, because they might contain "signals" of changed attitudes, even though one must assume that, as far the two super-powers themselves are concerned, their intensive contacts as co-chairmen would have preindicated any modifications in positions. The press eagerly analysed statements, in particular of the United States and the Soviet Union representatives, for signs of such modifications. Press conferences occasionally given by the representatives of the Soviet Union and the United States have always enjoyed heavy attendance.

In contrast with the ENDC disarmament negotiations, the trade negotiations of the Kennedy Round were characterized by the almost total absence of statements as a negotiating or signalling medium. Yet the press followed the Kennedy Round attentively, highlighting any rumours of discord between the principal delegations, those of the United States and the European Economic Community. Press briefings were occasionally given by the principal delegations and also by the Director-General of GATT as chairman of the Trade Negotiations Committee. The leaders of the United States negotiating team, including its head, the cabinet-level United States Representative for Trade Negotiations had at times to make statements to committees of the United States Congress. Such statements were of course carefully worded in the knowledge that they would reach the other principal negotiating partners. They tended to emphasize the "tough attitude" the United States would take, aiming at important concessions from the other participants. At times these statements served as "signals". For example, between six and twelve months before the date of expiry of the U.S. Trade Expansion Act, June 30, 1967, which was also the extreme limit of the Kennedy Round, rumours started to circulate that the U.S. Administration might be inclined to ask the U.S. Congress for a short extension of the Trade Expansion Act, say till December 31, 1967. Alternatively it was speculated that the Kennedy Round would be limited to concluding an agreement on industrial tariffs, leaving the difficult negotiations on agricultural questions till later. The United States counteracted these rumours and speculations not only with denials in the negotiations, but also with public statements in speeches, press conferences and statements to Congressional Committees to the effect that there was no question of requesting the U.S. Congress to authorize a short extension in the absence of concrete results that might possibly have justified such an extension. With equal force the United States denied that it could accept an "industrial deal" without simultaneous results in what it considered a key sector of the Kennedy Round, namely agriculture.

h. *The influence of the private sector*

Both trade and disarmament negotiations are conducted by governments. The role and conduct of the private sector is, however, fundamentally different in trade as compared with disarmament negotiations. In trade negotiations the position of private industry, agriculture and trade is directly affected in that their operations will be influenced by the positions taken and the concessions offered by governments. Precisely because these offers remain secret, private groupings, wishing to protect themselves against the unknown, will exert pressure.

In some countries, for example the United States, the government must ascertain under procedures laid down by law, in so-called hearings, the views and wishes of private groups and persons. In other countries the government will obtain these views through established, though less formal contacts with private organizations. In either case the position of the private sector may have an impact on the negotiating position to be taken by the government. The experience has been that groups which oppose some concession which will result in greater imports, i.e. in more competition, are more outspoken and active in their lobbying with governments than groups that are interested in exports to third markets, and hence in reductions in levels of protection in other countries which can only be obtained by making concessions oneself. The conspicuous position of the private sector in relation to trade negotiations and the differences in procedures under which each government consults this sector in view of on-coming trade negotiations have led to the belief by some observers [14] that the private sector should be associated in some way with future international trade negotiations under internationally agreed procedures.

In contrast with trade negotiations disarmament negotiations are not directly affected by private industry. However, in the largest countries the "military-industrial complex", as President Eisenhower called it in his farewell address, has an economic or professional interest in maintaining a strong defence industry. The concern expressed in industrial circles of non-nuclear countries regarding effects of a treaty providing for non-proliferation of nuclear arms on the development of a peaceful nuclear industry in these countries is a form of industrial opposition. However, the opposition is not against non-proliferation of nuclear arms itself. Once the nuclear powers have succeeded in convincing the non-nuclear countries that their industries will not be discriminated against in comparison with industry in the nuclear countries, the opposition will dwindle. Lists of communications from non-governmental organizations and persons received by the Secretariat of the ENDC (cf. docs. ENDC/NGC/21 and 22) reveal no pressure from business groupings. It is, of course, possible that any pressure against disarmament measures takes more subtle forms, not recognizable in published documents. The public in general, through national parliaments and private associations, takes a varying interest in disarmament and arms control negotiations. Obviously, certain issues interest public opinion more intensely than others. For example, when during the early 1960's resumed Soviet Union and United States atomic atmospheric testing resulted in increased levels of radioactive fall-out, private organizations all over the world expressed concern on the effects of this increased radio-activity on human, animal and plant life.

i. *The role of experts*

We have referred above to some of the technical conferences held in the disarmament context. One of the principal issues on which scientific arguments were invoked was the need, or its absence, to verify the observance of a test ban treaty by on-the-spot-inspections. Gradual scientific progress made it possible to conclude the 1963 Test Ban Treaty without any international verification system.

In the early phase of disarmament negotiations after the Second World War, scientists felt strongly that "if only disarmament negotiations were left to scientists, who would concentrate on the technical merits of the issue, rather than to power-blinded diplomats, then the millennium, if not actually at hand, could at least be reached by stages".[15]

It has been shown that when scientists were used as negotiators, they were able to do a good job when given a narrowly defined task, but faced "an obviously impossible task" when "asked to solve the deep controversies which plagued the negotiations" (on a test-ban treaty).[16] Scientists appear to have played a role in disarmament negotiations in the following ways:

(*a*) outside the negotiations proper: in preparing and advising on positions of their governments. In the United States and elsewhere scientists have helped to provide the scientific data needed to formulate policies;

(*b*) also outside the negotiations, in meetings with scientists from other countries. The most conspicuous example of this has been the so-called Pugwash Conferences on Science and World Affairs. After the tenth Pugwash Conference (1962) six scientists, three from the United States and three from the Soviet Union, issued a statement proposing that the use of sealed, automatic recording stations, (later dubbed "black boxes") might prove a way out of the test ban impasse;

(*c*) in discussing and if possible elaborating agreed solutions with scientists from "the other side" on specific problems in which considerations of a technical and scientific consideration are deemed to dominate. The 1958 Conference of Experts, which discussed technical aspects of bomb tests and of their possible cessation, "represented the first instance in which a group of scientists, under the rubric of a technical investigation, was given an independent, specific negotiating task which proved of paramount importance as a link in a chain of vital diplomatic negotiations";[17]

(*d*) as members of, or advisers to, delegations on disarmament. In this case the scientist may himself become a negotiator, and his specialized knowledge at times be an asset, at other times a liability.[18]

As to the role of lawyers in the disarmament negotiations Gotlieb has stressed that "the occasions are few when legal principles may be cited or legal precedents applied in the traditional meaning of those terms. ... The discussions of issues which may, perhaps, be classified as primarily *legal* are the exception; there are relatively few topics in either of the two disarmament plans or proposals for collateral or initial measures which can readily be characterized as 'legal'. In fact the distinction between what is 'legal' and what is 'political' seems artificial in the context of many problems that arise in the United Nations, especially its political, economic and social bodies, presenting, as they often do, issues involving a complex combination of elements which exceed the limits of any one aspect of international affairs or the ambit of any one discipline or sphere of activity".[19]

In trade negotiations scientific interventions have played a much smaller role. True, economists have calculated, on the basis of known or estimated elasticities of demand and supply, the expected effect of a certain reduction in import tariffs. During the Kennedy Round one country is reported to have used computer techniques in order to evaluate the significance of its own and others' offers for tariff concessions. But such calculations have not exercised a strong influence on the negotiations in any way comparable to that of the scientists who in private or governmental conferences have endeavoured to come to certain common conclusions on disarmament or arms control questions. Perhaps the scientific influence on trade negotiations is mostly visible in an important new sector of trade policies: policies concerning less-developed countries. In academic, research, and other organizations (including UNCTAD, OECD and GATT) efforts are being made to provide a scientific basis for the trade policies of less-developed countries, and of developed countries in relation to the less-developed world.

One of the reasons why the impact of economic science on trade negotiations must be deemed less than that of physics or seismology on disarmament negotiations is that for the latter effects can be calculated with considerable precision, in terms of the impact on defense levels of a nation. In trade negotiations the national impact is the sum total of the effects on specific branches of industry and agriculture. This makes calculations more complex, and more uncertain.

4. *A small intergovernmental conference: aid to a less-developed country*

To demonstrate the importance of conference diplomacy techniques we shall give the example of the "Intergovernmental Group on Indonesia" which met in Amsterdam on February 23 and 24, 1967, to consider, in the terms of the press communiqué issued at the end of the meeting, "the economic and financial situation of Indonesia and to exchange views on the possibilities of assistance to Indonesia in the implementation of its stabilization and rehabilitation programme." Members of the Group were Australia, Belgium, France, Federal Republic of Germany, Indonesia, Italy, Japan, the Netherlands, United Kingdom and United States. There were observers from Austria, Canada, New Zealand, Norway and Switzerland. Certain organizations active in international economic assistance also participated: the International Monetary Fund, the International Bank for Reconstruction and Development, the Organization for Economic Co-operation and Development, the Asian Development Bank and the U.N. Development Programme. The conference was organized by the Netherlands Government, through its Ministry of Foreign Affairs.

Since October 1965, when there was a change of government in Indonesia, the country had started efforts to overcome economic stagnation and severe inflation which had been permitted to become rampant over a long period. It had quickly become evident that even with drastic domestic measures to stabilize the economy, large amounts of external assistance would be necessary. During 1966 informal consultations were held by a number of governments who were large creditors of Indonesia and who had a special interest in a consolidation of Indonesia's large external debt and thereby in assisting the restoration of the Indonesian economy. During earlier consultations held in Tokyo and

Paris, the Netherlands Government suggested that all countries potentially interested in extending financial aid to Indonesia should meet
together with representatives of the Indonesian Government and the
principal international organizations concerned. The suggestion was
approved at the Paris meeting (December 1966). Invitations were sent
out by the Netherlands Government.

In spite of the short time available the meeting was carefully prepared.
The organizers of the Conference had agreed well in advance with the
Indonesian Government, the International Monetary Fund and the International Bank which documents each of them would prepare for
distribution (after translation) prior to the opening of the Conference.
A small task force in the Ministry of Foreign Affairs, separate from
the Conference Secretariat, coordinated all technical conference details.
The meeting was held in a large hotel in Amsterdam, in which the delegates were also lodged.

Such unity of meeting place and hotel is of considerable importance
in conferences as brief as the two-day meeting of the Intergovernmental Group on Indonesia. The two-fold advantage is that time otherwise lost in transport to and from meetings is gained and that more
frequent informal encounters between delegates are automatically facilitated.

The task force arranged for a team of simultaneous interpreters and
précis-writers, recruited with the assistance of international organizations
in Geneva and Paris. The agenda, which had been sent to governments with the invitation to attend, had been kept simple. Its main points
were the balance of payments of Indonesia for 1967, the mechanism
and conditions for external aid to Indonesia, and aid given during 1966.

The meeting opened with a statement of the Dutch Minister of Development Aid, who was elected chairman and presided over the opening
and closing sessions; a senior official of the Netherlands Ministry of
Foreign Affairs chaired the other sessions. After the chairman's opening
statement, the representatives of Indonesia and of the International
Monetary Fund (which had just had an expert mission in Indonesia
to review the financial and economic situation) and of the International
Bank delivered statements, introducing the reports they had prepared
and presenting the essential facts of the state of the Indonesian economy and the progress of the stabilization and rehabilitation programme.
In the ensuing discussions three principal points came into focus: the
mechanism of the Indonesian stabilization and financial control system
(including methods for allocating scarce foreign exchange), the immediate needs for 1967, expressed as the "foreign exchange gap", and the
terms of new external assistance to Indonesia, taking into account amor-
tization possibilities. The first subject, the mechanism of the Indonesian

financial and foreign exchange system, was mostly dealt with through an exchange of views, including questions to and answers by the Indonesian delegation. It was evidently not a subject on which the group was expected to arrive at any common conclusions. The press communiqué went on record that the Group "expressed its confidence in Indonesia's stabilization programme, including the new foreign exchange market system". The foreign exchange system had been arrived at after careful study by the Indonesian authorities and had the blessing of the International Monetary Fund experts. It constituted a set of given facts. On the other hand any agreed view emanating from the group on the estimated foreign exchange gap for 1967 was to have considerable significance, because even though the meeting was not intended to commit governments, it was a meeting of existing and potential donor countries. Therefore, an agreed view on Indonesia's foreign exchange needs for such a short term specific period as the calendar year 1967, would imply some sort of moral support by the governments represented at the meeting of common efforts to bridge the estimated foreign exchange gap by financial aid at terms and under conditions commensurate with Indonesian repayment capacity. Most of the discussions on this estimated gap took place in informal encounters, including luncheons and dinners. With the help of the representatives of the international organizations, some of whom worked the entire night of February 23 in order to compute a summary of the latest data available, the group was able to come to an agreed point of view, which is reflected in the following key paragraph of the press communiqué:

"... the Intergovernmental Group estimated Indonesia's foreign exchange gap to be now in the order of magnitude of $ 200 million in calendar year 1967. It also agreed on the need for new assistance on as soft terms as possible in view of Indonesia's serious balance of payments situation and the need to provide such assistance rapidly, if possible through agreements to be entered into during the first half of 1967, so as to assure Indonesia of a steady flow of imports throughout the year".

This carefully worded text did not mention specific amounts of assistance to Indonesia but the next paragraph of the press communiqué indicates that another meeting of the group would take a look at new promises of external assistance:

"It was agreed that the Group would hold a further meeting before the summer to review progress and performance under the stabilization programme and receive information on aid commitments and deliveries furnished in support of this programme. In this connection, the Group also agreed that all participating countries would inform the Chairman of the Group as promptly as possible of their decisions on assistance to Indonesia".

In conclusion, the meeting on February 23/24 of the Intergovernmental Group on Indonesia is a good example of how the desire of governments to cooperate on a set of specific questions can be transformed into concrete positive results with the assistance of the right conference diplomacy techniques:

—careful preparation of the conference, including an agenda which does not provoke unnecessary difficulties;

—the right type of documents, neither too voluminous nor too brief;

—unity of meeting place and residence of delegates;

—efficient conference services, in particular interpretation and availability of drafts;

—efficient chairmanship;

—reaching for an objective which, given the limited time available, was not too far-fetched;

—full cooperation of important international organizations having an interest in the subjects discussed.

NOTES

Chapter I

¹ Quoted in J. Saxon Mills, *The Genoa Conference*, London 1923, p. 18. Conferences before and just after the First World War can be found described in the following three works: F. S. Dunn, *The Practice and Procedure of International Conferences*, Baltimore 1929, Norman L. Hill, *The Public International Conference*, Stanford 1922, Ernest Satow, *International Congresses*, London 1920.

Impressions from the Paris Peace Conference and other personal experiences are related in Lord Hankey, *Diplomacy by Conference*, London 1946.

² Cf. H. Nicolson, *The Evolution of Diplomatic Method*, London 1954, p. 90.

³ This simple definition is given by William Sanders, in "Multilateral Diplomacy", *Department of State Bulletin*, Vol. XXI, no. 527 (August 8, 1949). See also Inis L. Claude Jr., "Multilateralism—Diplomatic and Otherwise", *International Organization*, Vol. XII, 1958, p. 43, who created the term "multiplomacy".

⁴ Dean Rusk, "Parliamentary Diplomacy—Debate versus Negotiation", *World Affairs Interpreter*, XXVI, 1955, p. 121-122.

⁵ Cf. Fred Charles Iklé, *How Nations Negotiate*, New York 1964, p. 2. According to Iklé "two elements must normally be present for negotiation to take place: there must be both common interests and issues of conflict. Without common interest there is nothing to negotiate for, without conflict nothing to negotiate about".

⁶ Cf. J. W. Beyen, "Diplomacy by conference", in *Contemporary Diplomacy*, Contributions from the International Diplomats Seminar, Klessheim, Vienna 1959, p. 64: "What we have today is not so much 'diplomacy by conference'. . ., it is rather diplomacy by regular board-meeting".

⁷ Cf. Harold Nicolson, *The Congres of Vienna*, London 1946, in particular chapter IX, The Problem of Procedure, and C. K. Webster, *The Congress of Vienna*, London 1937.

⁸ Hill, *op. cit.*, p. 18.

⁹ *Second Report of the Ad Hoc Committee of Experts to Examine the Finances of the United Nations and the Specialized Agencies*, GAOR, Twenty-first session, 1966, Annexes, document A/6343, par. 97.

¹⁰ Cf. C. A. Riches, *Majority Rule in International Organization, a Study of the Trend from Unanimity to Majority Decision*, Baltimore, 1940;

A. J. P. Tammes, "Decisions of International Organs as a Source of International Law", *Recueil des Cours of the Academy of International Law*, The Hague 1958-II, Leyden, A. W. Sijthoff, 1959, p. 265-364.

¹¹ Vladimir D. Pastuhov, *A Guide to the Practice of International Conferences*, Washington D.C., Carnegie Endowment for International Peace, 1945, deals with various aspects, including conference objectives. *The Technique of International Conferences*, Vol. V, no. 2 (1953) of the UNESCO International Social Science Bulletin, deals with a number of problems and issues involved in international conferences, mostly in terms of future research.

Chapter II

[1] The normal procedures at United Nations conferences can be found described in:

Sydney D. Bailey, *The General Assembly of the United Nations, A Study of Procedure and Practice,* London, Stevens, 1960;

Andrew Boyd, *United Nations: Piety Myth and Truth,* Penguin Books, 1962;

John G. Hadwen and Johan Kaufmann, *How United Nations Decisions Are Made,* Second Revised Edition, Leyden and New York, A. W. Sijthoff and Oceana, 1962;

H. G. Nicholas, *The United Nations As a Political Institution,* second edition, London, Oxford University Press, 1962.

For other organizations information on the decision-making process can be found in the books dealing with specific agencies some of which are listed in note 2 to chapter VI.

Various voting arrangements and consensus procedures are discussed in C. W. Jenks, "Unanimity, the veto, weighted voting, special and simple majorities and consensus as modes of decision in international organizations", in *Cambridge Essays in International Law, Essays in Honor of Lord McNair,* London 1965, p. 88-154.

[2] A. J. P. Tammes, "Decisions of International Organs as a Source of International Law", *op. cit.,* p. 287.

[3] For an analysis of the "no-objection" procedure see J. Charpentier, "La procédure de non objection", *Revue générale de Droit International Public,* Oct.-Dec. 1966, p. 862-877. The art. 19 crisis is discussed in Robert Keohane, "Political Influence in the General Assembly", *International Conciliation,* March 1966 (no. 577).

[4] Special Committee on Peace-Keeping Operations, *Summary Record of the First Meeting,* doc. A/AC. 121/SR. 1 of October 22, 1965.

[5] GAOR, 21st session, Annexes, agenda item 87, document A/6230, *Report of the 1966 Special Committee on Principles of International Law concerning Friendly Relations and Co-operation among States,* par. 571.

[6] Bailey, *op. cit.,* p. 154/155.

Chapter III

[1] The literature on the organization of international conferences in general is still relatively scarce. Apart from the older works by *Dunn* and *Hill,* mentioned in note 1 to chapter I, the principal comprehensive outline still appears to be: Vladimir D. Pastuhov, *A Guide to the Practice of International Conferences, op. cit.,* which mainly describes technical problems in the preparation for and conduct of international conferences.

[2] Cf. Richard N. Gardner, *Sterling-Dollar Diplomacy,* Oxford 1956.

[3] Cf. Bernard G. Bechhoefer, "Negotiating the Statute of the International Atomic Energy Agency", *International Organization,* Vol. XIII, 1959, p. 38.

[4] GAOR, Eighth session, *Report of the Special Committee on Measures to Limit the Duration of Regular Sessions of the General Assembly,* document A/2402, par. 41. Earlier in 1949, the General Assembly had approved various recommendations of the Special Committee on Methods and Procedures (GAOR, Fourth session, 1949, Suppl. no. 12, document A/937).

Cf. also Bailey, *op. cit.,* 1960, p. 127-140, and S. E. Werners, *The Presiding Officers in the United Nations,* Haarlem 1967, chapter III.

For a penetrating analysis of the U.N. General Assembly rules of procedure see Philip C. Jessup, "Parliamentary Diplomacy, An Examination of the Legal Quality of the Rules of Procedure of Organs of the United Nations", in *Recueil des Cours,* Académie de Droit International, The Hague, 1956-I, pp. 185-318, A. W. Sijthoff, Leyden 1957.

⁵ In meetings of the European Economic Community the first letter of each country's name in its own language determines the order of seating.

⁶ Cf. Chadwick F. Alger, "Inter-action and Negotiation in a Committee of the United Nations General Assembly", paper presented at the third North American Peace Research Conference, Peace Research Society (International), Philadelphia, November 1965.

⁷ Marya Mannes, "U.N., The Fine Art of Corridor Sitting", *The Reporter,* January 12, 1956.

⁸ Resolution GC(X) Res/214 of 28 September 1966, The Future of the International Centre for Theoretical Physics at Trieste. A summary of the discussion is found in IAEA documents GC(X) Com. 1/OR. 71 and 72, paras. 46-80 and 1-19 respectively.

Chapter IV

¹ Part II, "Cooperation and Conflict" of *The United Nations in the Balance, Accomplishments and Prospects,* edited by Norman J. Padelford and Leland M. Goodrich (New York 1965) reviews 20 years of U.N. history.

² Cf. Harry G. Johnson, *Economic Policies Towards Less Developed Countries,* Washington D.C. and London 1967, Appendix B, UNCTAD Principles Governing International Trade.

³ Wilson himself did not even follow this precept at the Paris Peace Conference; cf. Philip C. Jessup, *op. cit.,* p. 238.

⁴ H. Nicolson, *The Evolution of Diplomatic Method,* London 1954, p. 89.

⁵ Dag Hammarskjöld, The Role of the United Nations, in *Diplomacy in a Changing World,* ed. S. D. Kertesz and M. A. Fitzsimmons, Notre Dame, University of Notre Dame Press, 1959, p. 369/370.

Chapter V

¹ The literature on presiding officers is mostly limited to the U.N. Cf.:
S. E. Werners, *The Presiding Officers in the United Nations, op. cit.*
Bailey, *op. cit.,* especially p. 121-126;
J. P. Quénendec, "Le Président de l'Assemblée Générale des Nations Unies", *Revue Générale de Droit International Public,* Oct.-Déc. 1966, pp. 878-915;
Jessup, *op. cit.* Some presidents of the U.N. General Assembly have written about their experience:
Leslie Munro, *United Nations, Hope for A Divided World,* New York, H. Holt and Company, 1960;
M. Zafrulla Khan, "The President of the General Assembly of the United Nations", *International Organization,* vol. XVIII, no. 3, Spring 1964, pp. 231-240;
Charles Malik, *Man in the Struggle for Peace,* New York, Harper & Row, 1962.

² Andrew W. Cordier, "The General Assembly," in *Annual Review of United Nations Affairs, 1953,* New York University Press, New York 1954, p. 65.

³ Jessup, *op. cit.,* p. 266.

⁴ Bailey, *op. cit.,* p. 121.

⁵ Cf. Werners, *op. cit.,* pp. 44-47.

⁶ UNCTAD, Trade and Development Board, *Official Records,* Second Session, 1965, 41st to 48th meeting.

⁷ Executive Committee of the High Commissioner's Programme, Fourteenth Session, 1965, *Summary Record,* 124th meeting.

⁸ *Plenipotentiary Conference of the International Telecommunication Union,* Montreux 1965, Minutes, Second to Seventh Plenary Meeting (published by the General Secretariat of the ITU, Geneva, 1966).

⁹ International Labour Conference, *Forty-sixth Session,* 1962, Record of Proceedings, p. 247.

¹⁰ International Labour Conference, *Forty-seventh Session,* 1963, Record of Proceedings, p. 76 and p. 160.

¹¹ International Labour Conference, *Forty-eighth Session,* 1964, Record of Proceedings, p. 111.

¹² International Labour Conference, *Forty-ninth Session,* 1965, Record of Proceedings, p. 171.

¹³ International Labour Conference, *ibid.,* p. 82.

¹⁴ International Labour Conference, *Fiftieth Session,* 1966, Record of Proceedings, p. 234, p. 246 and p. 247.

¹⁵ Fourth Report of the Working Party of the Governing Body of the International Labour Office on the Programme and Structure of I.L.O., issued as Supplement to part II of Report I of the Director-General, *International Labour Office,* Geneva 1967, p. 18.

¹⁶ International Labour Conference, *Fifty-first session,* Record of Proceedings, 9 June 1967.

¹⁷ Cf. Hadwen and Kaufmann, *op. cit.,* Chapter V.

¹⁸ Cf. GAOR, 22nd session, Annexes, UNCTAD, Report of the Trade and Development Board (25 September 1966-9 September 1967), par. 30.

¹⁹ Andrew Boyd, *op. cit.,* pp. 64-65.

Chapter VI

¹ Gunnar Myrdal, *Realities and Illusions in Regard to Intergovernmental Organizations,* London 1955.

² There exists a large number of studies on the Secretary-General and the Secretariat of the United Nations of which we mention:

Sydney D. Bailey, *The Secretariat of the United Nations,* Carnegie Endowment for International Peace, United Nations Study nr. 11, New York 1962;

Leland M. Goodrich, "The Political Role of the Secretary-General", *International Organization,* Vol. XVI, nr. 4, Autumn 1962, pp. 720-735;

Leon Gordenker, *The U.N. Secretary-General and the Maintenance of Peace,* New York, 1967;

Dag Hammarskjöld, *The International Civil Servant in Law and in Fact,* lecture at Oxford University, May 30, 1961, reprinted in *The Servant of Peace, A Selection of the Speeches and Statements of Dag Hammarskjöld,* edited and introduced by Wilder Foote, London and New York 1962, pp. 329-353;

Trygve Lie, *In the Cause of Peace,* New York 1954;

Stephen M. Schwebel, *The Secretary-General of the United Nations,* Cambridge, Mass. 1952;

Michel Virally, *Le Rôle Politique du Secrétaire-Général des Nations Unies*, Annuaire Français de Droit International, Paris, Vol. IV, 1958, pp. 360-399.

The following works deal with international secretariats generally or include chapters on secretariat activities:

A. Boyd, *op. cit.*, chapter 5, "Tough at the Top";

Inis L. Claude, *Swords into Plowshares: The Problems and Progress of International Organization*, revised edition, New York, Random House, 1964, chapter 10 "The Problem of the International Secretariat";

Hadwen and Kaufmann, *op. cit.*, pp. 20-22 and pp. 144-150;

G. Langrod, *The International Civil Service*, Leyden, 1963;

A. Loveday, *Reflexions on International Administration*, Oxford, 1956;

H. G. Nicholas, *op. cit.*, chapter VII, "The Secretariat";

Jean Siotis, *Essai sur le Secrétariat International*, Geneva, 1963.

There exists a voluminous literature, in books and articles, on the European Economic Community and its executive organ, the Commission.

Secretariat activities of U.N. specialized agencies are analysed in:

C. H. Alexandrowicz, *World Economic Agencies: Law and Practice*, London and New York 1962;

Hans Aufricht, *The International Monetary Fund: Legal Aspects, Structure, Functions, 1945-63*, New York 1964;

R. Berkov, *The World Health Organization, A Study in Decentralized International Administration*, Geneva, 1957;

Eugene R. Black, *The Diplomacy of Economic Development*, Cambridge, Mass. 1960 (on the World Bank, by its former President);

G. A. Codding Jr., *The International Telecommunication Union*, Leyden, 1952;

Luther H. Evans, "Some Management Problems of UNESCO", *International Organization*, Vol. XVII, no. 1, Winter 1963, pp. 76-90;

Ernst B. Haas, *Beyond the Nation-State, Functionalism and International Organization*, Stanford, 1964 (mostly on the ILO);

G. Hambridge, *The Story of FAO*, New York, 1955;

W. H. C. Laves and C. A. Thomson, *UNESCO, Purpose, Progress, Prospects*, Bloomington 1957;

J. Morris, *The World Bank*, London 1963 (published in New York under the title *The Road to Huddersfield*);

T. V. Sathyamurthy, *Politics of International Co-operation: Contrasting Conceptions of UNESCO*, Geneva and Paris, 1964;

T. V. Sathyamurthy, "Twenty Years of UNESCO: An Interpretation", *International Organization*, vol. XXI, nr. 3, Summer 1967, pp. 614-633;

J. Schenkman, *The International Civil Aviation Organization*, Geneva 1955;

Andrew Shonfield, *The Attack on World Poverty*, London and New York 1960 (discusses World Bank policies);

Jean Thomas, UNESCO, Paris 1962.

[3] Cf. Dag Hammarskjöld's statement before the Security Council on October 31, 1956, when he said—in relation to the Suez Crisis—that he would have called for an immediate meeting of the Security Council had not the United States Government already taken the initiative. (*The Servant of Peace, op. cit.*, p. 123/124).

[4] Cf. Schwebel, *op. cit.*, chapter 9; A. C. Breycha-Vauthier, in "Le Fonctionnaire International" (article in *Contemporary Diplomacy, Contributions from the International Seminar for diplomats at Klessheim*, Vienna 1959, p. 266) recalls this distinction and also relates the often repeated story, according to which a newly arrived delegate, to whom are explained the functions of the chairman

and of the secretary of a committee, asks: "Do you really think that the chairman is necessary". C. Wilfred Jenks, "Some Constitutional Problems of International Organization", *British Yearbook of International Law*, XXII (1945), suggested that one might distinguish between "parliamentary" and "secretarial" leadership in relation to executive heads.

⁵ Inis L. Claude, Jr., *op cit.*, pp. 176/177.

⁶ Cf. *The Servant of Peace, op. cit.*, p. 330.

⁷ UNESCO, *Records, General Conference, Thirteenth Session*, Resolutions (Annexes), Paris 1964, p. 165.

⁸ Hammarskjöld, in *The Servant of Peace, op. cit.*, p. 342.

⁹ *The Servant of Peace, op. cit.*, p. 150.

¹⁰ Delivered at Oxford University, 30 May 1961, reprinted in *The Servant of Peace, op. cit.*, p. 329-353.

¹¹ GAOR, 21st session (Supplement 1 A, doc. A/6301/add. 1).

¹² Lie, *op. cit.*, chapters XVII and XVIII.

¹³ Robert W. Cox, *The Executive Head: an essay in the comparative study of heads of international organizations*, Geneva, September 1964.

¹⁴ This account is based on, and the quotations are from, A. Broches, "Development of International Law by the International Bank for Reconstruction and Development", in *Proceedings, American Society of International Law*, Washington D.C., April 1965.

Chapter VII

¹ Most modern books on diplomacy or international law give attention, sometimes considerable, to the composition and working methods of delegations and permanent missions. Cf. for example:

Philippe Cahier, *Le Droit Diplomatique Contemporain*, Genève, Librairie Droz, 1964, Part II, Ch. IV;

H. G. Nicholas, *op. cit.*, chapter 8;

also: Hadwen and Kaufmann, *op. cit.*, chapter II, The Organization and Methods of Delegations;

Richard F. Pedersen, "National Representation in the United Nations", *International Organization*, Spring 1961, pp. 256-266.

A systematic inquiry into the composition and functions of permanent missions in Brussels, Geneva, New York and Paris is being conducted by the Carnegie Endowment for International Peace.

C. Labeyrie-Ménahem, *Des Institutions Spécialisées; Problèmes Juridiques et Diplomatiques de l'Administration Internationale*, Paris, Pedone, 1953 and H. G. Schermers, *De Gespecialiseerde Organisaties, Hun Bouw en Inrichting* (The Specialized Agencies, their Structure and Organization), (with summary in English), Leyden 1957, have compared the composition of delegations to conferences of different specialized agencies.

² Cf. Rosalyn Higgins, *The Development of International Law Through the Political Organs of the United Nations*, London, Oxford University Press, 1963, part III, Recognition, Representation and Credentials in United Nations Practice.

³ See GAOR 21st session, supplement no. 9 (document A/6309, rev. 1), Report of the International Law Commission on the second part of its 17th session (January 1966) and the first part of its 18th session (May-July 1966), p. 21.

⁴ Cf. A. E. F. Sandström, "Ad Hoc Diplomacy" (document A/CN.4/129 of

March 11, 1960), in *Yearbook of the International Law Commission 1960*, and M. Bartos, Report on Special Missions (document A/CN.4/166 of April 1st, 1964) in *Yearbook of the International Law Commission* 1964.

Cf. also Cahier, *op. cit.*, part II, chapter II, on *ad hoc* diplomacy.

5 Cf. Labeyrie-Ménahem, *op. cit.*, p. 99.

6 On summit diplomacy in general cf. Dean Acheson, *Meetings at the Summit, a Study in Diplomatic Method,* Durham, N.H., University of New Hampshire, 1958; Dean Rusk, "The President", *Foreign Affairs,* April 1960; Elmer Plischke, *Summit Diplomacy, Personal Diplomacy of the President of the United States,* College Park, Maryland, University of Maryland, 1958. Summit diplomacy at the first part of the 15th session of the U.N. General Assembly is discussed in Hadwen and Kaufmann, *op. cit.*, pp. 136-144.

7 Cf. Pitman B. Potter, *Permanent Delegations to the League of Nations,* Geneva 1930, and

F. P. Walters, *History of the League of Nations,* London and New York 1952, vol. 1, p. 199.

8 *The Servant of Peace, op. cit.*, p. 201; see also *ibid.*, p. 224: "The permanent representation at Headquarters of all Member nations, and the growing diplomatic contribution of the permanent delegations outside the public meetings—often in close contact with the Secretariat—may well come to be regarded as the most important 'common law' development which has taken place so far within the constitutional framework of the Charter" (from the Introduction to the Annual Report 1958-1959).

9 Cf. Chadwick F. Alger, "Non-resolution consequences of the United Nations and their effect on international conflict", *Journal of Conflict Solution,* Vol. V, no. 2, June 1961.

10 Cf. Bailey, *op. cit.*, p. 18.

Chapter VIII

1 Abraham de Wicquefort, *Mémoires Touchant les Ambassadeurs et les Ministres Publics, avec des Réflexions faites sur eux et une Réponse au Ministre Prisonnier,* Cologne 1677. The earlier quotation on p. 130 is from O. Maggi, *De Legato* (1956), cited in Nicolson, *Diplomacy,* 3rd ed., London, Oxford University Press, 1963, p. 106. The best known old book discussing qualifications for those who are sent out by their Prince to negotiate with other Princes (the term diplomat did not yet exist) is: François de Callières, *De La Manière de Négocier avec les Souverains, De l'Utilité des Négociations, du Choix des Ambassadeurs et des Envoyez, et des Qualités Nécessaires pour Réussir dans ces Employs,* Amsterdam 1716 (English translation, London 1919). Extracts can be found in English translation in Nicolson, *op. cit.*, chapter V, and in French in E. Satow, *A Guide to Diplomatic Practice,* 4th ed. by N. Bland, London 1964, chapter IX. Cf. also Jules Cambon, *Le Diplomate,* Paris 1926, especially Ch. II. The requirements for diplomats involved in assistance to developing countries are discussed in Michael H. Cardozo, *Diplomats in International Cooperation: Stepchildren of the Foreign Service,* Ithaca, N.Y., Cornell University Press, 1962.

2 Cf. Hadwen and Kaufmann, *op. cit.*, p. 98., and James Patrick Sewell, *Functionalism and World Politics, A Study Based on United Nations Programs Financing Economic Development,* Princeton, N.J., Princeton University Press, 1966, chapter V.

3 Nicolson, *Diplomacy, op. cit.,* p. 113.
4 Cambon, *op. cit.,* p. 10.
5 Nicolson, *Diplomacy, op. cit.,* p. 119.
6 Andrew Boyd, *op. cit.,* p. 57.
7 Inis L. Claude, Jr., *Swords into Plowshares, op. cit.,* p. 180.

Chapter IX

1 Well known recent studies are:
Thomas Hovet Jr., *Bloc Politics in the United Nations,* Cambridge, Mass., Harvard University Press, 1960;
Hayward R. Alker Jr. and Bruce M. Russett, *World Politics in the General Assembly,* New Haven and London, Yale University Press, 1965;
Arend Lijphart, "The Analysis of Bloc Voting in the General Assembly", *American Political Science Review,* Vol. 57 (1963), pp. 902-917.
2 Bailey, *op. cit.,* p. 28.
3 Hadwen and Kaufmann, *op. cit.,* p. 64.
4 Hovet, *op. cit.,* p. 30.
5 On the non-aligned states see:
L. W. Martin (ed.), *Neutralism and Nonalignment,* New York, Frederick A. Praeger, 1962, in particular the article by Francis O. Wilcox, "The Nonaligned States and the United Nations";
Arthur Lall, "The Asian Nations and the United Nations", and John Karefa-Smart, "Africa and the United Nations", in *The United Nations in the Balance, Accomplishments and Prospects* (ed. by Norman L. Padelford and Leland M. Goodrich), New York, Frederick A. Praeger, 1965;
Robert L. Rothstein, "Alignment, Nonalignment, and Small Powers", *International Organization,* Vol. XX, no. 3, Summer 1966, pp. 397-418.
6 Cf. Frans A. M. Alting von Geusau, "The External Representation of Plural Interests, The European Community and its Members in the Conduct of External Relations", *Journal of Common Market Studies,* Vol. V, no. 4, June 1967, pp. 426-454.
7 Cf. J. Siotis, "ECE in the Emerging European System", *International Conciliation,* January 1967, p. 11.
8 Hovet, *op. cit.,* p. 112.
9 Cf. Henry S. Bloch, *The Challenge of the World Trade Conference,* Occasional Paper, Columbia University, New York 1964-65.

Chapter X

1 For a general discussion of tactical moves, see Thomas C. Schelling, *The Strategy of Conflict,* New York, Oxford University Press, 1963, in particular chapters 2, 3, 7 and 8, and F. C. Iklé, *How Nations Negotiate,* New York, Harper & Row, 1964, in particular chapters 4, 5, 6 and 7.
2 Cf. A. Boyd, *United Nations: Piety, Myth, and Truth, op. cit.,* which gives under the heading "Offstage" (p. 66-73) a vivid description of the informal processes of the United Nations.
See also Hadwen and Kaufmann, *op. cit.,* p. 49-54, and Chadwick F. Alger, "Personal Contact in Intergovernmental Organization", in Herbert Kelman, ed., *International Behavior,* New York, Holt Rinehart and Winston, 1965, pp. 523-547.

³ Satow, *A Guide to Diplomatic Practice, op. cit.,* p. 143.

⁴ A. Lall, *Modern International Negotiation,* New York, Columbia University Press, 1966, pp. 328-329.

⁵ UNESCO, *The technique of international conferences, A progress report on Research Problems and Methods,* UNESCO, doc. SS/3, 1951, p. 28.

⁶ Oppenheim, *International Law,* vol. 2., p. 12 (7th ed. by Lauterpacht).

⁷ For a full account of the "chicken war" see Herman Walker, "Dispute settlement: The Chicken War", *American Journal of International Law,* Vol. 58, no. 3, July, 1964, pp. 671-685.

⁸ O. Schachter, in *Annual Review of United Nations Affairs 1963-1964,* New York, Oceana Publications and New York University Press, 1965, p. 126.

Chapter XI

¹ A full history of disarmament discussions and measures after the Second World War is given in *The United Nations and Disarmament 1945-1965,* United Nations, New York 1967. Cf. also Bernhard G. Bechhoefer, *Postwar Negotiations for Arms Control,* Washington D.C., Brookings Institution, 1961.

² W. Epstein, "General Survey of Disarmament", *Acts of the International Summer School in Disarmament and Arms Control,* Rome, June 1966.

³ *GATT, What it is ... what it does ... how it works,* GATT Secretariat, Geneva 1968, p. 6.

⁴ For a summary of the results of the Kennedy Round See GATT Press Release 992 of June 30, 1967; also E. Wyndham White, "The Kennedy Round of Trade Negotiations", *Inter-Parliamentary Bulletin,* 1967, No. 3, pp. 102-107.

⁵ Cf. John W. Evans, *U.S. Trade Policy, New Legislation for the Next Round,* New York, Council on Foreign Relations, 1967, chapter IV, "The Two Faces of Reciprocity". This book contains an excellent review of the issues which dominated the Kennedy Round.

⁶ Cf. Sir John Slessor, "Western Preconditions for Disarmament and Arms Control", in *First Steps to Disarmament,* ed. E. Luard, London, Thames and Hudson, 1965, p. 51.

⁷ H. K. Jacobson and E. Stein, *Diplomats, Scientists and Politicians, the United States and the Nuclear Test Ban Negotiations,* Ann Arbor, University of Michigan Press, 1966, pp. 498-499.

⁸ Lord Chalfont, "The Politics of Disarmament", *Encounter,* October 1966, reprinted in *Survival,* November 1966.

⁹ Introduction to the Annual Report of the Secretary-General on the Work of the Organization, 16 June 1961-15 June 1962, GAOR, 17th session, supplement No. 1A. The Canadian initiative on non-orbiting of nuclear weapons is described in A. E. Gotlieb, "Nuclear Weapons in Outer Space", *Canadian Yearbook of International Law 1965.*

¹⁰ Jacobson and Stein, *op. cit.,* p. 498.

¹¹ Cf. Allan Gotlieb, *Disarmament and International Law,* Toronto 1965, p. 66.

¹² Cf. G. Curzon, *Multilateral Commercial Diplomacy, The General Agreement on Tariffs and Trade and its Impact on National Commercial Policies and Techniques,* London 1965, pp. 48-51.

¹³ The negotiating mechanism of the EEC in the Kennedy Round, has been analyzed by Norbert Kohlhase, "Die Kennedy-Runde als Präzedenzfali", in *Europa Archiv,* 13, 1967.

[14] Participation of the private sector in trade negotiations has been suggested by Robert B. Schwenger, *Rethinking Foreign Trade Policy*, Washington D.C., February 1966 (private circulation); also J. Kaufmann, "Trade policies for less developed countries", in H. B. Chenery c.s., *Towards a Strategy for Development Co-operation*, Rotterdam, Rotterdam University Press, 1967, p. 46.

[15] Ernst B. Haas, *Beyond the Nation State, op. cit.*, p. 17.

[16] Jacobson and Stein, *op. cit.*, p. 489.

[17] Jacobson and Stein, *op. cit.*, p. 53.

[18] Cf. R. Gilpin, *American Scientists and Nuclear Weapons Policy*, Princeton 1962, p. 219; also Jacobson and Stein, *op. cit.*, pp. 486-493.

[19] Gotlieb, Disarmament and International Law, *op. cit.*, p. 29.

INDEX

A

Adaptability, 134, 135
Ad Hoc Committee of Experts on Finances of U.N. and Specialized Agencies, 60
Adjournment of meeting, 51, 158
Advisory Committee on Administrative and Budgetary Questions, U.N. (ACABQ), 71
African group, 142
Agenda, 49, 87, 145-146
Agreement, 40-44, 146-148
Algeria, 100
Anger, 75, 76
Arab League, 143
Argentina, 187, 193
Arrangement of business, 87
Asian Development Bank, 200
Asian group, 142
Atomic Energy, U.N. Conferences on the Peaceful Uses of, 28
Atomic Energy Commission, U.N., 173
Australia, 187, 193, 194, 200
Austria, 193, 200

B

Bailey, Sydney, 43, 141
Bargaining, *see* Negotiations
Belgium, 36, 115, 116, 145, 158, 179, 200
Benelux, 116, 143, 179
Bilateral negotiations, 185
Brazil, 88, 89, 174, 194
Bretton Woods Conference (1944), 26, 47
British Guiana, 93
Broches, A., 111
Budgets, Budgetary procedures, 26, 70-72, 151, 167
Bulganin, N.A., 174
Bulgaria, 174, 195
"Bureau", 84, 85
Bureaux Internationaux Réunis pour la Propriété Intellectuelle (BIRPI), 122
Burma, 174, 194

C

Callières, François de, 75, 131, 133, 134
Calm, 133
Cambon, Jules, 133
Canada, 43, 79, 143, 173, 174, 186, 187, 193, 194, 195, 200
CERN (European Organization for Nuclear Research), 121, 122
Chairmen, *see* Presiding Officers
Charter, U.N., *see* U.N. Charter
"Chicken War", 169
Chile, 89
China, 68, 115, 156
Closure of debate, 51, 158, 159
Co-chairmen, 85, 176, 185, 186, 194
Commission, European, 106, 190-192, 194
Committees, 48-50
Commodity conferences 57, 100, 144
Commonwealth, 143
Communication, 162-164
Compromise solutions, texts, 79, 99-100
Conciliation, 168-171
—in GATT, 169
—in U.N., 168
—in UNCTAD, 170-171
Conference diplomatic language, 167-168
Conference diplomats, 136-140
—characteristics, 136-138
—professional background, 138-140
—qualifications, 130-136
Conferences, international
—geo-climatological aspects, 62-63
—hierarchical position, 63-65
—lobbies, 56
—objectives, 25-28
—organization, 48-50, 86-87
—periodicity and length, 59-61

—preparation, 45-47
—procedures, 29-44, 50-52, 86-97, 158
—scope, 57
—secretariat services, 52-55
—size and membership, 57-59
Conference rooms, 55-56
Confidence, 75-76
Conflicts, 66-74
—budgetary, 70-72
—"demand-offer", 150
—economic, 69-70
—elections, 73-74
—political, 69
—role of chairman, 97-101
Congo, 41, 109, 132
Congress of Vienna (1815), 23, 24
Consensus, 40-44
Conservation of the Resources of the
    Sea (1954), Conference on, 60
Cordier, A. W., 83
Co-sponsors (of draft resolutions), 31,
    154
Council of Europe, 121
Courage, 136
Cox, Robert W., 111
Credentials, 59, 114-115, 121
Cuba, 194
Cyprus, 67, 147
Czechoslovakia, 158, 174, 195

D

Debate, 29, 164-167
—adjournment, 51
Decisions, 29-44
—consensus, 40-44
—voting, 29-40
Delegations, 113-129
—allocation of tasks, 129
—composition, 114-120
—credentials, 114, 115
—definition, 113-114
—delegation meetings, 127-128
—experts, 117, 120
—joint, 116
—leadership, 76-79, 117-120, 127
—nationality, 115, 116
—parliamentary members, 117
—permanent missions, 121-126
—press attaché, 129
—public members, 117
—reporting, 128, 129

—secretary-general of, 129
—specialists, 117, 120, 126
Denmark, 116, 142, 193
Development, problems of economic,
    69-70, 200-203
Dillon Round of trade negotiations,
    178, 180
Diplomacy
—conference diplomacy, 15-17, 21-22
—multilateral diplomacy, 22
—parliamentary diplomacy, 22
—summit diplomacy, 120, 173-174
Direct Communications Link, 175, 185
Disagreements, *see* Conflicts
Disarmament Commission, U.N., 173,
    174
Disarmament negotiations, 44, 60, 82,
    172-177, 183-200
Discontinuance of Nuclear Weapons
    Tests, Conference on, 174
Division, Motion for, 33, 86
Documents, 47-48
Documents officer, 55
Drug Supervisory Body, U.N., 122
Drummond, Sir Eric, 107
Duguet, Abbé, 130

E

East-West trade, 64
Economic Commission for Europe
    (ECE), 43, 64, 67, 82, 117, 119, 122
—Committee on Development of
    Trade, 64, 99, 158
—groups, 145
—length of meetings, 61
Economic Commission for Latin
    America (ECLA), 63
Economic and Social Council, U.N.
    (ECOSOC), 25, 49, 54, 57, 58, 59,
    63, 64, 65, 68, 71, 73, 77, 78, 81,
    113, 116
—delegations, 113, 116
—functional commissions, 114, 125
—reports, 54
—rules of procedure, rule 10: 105
    rule 18: 113
    rule 30: 105
Economists, 139, 199
—in trade negotiations, 199-200
Eighteen-Nation Committee on Dis-
    armament, Conference of the

(ENDC), 44, 50, 57, 60, 77, 82, 123, 175-177,183-200
Eisenhower, Dwight D., 173, 197
Elections, 73-74, 132, 146-147, 160
Endurance, physical, 136
Ethiopia, 174, 194
European Atomic Energy Community (EURATOM), 187, 195
European Economic Community (EEC), 82, 106, 116, 121, 123, 143, 146
—"chicken war", 169
—Commission, 106, 190-194
—trade negotiations, 177-200
—voting rules, 36, 38
European Free Trade Association (EFTA), 122, 143, 179, 193
Evans, John W., 182
Experts
—groups of, 120
—in delegations, 117-119
—in trade and disarmament negotiations, 198-200
Explanation of vote, 34, 131, 166-167

F

Finland, 116, 142, 193
"Fire Brigades", 79
Food and Agricultural Organization of the United Nations (FAO), 25, 60, 119, 123
France, 36, 89, 145, 173, 174, 175, 179, 195, 200
Functional Commissions, ECOSOC, 114, 125

G

General Agreement on Tariffs and Trade (GATT), 27, 43, 47, 70, 116, 122, 200
—chairmanship of committees, 85
—conciliation, 169
—date and length of meetings, 61, 102
—postal ballot, 39-40
—reports, 54
—residual restrictions, 67
—secretariat, 106, 189
—trade negotiations, 44, 80, 82, 177-200
General Assembly, U.N., *passim*
—committees, 49

—delegations, 113, 117-118, 127, 128
—disarmament questions, 173-176, 188
—General Committee, 85
—reports, 54
—rules of procedure, rule 25: 113
    rule 38-44: 85
    rule 69: 37
    rule 70: 92
    rule 74: 167
    rule 79: 51
    rule 80: 31
    rule 82: 33
    rule 85: 37
    rule 89: 39
    rule 91: 86
    rule 92: 33
    rule 115: 167
    rule 123: 33
—seating, 52
—starting date, 61
—Vice-Presidents, 84, 146, 147
General Debate, 165
Geographical Names, U.N. Conference (1967) on the Standardization of, 57
German Democratic Republic, 67, 185
Germany, Federal Republic of, 36, 123, 145, 169, 179, 187, 200
Gotlieb, A., 199
Greece, 143, 147
Groups, 141-152
—and negotiating process, 148-152
—common interest, 144, 145
—definitions, 141
—economic, 143, 144
—functions, 145-148
—"Group of 77", 144, 150
—"group B", 146, 147
—in ILO, 151
—in UNCTAD, 144
—in WHO, 151-152
—informal, 98, 99
—inner circles, 78
—leadership, 79
—political, 143
—regional, 142
—relations with secretariats, 149
—role in disarmament and trade negotiations, 192-195
—types, 142-145

H

Hammarskjöld, Dag, 80, 107-109, 125, 132
Headquarters sites, elections for, 74, 88-90
Historians, 139-140
Holy See, 58, 144
Honesty, 131-132
"Hot Line" (Direct Communications Link), 175, 185
Hovet, Thomas, 141, 149, 150
Human Rights Covenants, 27
Hungary, 158

I

India, 131, 174, 194
Indonesia, 43, 44, 200
—Intergovernmental group on, 200-203
Information, public information media, 79-82
Inner circles, 78
Instructions, 119, 160-162
Intellectual arguments, 154
Intergovernmental Committee for European Migration (ICEM), 82, 122
International Atomic Energy Agency (IAEA), 58, 64, 173
—Inspectors, 106
—Statute Conference (1956), 26, 48, 49, 68, 78
International Bank for Reconstruction and Development (IBRD), 25, 26, 36, 47, 200
—Center for Settlement of Investment Disputes, 111-112
—Executive Board, 26, 65, 85, 111-112
—Governors' Annual Meeting, 62, 112
International Centre for Theoretical Physics, 64
International Coffee Agreement, 38
International Court of Justice, 27, 58
International Development Association (IDA), 25, 111
International Finance Corporation (IFC), 25, 111
International Labour Organization (ILO), 23, 25, 27, 43, 49, 50, 122, 124, 167
—budget procedure, 71

—Conference, 29, 39, 50, 59, 61, 63, 76, 113, 138, 165
—Constitution, 105, 106, 113
—delegations, 113, 114, 118
—Director-General, 29, 105, 106
—Governing Body, 26, 61, 63, 82
—groups, 141, 151
—irrelevant remarks at Conference, 92-97
—powers of President of Annual Conference, 86, 92-97
—Standing Orders of Conference
  —art. 13: 92
  —art. 14: 92
  —art. 17: 30
  —art. 20: 37
—tripartite structure, 36, 113, 141
International Law Commission, 115
International Monetary Fund (IMF), 25, 26, 36, 47, 63, 123, 200
—Executive Board, 26
—Governors' Annual Meeting, 62
International Narcotics Control Board, 122
International Red Cross Committee (CICR), 122
International Telecommunication Union (ITU), 25, 59, 119, 122, 124
—Administrative Council, 26
—African Broadcasting Conference (1964), 67
—Plenipotentiary Conferences, 59, 87, 90-91
—World Administrative Radio Conference (1967), 57
International Trade Organization (ITO), 48, 177, 189
Interpreters, interpretation, 55, 164
Ireland, 77-78
Irrelevant remarks, 92-97
Israel, 80, 81
Italy, 36, 145, 174, 179, 186, 195, 200

J

Jacobson, H. K., 185
Japan, 143, 181, 193, 194, 200
Jessup, Philip J., 84
Jordan, 41

K

Kennedy Round of trade negotiations, 80, 116, 148, 180-200
Korean conflict, 156, 162
Krishna Menon, V.K., 162

L

Labeyrie-Ménahem, C., 117
Lall, Arthur, 162
Languages, 136, 145, 163, 164
Latin American caucus, 142
Law of the Sea, Conferences on, (1958, 1960) 26, 60
Law of Treaties, International Conference on, (1968, 1969), 58
Lawyers, 138, 199
Leadership, 76-79
—by delegations, 76-78
—by groups, 79
—by inner circle, 78
—by president, 78
—by secretariat, 79
League of Arab States, 143
League of Nations, 23, 24, 106, 107, 121, 137
Lebanon, 43, 74
Length of speeches, 167
Liaison offices, 123
Lie, Trygve, 110
Liechtenstein, 58, 144
Lloyd George, David, 21
Lobbies, lobbying, 55, 56, 129, 137, 159-160, 197-198
Loyalty, 135
Luncheons, 56, 83, 159, 160, 163
Luxemburg, 36, 116, 145, 179

M

Majority requirements, 37-38
Mali, 41
Malik, Charles, 74
Mediation, 100
Membership, 58-59
Mexico, 174, 194
Middle East, 41
Modesty, 133-134
Monaco, 58
Munro, Leslie, 100
Myrdal, Gunnar, 102

N

Negotiations, 98-100
—definition, 23
—disarmament, 172-177, 183-200
—trade, 177-200
Nehru, J., 162
Netherlands, 36, 77, 116, 118, 145, 179, 200-203
New Zealand, 100, 144, 187, 200
Nicolson, Harold, 80, 132, 134
Nigeria, 89, 174, 194
Non-aligned nations, 43, 143, 176, 194
Non-governmental organizations, 59, 82, 198
Non-proliferation of nuclear arms, 77, 175, 185, 195, 198
Nordic countries, 116, 142, 193
North Atlantic Treaty Organization (NATO), 121, 143, 173, 195
Norway, 116, 142, 193, 200

O

Objectives of conferences, 25-28
Observers, 58, 59, 123
Organization for Economic Co-operation and Development (OECD), 38, 121, 132, 143, 146, 200
Organization of American States (OAS), 143
Outer Space, U.N. Committee on the Peaceful Uses of, 26, 64
—Treaty on Exploration of, 175

P

Palais des Nations, 24, 56
Paris Peace Conference (1919), 60
Parliamentarians, 140
Parliamentary diplomacy, 22
Patience, 133
Periodicity of conferences, 60-61
Permanent delegations and missions, 121-129
—definition, 121
—functions, 123-126
—in Geneva, 121-122
—in New York, 121
—internal organization and working methods, 126-129
Permanent Observers, 123

Permanent Representatives, 121-126, 191, 193
Points of order, 51-52, 92, 93, 97
Poland, 47, 174, 195
Political scientists, 139
Portugal, 147, 193
Postal ballot, 39-40
Prebisch, Raúl, 48
Précis-writers, 45, 46, 55
Precision, 132
Presiding officers, 83-101, 135, 176
—appointment of committee members, 97-98
—general characteristics, 78, 83-85
—procedural functions, 86-91
—reversal of presidential ruling, 90-91
—ruling on irrelevant remarks, 92-97
—substantive functions, 97-101
Privacy of meetings, 81-82
—in disarmament and trade negotiations, 195-197
Private sector, 119, 197-198
Procedural motions, 51, 158
Procedure, normal, 29-34, 50-52, 86-87
—rules of specific organs, *see* under General Assembly, etc.
Promises, 154
Proposals, 29-35, 153-159
Protocol, 52
Pseudo-diplomats, 117
Publicity, 79-82
—in trade and disarmament negotiations, 195-197
Pugwash Conferences on Science and World Affairs, 199

Q

Quorum, 36-37

R

Rapporteur (elected), 54-55
Rapporteur (expert), 120
Receptions, 159-160, 163
Recommendations, 25, 70
Records, 53
Refugees, U.N. High Commissioner for, 28, 72, 122
—Executive Committee, 26, 90, 159

Reply, right of, 52
Reports, 53-55, 128
Resolutions, normal procedure, 29-44
—amendments, 32-33
—sponsors, 31, 154
Rey, Jean, 194
Roll-call vote, 39
Rome, Treaty of (1957) 36, 38, 121, 190-192
Romania, 73, 174, 195
Rules of Procedure, 43, 50-52
(*see also* Economic and Social Council, General Assembly, International Labour Organization)
Rusk, Dean, 22

S

San Francisco Conference (1945), 26
San Marino, 58, 144
Satow, Ernest, 160
Schachter, O., 171
Science and Technology, U.N. Conference on the Application of—for the Benefit of the Less-Developed Areas (1963), 28, 54, 58, 60, 102
Scientists, role in disarmament and trade negotiations, 198-200
Sea, Conferences on the Law of the—, (1958, 1960), 26, 60
Secret ballot, 39
Secretariats
—constitutional position of head of secretariat, 104-106
—leadership, 79
—personality of head of secretariat, 102-104, 107-108
—relation with groups, 149, 151-152
—role in activities of organizations, 104, 109-112
—role in disarmament negotiations, 188-189
—role in political conflicts, 108-109
—role in trade negotiations, 189
—secretariat services, 52-55
Secretary-General, U.N., 42, 43, 83, 103, 105, 108-110, 121, 188-189
Security Council, 21, 44, 57, 66-67, 69, 74, 81, 93, 95, 105, 132, 156, 173, 188
—elections, 38, 41, 73
—rules of procedure, 85

Social functions, 159-160
South Africa, Union of, 76, 90, 156
Soviet Union, 41, 68, 73, 78, 113, 142, 156, 158
—in disarmament negotiations, 172-177, 184-200
Spain, 93
Special U.N. Fund for Economic Development, (SUNFED), 157
Speeches, *see* Statements
Speed, 136
Sponsorship of draft resolutions, 30-33, 154, 165
Statements, 137, 162-168
—explanations of vote, 34, 166-167
—general debate, 164-165
—length, 167
—on specific items, 165
—points of order and procedural motions, 51-52, 166
—to introduce draft proposal, 31, 165
Stein, E., 185
Summit Diplomacy, 120, 173-174
Suez crisis, 79
Surinam, 118
Surprise Attack, Conference of Experts on (1958), 174
Sweden, 116, 142, 158, 174, 186, 193, 194
Switzerland, 123, 187, 193, 194, 200
Syria, 43

T

Tactics, 153-159
—to get a proposal adopted, 153-155
—to get a proposal rejected, 155-159
Tammes, A. J. P., 40
Talleyrand, 134
Tanzania, United Republic of, 88
Ten-Nation Disarmament Commission, 174
Test Ban Treaty, Partial, 175, 185, 186, 187, 192, 198-199
Thant, U, 110, 186
Thomas, Albert, 107
Threats, 155-157
Time, Timing, 61-62, 189-190
Trade Negotiations, 44, 82, 177-200
Translators, 55
"Trial Balloons", 80
Truthfulness, 131-132

Turkey, 43, 143
Two-thirds majority, 37

U

Ultimatums, 156
Unanimity, 38, 40
United Arab Republic, 80, 90, 91, 174, 194
United Kingdom, 89, 90, 93, 145, 173, 181, 193, 194, 195, 200
United Nations
—Atomic Energy Commission, 173
—Budget procedures, 71
Charter, 37, 41, 42, 43, 63, 96, 105, 108, 121, 168, 169, 188
United Nations Capital Development Fund, 131, 157
United Nations Children's Fund (UNICEF), 72
United Nations Commission for Conventional Armaments, 173
United Nations Conference on the Application of Science and Technology for the Benefit of the Less Developed Areas (UNCSAT), (1963), 28, 54, 58, 60, 102
United Nations Conference on Trade and Development (UNCTAD), (1964), 23, 27, 41, 48, 58, 63, 70, 113, 119, 122, 144, 145, 200
—Board, 75-76, 87, 88-90, 99-100, 147
—conciliation procedure, 170-171
—group behaviour, 141, 145, 148, 150-151, 152
—principles governing trade relations, 69-70
—procedural discussion, 88-90
United Nations Development Programme (UNDP), 28, 74, 200
—Governing Council, 26, 42, 72, 74
United Nations Disarmament Commission, 173, 174
United Nations Economic and Social Council, *see* Economic and Social Council
United Nations Educational, Scientific and Cultural Organization (UNESCO), 25, 26, 60, 107, 114, 123
United Nations Emergency Force (UNEF), 79, 80

United Nations General Assembly, *see*
General Assembly
United Nations Industrial Development
Organization (UNIDO), 27, 28, 74
United Nations Panels for Inquiry and
Conciliation, 169
United Nations Peacekeeping Force in
Cyprus (UNFICYP), 67
United Nations Regional Economic
Commissions, 57, 82
see also Economic Commission for
Europe, Economic Commission for
Latin America
United Nations Research Institute for
Social Development, 77
United Nations Scientific Advisory
Committee, 80
United Nations Scientific Committee
on the Effects of Atomic Radia-
tion, 115
United Nations Secretary-General, *see*
Secretary-General
United Nations Security Council, *see*
Security Council
United Nations Special Committee on
Peacekeeping Operations, 43
United Nations Special Committee on
Principles of International Law
concerning Friendly Relations and
Co-operation among States, 43
United Nations Special Fund, 74, 98,
131
United States of America, 41, 68, 77,
91, 123, 131, 157, 200
—"chicken war", 169
—in disarmament negotiations, 172-
177, 184-200
—in trade negotiations, 177-182, 184-
200
Universal Postal Union (UPU), 23, 58
U.S.S.R., *see* Soviet Union

V

Vice-Presidents, 84
—of General Assembly, 146, 147
Vienna, Congress of (1815), 23, 24
Viet-Nam, 165
Voluntary programmes, 72
Voting, 36-40, 112

—dual, 38
—majority requirements, 37, 38
—methods of, 38-40
—postal ballot, 39
—quorum, 36, 37
—roll-call, 39
—secret ballot, 39
—show of hands, 38
—weight, 36

W

Warnings, 155-157
Warsaw Pact, 143, 173
Western European group, 142
"Western European and other" group,
147
Western European Union, 143, 145
Wicquefort, Abraham de, 130
Wilson, Woodrow, 79
Work programmes, 70-72
World Food Programme (WFP), 28,
72, 82
World Health Organization (WHO),
25, 43, 106, 122, 124, 159
—Assembly, 39, 50, 59, 113, 114, 151-152
—budget, 71, 106, 151
Constitution, 106, 114, 118
—delegations, 113, 114, 118
—Director-General, 106, 151, 152
—Executive Board, 26, 61
—groups, 151-152
World Intellectual Property Organiza-
tion (WIPO), 26, 122
World Meteorological Organization
(WMO), 25, 26, 58, 105, 122, 123,
124
—Congress, 59, 123
—Constitution, 114
WMO/UNESCO Symposium on Hy-
drological Forecasts (1967), 63
Wyndham White, E., 189, 193

Y

Yugoslavia, 147

Z

Zeal, 134

DATE DUE

GAYLORD			PRINTED IN U.S A.